Rational Choice and Democratic Deliberation
A Theory of Discourse Failure

This book offers the first comprehensive and sustained critique of theories of deliberative democracy. In public political deliberation, people will err and lie in accordance with definite patterns. Such discourse failure results from behavior that is both instrumentally and epistemically rational. The deliberative practices of a liberal democracy (let alone repressive or nondemocratic societies) cannot be improved so as to overcome the tendency for rational citizens to believe and say things at odds with reliable propositions of social science. The theory has several corollaries. One is that much contemporary political philosophy can be seen as an unsuccessful attempt to vindicate, on symbolic and moral grounds, the forms that discourse failure takes on in public political deliberation. Another is that deliberative practices cannot be rescued even on non-epistemic grounds, such as social peace, impartiality, participation, and equality. To alleviate discourse failure, this book proposes to reduce the scope of majoritarian politics and enlarge markets.

Guido Pincione is a professor of law and professor of philosophy at the Universidad Torcuato Di Tella, Buenos Aires. He has been a visiting scholar at the Center for Ethics and Public Affairs, Murphy Institute, Tulane University, and at the Social Philosophy and Policy Center, Bowling Green State University.

Fernando R. Tesón is a leading scholar in the field of international law and ethics. He is the author of *Humanitarian Intervention* and *A Philosophy of International Law*.

Rational Choice
and Democratic Deliberation

A Theory of Discourse Failure

GUIDO PINCIONE

Universidad Torcuato Di Tella, Buenos Aires

FERNANDO R. TESÓN

Florida State University College of Law

CAMBRIDGE
UNIVERSITY PRESS

CAMBRIDGE UNIVERSITY PRESS
Cambridge, New York, Melbourne, Madrid, Cape Town, Singapore, São Paulo

Cambridge University Press
32 Avenue of the Americas, New York, NY 10013-2473, USA

www.cambridge.org
Information on this title: www.cambridge.org/9780521862691

First published 2006

Printed in the United States of America

A catalog record for this publication is available from the British Library.

Library of Congress Cataloging in Publication Data

Pincione, Guido.
Rational choice and democratic deliberation : a theory of discourse failure /
Guido Pincione and Fernando R. Tesón.
p.   cm.
Includes bibliographical references and index.
ISBN-13: 978-0-521-86269-1 (hardback)
ISBN-10: 0-521-86269-8 (hardback)
1. Rational choice theory.   2. Democracy.   I. Tesón, Fernando R., 1950–   II. Title.
HM495.P56   2006
321.801–dc22   2005031121

ISBN-13   978-0-521-86269-1 hardback
ISBN-10   0-521-86269-8 hardback

Contents

Preface   *page* vii

Acknowledgments   xi

1. Introduction   1
    1.1. The Allure of Deliberation   1
    1.2. Rational Choice and Political Discourse   5

2. The Epistemic Argument for Deliberation   8
    2.1. Political Illiteracy: An Illustration   8
    2.2. Discourse Failure   13
    2.3. Patterns of Political Belief   21
    2.4. Discourse Failure and Cognitive Psychology   40
    2.5. Persuasive Definitions   44
    2.6. Discourse Failure and Desert   50
    2.7. The Cost of Dissent   53

3. The Rational Choice Framework   65
    3.1. Instrumental and Epistemic Rationality   65
    3.2. Rational Choice and Morality   78
    3.3. Why Our Argument Is Not Ad Hominem   82
    3.4. A Note on Empirical Testing   83

4. The Resilience of Discourse Failure   87
    4.1. Reliable Social Science and Opacity   87
    4.2. Deliberative Institutions   92
    4.3. Good Policies, Bad Reasons   98
    4.4. Shortcuts   105
    4.5. Deliberation, Free Speech, and Truth   108
    4.6. Deliberation as a Regulative Ideal   113
    4.7. Deliberative Democracy, Condorcet, and Bayes   117

5. Symbolism in Political Argument   123
    5.1. Self-Defeatingness as Symbolism   123
    5.2. Symbolic Behavior in Politics   124
    5.3. Symbolic and Causal Utility: Nozick's Challenge   126
    5.4. Symbolizing as the Intended Outcome   129
    5.5. Are Self-Defeating Reformers Rational?   132
    5.6. Why Political Deliberators Appear to Neglect Consequences   137

6. Discourse Failure and Political Morality   142
    6.1. The Moral Turn   142
    6.2. Balancing, Deontology, and the Display Test   150
    6.3. Direct Involvement in Evildoing   161
    6.4. Split Responsibility   166
    6.5. Causal Complexity in Political Argument   168
    6.6. Moral Error   170
    6.7. Enforcement and Causation   173
    6.8. A Note on Religious Morality   176
    6.9. A Note on the Minimum Wage and Employment   179
    6.10. Types of Discourse Failure: A Summary   181

7. Non-Epistemic Defenses of Deliberation   183
    7.1. Deliberation as the Exercise of Autonomy   183
    7.2. Sincerity in Deliberation   186
    7.3. Deliberation and Social Conflict   189
    7.4. Deliberation and Impartiality   192
    7.5. Deliberation, Participation, and Equality   194
    7.6. Is Discourse Failure Always Bad?   198

8. Deliberation, Consent, and Majority Rule   204
    8.1. Consent and Reasonableness   204
    8.2. Deliberation, Justice, and Rights   211
    8.3. Deliberation and Majority Rule   213
    8.4. Vote Indeterminacy   217
    8.5. The Courtroom Analogy   221
    8.6. Substantive Principles and Deliberative Politics   224

9. Overcoming Discourse Failure: Voluntary Communities   228
    9.1. A Contractarian Society   228
    9.2. Contracts and Truth   230
    9.3. Contracts and Compromise   232
    9.4. The Paradox of Contract   234
    9.5. Further Objections and Replies   238
    9.6. Discursive Advantages of Voluntary Communities   242
    9.7. Loose Ends   246

Index   249

Preface

Much has been said about the disenchantment that people have with democratic politics. Many have voiced their concerns about the excessive influence of money or special interests, or the role of the media, or partisanship, or lack of accountability, or the cumbersome and even corrupt nature of the workings of legislatures, or politicians' breaching promises or deceiving the public. People may differ on their diagnoses or may place different emphases on the factors responsible for democratic degradation. But everyone seems to agree that democratic societies need to *promote* deliberation, participation, and civic education. Whatever else we can do to improve our democratic practices, surely facilitating access to deliberative fora so that citizens can debate, confront one anothers' ideas, and thus ultimately move toward the political truth, or at least increase our chances of enacting wise public policies, is primordial.

This book dissents. It offers a sustained critique of theories of deliberative democracy. Its theme is that public political deliberation will inevitably display certain patterns of error that we call *discourse failure*. As we developed our thoughts, we realized that our theory of discourse failure would not serve its polemical purposes unless we defended its assumptions about epistemic and instrumental rationality. Why do people say the false things they say in political contexts? Do they believe those things? And, if they don't believe them (if they know better), why do they persist in publicly displaying them? Our book tries to solve this puzzle by offering a comprehensive theory of political discursive behavior. People err because it is rational for them to err. Politicians lie because it is rational for them to lie. And, interestingly, they don't err or lie in a random way: Public political utterances conform to identifiable patterns. Moreover,

we came to the conclusion that no feasible improvement in the deliberative practices of a liberal democracy, let alone illiberal or nondemocratic
states, can overcome rational citizens' propensity to believe and say things
at odds with the most reliable propositions of social science. Our theory
has several corollaries. One is that much contemporary political philosophy, whether explicitly deliberativist or not, can be seen as an unsuccessful
attempt to vindicate, on symbolic or moral grounds, the forms that discourse failure takes on in public political deliberation. Another is that
deliberative practices cannot be saved even on non-epistemic grounds,
such as social peace, impartiality, participation, and equality.

So we ended up writing an interdisciplinary book. By this we do not
mean that we approach a subject from different angles, but rather and,
we hope, more interestingly, that we offer a unified theory whose propositions conventionally pertain to moral and political philosophy, political
science, and economics (in particular, the foundations of rational choice
theory).

As we said, our conclusion is grim: Political deliberation does not serve
cognitive goals, and it often drives us further from the truth. One natural
reaction is to say that democracy is morally unavoidable; to paraphrase
Churchill, bad as democratic politics are, everything else is worse. Our
answer is that, because the propensities to err and posture are intimately
tied to the subjection of a vast area of peoples' lives to majoritarian distributive politics, we could overcome discourse failure by enlarging markets and reducing politics. Even though the psychological factors that
make people believe or say falsehoods cannot be easily eradicated, eliminating or reducing the incentives to err and posture can in general bring
people's discursive behavior closer to the truth. In other words, designing institutions so that people will internalize the costs of their discursive
mistakes will lead to fewer such mistakes.

Writing this book has taken us several years. Our philosophical conversations go as far back as our friendship, more than twenty-five years.
This book, however, started in 1999 with an idle talk about Robert Nozick
and symbolism over a cup of coffee on a cold night in Mar del Plata, on
the Argentine coast. The idea of discourse failure matured throughout
several years on three continents, but mostly in prolonged periods of
collaboration in the United States and Argentina, a lot of it over long
after-dinner conversations (the fabled Argentine *sobremesa*). We would
like to acknowledge several audiences that heard joint presentations of
parts of the book. In the United States, we talked to the Arizona State
University Moral, Political, and Legal Philosophy Discussion Group and

to the University of Arizona Philosophy Department. In Argentina, the Universidad Torcuato Di Tella Law School heard presentations at the Conference on Moral Philosophy (1999) and at its regular seminar. We also delivered drafts to the Argentine Society for Philosophical Analysis and to the Universidad del CEMA Political Science Department. Finally, we talked to the Economics, Ethics and Law Workshop of the 22nd World Congress of the International Association for Philosophy of Law and Social Philosophy, held at the University of Granada, Spain (2005). We thank all these audiences for helpful comments and criticisms. We owe special thanks to Geoff Brennan, Loren Lomasky, Joseph Raz, Eduardo Rivera López, Seana Shiffrin, and Horacio Spector for their valuable comments on earlier drafts. Last, but not least, we thank two reviewers for Cambridge University Press, whose trenchant criticisms helped us to improve the argument dramatically.

Guido Pincione spent the academic year 2003–4 working on this book (with his co-author in Florida, through the marvels of NetMeeting technology) as visiting Fellow at the Center for Ethics and Public Affairs, Murphy Institute, Tulane University. While in that stimulating environment, he was able to do his most substantial work on this book. He especially thanks Jerry Gaus for his characteristically acute and thought-provoking suggestions, and an audience at both the Center and the Tulane Philosophy Department to which he presented an earlier version of Chapter 5. He also worked on this book as visiting scholar at Corpus Christi College (Oxford), the Research School of Social Sciences at Australian National University, Arizona State University College of Law, and Florida State University College of Law. A stay at the Social Philosophy and Policy Center at Bowling Green State University supplied him with an eleventh-hour opportunity to test our argument in exciting conversations with Fred Miller and Jeff Paul and allowed him to perform a final correction of the manuscript. He also expresses his gratitude to his home institution, the Universidad Torcuato Di Tella Law School, which awarded him generous leaves to visit all these places. His friend, colleague, Dean, and Provost Horacio Spector deserves credit for supporting our joint project and for promoting an intellectual environment where law, philosophy, and economics fruitfully interacted to the benefit of the project. Finally, he thanks the audiences at the Bowling Green State University Philosophy Department, the International Economics and Philosophy Society (Ninety-Ninth Annual Meeting of the American Philosophical Association, 2002), and the Torcuato Di Tella Law School, to which he presented earlier drafts.

Fernando Tesón thanks his institution, Florida State University College of Law, and especially Dean Don Weidner, for unflinching support of his scholarship. Starting in 2002, Tallahassee provided an ideal working environment to bring this project to fruition. He also thanks Arizona State University for supporting his research in various ways during the many years he spent there. He presented the core of the book to members of the law and philosophy faculties at Florida State University in the fall of 2004 and benefited from the criticisms and comments then offered. Special thanks go to Greg Mitchell, Jon Klick, Amitai Aviram, and Adam Hirsch. Like Guido Pincione, Fernando Tesón owes a special debt of gratitude to the Universidad Torcuato Di Tella Law School in Buenos Aires, where he has been a regular visitor for the past ten years, and to Dean and Provost Horacio Spector for his multifaceted support for our project. Most important, he thanks his wonderful family: his wife, Bettina; his children, Fernando, Marcelo, and Carolina; and, in faraway Buenos Aires, his mother and brother, Marta and Daniel. They provided tremendous support and strength throughout; without them this book would not exist.

As usual, no one except us is responsible for our mistakes.

Guido Pincione and Fernando R. Tesón
Buenos Aires and Tallahassee, September 2005

Acknowledgments

Chapter 5 largely reproduces our article "Self-Defeating Symbolism in Politics," *The Journal of Philosophy*, Vol. XCVIII, No. 12, December 2001, pp. 636–52.

Sections 6.1 through 6.8 present, in a version adapted to the argument of this book, our article "Rational Ignorance and Political Morality," forthcoming in *Philosophy and Phenomenological Research*.

We thank these two journals for permission to make use of material published there.

1

Introduction

1.1. The Allure of Deliberation

It is generally assumed that political deliberation is one of our most cherished values. Ideally, it precedes democratic decisions and enhances their legitimacy. Deliberative democracy, a form of political organization that fosters robust deliberation among citizens, is attractive because it appears as the only alternative to various undesirable things.[1] First, deliberative democracy excludes elitist conceptions of politics. Deliberation stands in

---

[1] The literature is extensive. Representative works include Thomas Christiano, *The Rule of the Many: Fundamental Issues in Democratic Theory* (Boulder, Colo.: Westview Press, 1996); Robert E. Goodin, *Reflective Democracy* (Oxford: Oxford University Press, 2003) (emphasizing internal deliberation, as well as deliberation with others); Amy Gutmann and Dennis Thompson, *Democracy and Disagreement* (Cambridge, Mass.: Belknap Press, 1996); Carlos Santiago Nino, *The Constitution of Deliberative Democracy* (New Haven, Conn.: Yale University Press, 1996); the essays in James Bohman and William Rehg, eds., *Deliberative Democracy: Essays in Reason and Politics* (Cambridge, Mass.: MIT Press, 1997); Jon Elster, ed., *Deliberative Democracy* (Cambridge: Cambridge University Press, 1998); and James S. Fishkin and Peter Laslett, *Debating Deliberative Democracy* (Oxford: Blackwell, 2003). Among political scientists, Benjamin Page and Robert Shapiro have expressed optimism about political deliberation. See Benjamin I. Page and Robert Y. Shapiro, *The Rational Public: Fifty Years of Trends in Americans' Policy Preferences* (Chicago: University of Chicago Press, 1991), esp. pp. 1–66 and 362–6. Not all epistemic defenses of *democracy* (understood as defenses of majority voting) are sympathetic to deliberation, however. In particular, some epistemic defenses of democracy based on the Condorcet theorem require independence of judgment, and thus little or no deliberation. For a discussion of this and related issues, see Luc Bovens and Wlodek Rabinowicz, "Complex Collective Decisions: An Epistemic Perspective," *Associations*, Vol. 7, No. 1 (2003), pp. 37–50. For a discussion of democracy centered on voting, see David Estlund, "Democracy Without Preference," *Philosophical Review*, Vol. 99, No. 3 (1990), pp. 397–423. We examine the Condorcet theorem in section 4.7.

the way of the ambitions of self-appointed philosopher-kings. It vindicates self-government and the views of ordinary citizens. Because everyone's opinion counts, and because everyone participates in the formulation of public policies, deliberative democracy evokes the values of autonomy and civic equality. Second, deliberative democracy rejects political irrationalism. By placing faith in rational argument, theories of deliberative democracy conjure up the image of a political forum analogous to the scientific forum, where critical thinking improves our beliefs and the decisions based on them. Just as scientific deliberation increases our knowledge of the world and improves our technologies, so political deliberation furthers our moral and factual understanding of society and the selection of policies based on that understanding.

The undoubted appeal of deliberation and its role in democracy has led many writers to cast it as the cornerstone of a good polity. They have attempted to substitute a deliberative model of democracy for traditional, liberal models of constitutional democracy – that is, of rights-constrained majority rule. The relationship between theories of deliberative democracy and theories of liberal democracy may assume various forms. Most versions of deliberativism declare themselves to be compatible with traditional liberalism; they simply insist that deliberation enhances the legitimacy of laws and policies.[2] Some deliberativists go further and question the attempt by traditional liberal philosophers to establish the priority of rights or justice over democracy.[3] At any rate, while various liberal models may assign varying degrees of importance to deliberation, they give pride of place to substantive principles such as rights, justice, consent, political representation, and the collective will. In those theories, principles of justice are prior to political discussion – they are not its outcome. The legitimacy of political decisions primarily depends on the satisfaction of those foundational principles.[4] And principles of justice constrain

---

[2] Notably Amy Gutmann and Dennis Thompson, and Carlos Nino (see citations in previous note).

[3] See Jürgen Habermas, *Between Facts and Norms*, William Rehg, trans. (Cambridge, Mass.: MIT Press, 1996), pp, 135–6, 159–60, and 463–90. For a full discussion of this issue, see Gerald Gaus, *Contemporary Theories of Liberalism* (London: Sage 2003), pp. 119–47.

[4] This liberal tradition, broadly understood, encompasses writers otherwise as diverse as John Locke, Immanuel Kant, Robert Nozick, and Ronald Dworkin. John Rawls is a special case. In *A Theory of Justice* (Cambridge, Mass.: Harvard University Press, 1971), he joins the traditional liberal camp (priority of justice over democracy), whereas in his more recent work he endorses some themes of deliberative democracy. See "Public Reason Revisited," reprinted in John Rawls, *The Law of Peoples* (Cambridge, Mass.: Harvard University Press, 1999), pp. 138–40.

democratic decisions, independently of how much deliberation preceded those decisions. In contrast, whatever their attitude toward foundational principles, theories of deliberative democracy argue that political deliberation ought to be promoted. Deliberativists urge more deliberation in existing fora, such as legislatures, and sometimes recommend the creation of new fora. Typically, deliberative theories claim that political deliberation enhances the legitimacy of political decisions, or otherwise improves the quality of political life and promotes the values of mutual respect and the quality and effectiveness of social policies.

Deliberativists often use an epistemic argument: Deliberation improves the empirical or normative soundness of our beliefs. Indeed, it would be odd for one to promote political deliberation if one thought of it as an exchange of ideas and arguments unrelated to the search for the truth. The idea of deliberation as a vehicle to truth is old and venerable. It was best put by John Stuart Mill in his defense of free speech: Vigorous and lively discussion leads to the survival of the better ideas in society.[5] Deliberative democrats regard deliberation as a means to enhance the legitimacy of political coercion by, among other things, approaching truth in politics as closely as can be feasibly done.[6] Though perhaps neither necessary nor sufficient for the legitimacy of political coercion, on this view deliberation contributes to that legitimacy by enlightening political discourse.

Deliberation enlightens us, it is thought, on two counts. On the one hand, it gets us closer to the truth. This is a central theme in the philosophy of science. By constantly probing into alternative hypotheses, the

---

[5] See John Stuart Mill, *On Liberty* (1859). Mill defends political deliberation in *Considerations on Representative Government* (1861) not on epistemic grounds but by reference to the value of participation. See Chapters II and VI. His view that institutions should ensure that the superior of mind should govern, however, does not seem particularly congenial to modern deliberativism. See *Representative Government*, especially Chapter VIII. At least one specialist claims that "Mill inclined to the view that the mass or multitude was not in a position to acquire a clear understanding of the appropriate criteria for public conduct." R. J. Halliday, *John Stuart Mill* (London: George Allen & Unwin, 1980), p. 69. As Gaus suggests, Mill's opposition to democratic equality is grounded in epistemic considerations. See Gaus, *Contemporary Theories of Liberalism*, p. 165. It seems fair to conclude that Mill was worried about the epistemic infirmities of political deliberation, notwithstanding his defense of the practice against nonparticipatory institutions (e.g., absolute monarchy and aristocracy).

[6] See Chapter 2, note 15. We explore in section 4.5 to what extent deliberative democrats can use arguments for free speech. We will also address (sections 8.1 through 8.4) the view that deliberation may mitigate, if not eliminate, the otherwise coercive nature of majority rule.

scientific community moves science in the direction of truth.[7] On the other hand, deliberation enables us to reach moral truths.[8] If we believe that moral progress is possible, then we will endorse continual discussion, revision, and refinement of our moral beliefs, thus again improving our practical reasoning with a view to behaving correctly or virtuously. Finally, deliberative democracy may be defended on non-epistemic grounds. Thus, some writers value the symbolic function that deliberation can fulfill. Others claim that deliberation realizes individual autonomy or the equal moral standing of persons, or that it helps prevent social conflict.

This book challenges those claims. None of these arguments or others we will address in due course provides a satisfactory defense of political deliberation. Political deliberation as a prelude to majority vote is plagued with deficiencies that undermine its aptitude to lead to better government. Those deficiencies are mainly epistemic. To put it simply, citizens will be systematically mistaken in their beliefs about the social world, and no realistic amount of deliberation can put them right. Further, typical political deliberation will undermine non-epistemic goals, such as various ideals of justice. We hasten to reaffirm the importance of the *freedom* to deliberate. But the reasons usually offered for political deliberation, understood as the public debate preceding political decisions in typical liberal democracies, are unconvincing.

We will proceed in the following sequence. In the next section, we locate our argument within the rational choice tradition in social science. In Chapter 2, we diagnose the pathologies that affect political deliberation. We introduce the key notion of discourse failure to explain those pathologies. Chapter 3 discusses the place of moral judgment within the rational choice framework, indicates how our use of rational choice assumptions combines with principles of epistemic rationality, and suggests directions for empirical testing of our theory. Chapter 4 replies to various attempts to save the epistemic credentials of deliberation. In Chapter 5, we show that standard rational choice assumptions accommodate apparently self-defeating political positions; in particular, we

---

[7] Similar views obtain if "higher predictive power" and other notions that need not be given a realist interpretation substitute "truth." Our assessment of the epistemic defense of deliberation will not turn on any particular account of science.

[8] Here again (see note 7), by writing "moral truths" we do not mean to endorse moral realism. The deliberative argument, and our critique, can be cast in realist, coherentist, expressivist, and perhaps other conceptions of moral judgment, provided that they allow for degrees of moral plausibility.

argue that counterproductive positions cannot be vindicated as symbolic behavior. Chapter 6 fends off attempts to save such positions as non-consequentialist moral outlooks. In Chapter 7, we reject non-epistemic defenses of deliberation, such as those relying on autonomy, impartiality, or equality. In Chapter 8, we explore the obscure relationships between deliberation, majority rule, and consent and show why theories of deliberative democracy find it difficult to bring those notions into a coherent whole. Finally, in Chapter 9 we outline a form of social order capable of overcoming deliberative flaws; we explain why, unlike the utopian features of deliberative democracy, the utopian features of our proposal are innocuous. We also underscore why allowing people to actually consent to institutional arrangements (in contradistinction to the nonconsensual features of modern democracy) will help reduce those deliberative flaws.

1.2. Rational Choice and Political Discourse

In this book we use rational choice theory to diagnose the flaws of deliberativism. Rational choice theory relies on an instrumental account of rationality. It assumes that agents pursue their goals (maximization of votes, glory, money, power, and so forth) at their lowest personal cost, given their beliefs. Local producers, for example, can easily see that protectionist measures are in their interest. Moreover, they can sometimes influence the political outcome in their favor – by lobbying, for example. Special-interest legislation results from strategies pursued by political actors who stand to gain by that legislation. Thus, agents will undertake rent seeking (a term used to denote gains obtained through political action, as opposed to action in private markets) as long as their expected benefits exceed their expected costs. This simple dynamic of self-interest in political decision making has been analyzed in detail in the literature.[9] Rational choice models yield predictions about the strategies of rent seekers. Among other things, the models broadly predict what positions they will publicly defend – for example, in their paid advertisements. Thus, within the instrumental rationality framework, local producers in our example will likely hire professionals (economists, journalists, lawyers, and others) who will publicly defend protectionist views.

Much rational choice analysis assumes that voters are self-interested. On this view, they vote for candidates who they think will support policies

---

9 See, for example, Glenn Parker, *Congress and the Rent Seeking Society* (Ann Arbor: University of Michigan Press, 1996).

that will benefit them. Such models often involve a narrow understanding of what is in someone's interest. Thus, a usual behavioral assumption is that political agents maximize wealth as much as traditional economic agents do. Things are not so simple, though. *When combined with those behavioral assumptions*, rational choice models of voting behavior have difficulty explaining voter turnout.[10] Why do so many people vote, given that the expected utility of voting is arguably negligible (or even negative, given the cost of going to the polling booth)? One way to address this concern is to relax the assumption of self-interest. People are motivated in multifarious ways. Some regard voting as a civic duty or as a means to express adherence to a value or principle. Alternatively, some voters may be wrong about the real impact of their vote or even about what rationality (moral or otherwise) requires them to do. The kind of rational choice theory that we adopt in this book may safely assume that most people make room for moral considerations in their decisions. This approach makes it easier to accommodate voting behavior: We should simply recognize that sometimes being moral can be costly. Of course, it is a matter of substantive morality whether individuals have an *obligation* to discharge their duty even at a prohibitive cost to themselves. What seems certain is that *more* people *will* discharge their duties if they can do so at low personal cost. As Geoffrey Brennan and Loren Lomasky argue, many citizens will express their civic commitments through voting because voting is cheap.[11] This twist on classical rational choice theory is of great importance, because it explains away an apparent anomaly in the theory. Once we understand that even morally motivated people are cost-sensitive, we can see why citizens will go to the polls, even though they know that their vote is inconsequential: They want to convey their commitment to values or principles by voting, and they use cost-effective means to achieve those expressive aims. Moreover, this broader understanding of voters' self-interest does not affect the theory's testability: We should expect morally committed voters (as indicated by independent empirical evidence) to vote in less proportions as their expected costs rise (because of, for example, new legislation increasing the probabilities

---

[10] The qualification in italics is frequently ignored in critiques of rational choice theory that point to voter turnout. An example is Donald P. Green and Ian Shapiro, *Pathologies of Rational Choice Theory: A Critique of Applications in Political Science* (New Haven, Conn.: Yale University Press, 1994), pp. 47–71.

[11] See Geoffrey Brennan and Loren Lomasky, *Democracy and Decision* (Cambridge: Cambridge University Press, 1993).

that voters will serve jury duty, on the assumption that they regard such service as onerous).[12]

We build upon these ideas to address heretofore-unexplored questions: Given the structure of incentives faced by political actors, will they engage in truth-sensitive deliberative practices? Is it possible to discern not just patterns of *political decisions* (how people vote or legislate, how much they will invest in which sorts of lobbying, and so on) but also patterns of *political beliefs* and *public positions?* We answer "no" to the first question and "yes" to the second. Citizens will predictably deliberate in a truth-*in*sensitive manner. As a result, defenses of deliberative democracy that rest on the presumed epistemic virtues of deliberation are utopian. Moreover, deliberative processes give competitive advantages to morally objectionable positions. It follows that the use of social coercion to implement majoritarian views under those circumstances will often be morally objectionable as well. Nor can political deliberation be saved by appealing to the expressive or symbolic value of publicizing certain political positions, or to the moral nature of such positions, in a sense of "moral" that exempts deliberators from scrutiny of complex causal claims. We will explore forms of social organization that may overcome the pathologies we identify in typical liberal democracies and better protect the liberal and egalitarian values that underlie many theories of deliberative democracy. We also reaffirm the importance of the right to free speech that makes deliberation possible. But we do challenge the view that a large segment of people's lives should be subject to rules for collective decision making that, in a sense we hope to clarify, are nonconsensual. The values espoused by theories of deliberative democracy, including the value of ideal deliberation, will be better served by a society in which most outcomes are the result of a highly decentralized, and so more consensual, decision-making structure.

---

[12] For further discussion of the cost of being moral, see sections 3.6 and 5.1.

2

The Epistemic Argument for Deliberation

2.1. Political Illiteracy: An Illustration

Consider one argument often given by people who defend trade barriers (e.g., quotas, tariffs, and subsidies). Protectionism is needed, they claim, to preserve domestic jobs. Domestic industries that lose out to foreign competitors have to downsize or go out of business, and thus lay off workers. Foreign workers and some local firms may gain from trade liberalization, but the welfare of our workers requires that we erect protectionist barriers. We owe a duty of solidarity to our fellow citizens in an economic context where what they lose, foreigners gain. If our goal is to preserve domestic jobs, we should protect industries threatened by foreign competition.[1]

The argument gains credibility from the obvious fact that domestic industries affected by foreign competition *do* suffer financially and so lay off workers. Who the precise losers and winners are is left obscure in

---

[1] Examples abound. During the 2004 presidential primary season in the United States, candidates received cheers from large audiences by opposing free trade in the name of protecting domestic jobs. In North Carolina, billboards read, "Lost your job to free trade or offshoring yet?" See Elizabeth Becker, "Globalism Minus Jobs Equals Campaign Issue," *New York Times*, January 31, 2004, A12, col. 1. One of the candidates, Senator John Edwards, made headlines when he said that trade was a "moral issue" and that it was not right "to drive up stock prices if it drives down wages." See "AFL-CIO: Looking for Unity," *New York Times*, February 20, 2004, A16, Col 1. On March 5, 2004, the U.S. Senate voted to bar most firms that win federal contracts from performing the work outside the United States ("outsourcing"), thus apparently endorsing the politicians' claim that outsourcing labor is harmful to the country. The chairman of the Federal Reserve Board, Alan Greenspan, did not seem to convince many senators with his pro–free-trade testimony. See "Greenspan Warns Congress Not to Create Trade Barriers," *New York Times*, March 12, 2004, C6, Col. 5.

this argument, but this much seems to be common to all protectionist positions: Trade is not mutually advantageous. Sometimes protectionists suggest that other nations' aggressive exporting strategies are unfair. This position is more moderate, as it would accept trade liberalization if trade volumes were roughly equivalent, or if everyone agreed not to protect.

Generally speaking, the protectionist argument from job loss is not supported by reliable economic theory or by empirical evidence.[2] To be sure, the relationship between trade liberalization and employment is quite complex. It seems fair, however, to draw the following conclusions from the literature:

1) Trade liberalization not only increases *aggregate* wealth in *each* trading partner but also benefits the poor as a class in each of them (we consider here, however, the argument from job loss only). These results are predicted by economic models that apply the well-established law of comparative advantages.[3] Trade liberalization,

---

[2] See, in addition to works cited in the notes that follow, Jagdish Bhagwati, *In Defense of Globalization* (New York: Oxford University Press, 2004), pp. 122–34.

[3] Explanations of the law of comparative advantages can be found in any textbook on international economics. It was first formulated by David Ricardo in his *Principles of Political Economy,* 1817. See, generally, Animash Dixit and Victor Norman, *The Theory of International Trade* (Cambridge: Cambridge University Press, 1980). For a more technical theoretical discussion, see Alan V. Deardorff, "The General Validity of the Law of Comparative Advantages," *Journal of Political Economy,* Vol. 88, 1980, pp. 941–57. Regarding empirical confirmation of the law, see James Harrigan, "Specialization and the Volume of Trade: Do the Data Obey the Laws?," working paper of the National Bureau of Economic Research, available at www.nber.org/papers, December 2001; and Jagdish Bhagwati and T. N. Srinivasan, "Trade and Poverty in the Poor Countries," *American Economic Review,* Vol. 92, no. 2, pp. 180–3. A country has a comparative advantage in producing a good if its *opportunity cost* (i.e., the value of goods forgone) of doing so is lower than that of other countries. Standard trade theory predicts that countries will export goods in which they have a comparative advantage and regards free trade as a necessary condition for global efficiency. The law of comparative advantages entails that even nations lacking an *absolute* advantage in the production of any commodity (i.e., nations that cannot produce any good more cheaply than their trading partners) can gain from free trade if they concentrate on producing commodities for which they have *comparative* advantages (i.e., goods in which they had the smallest disadvantage in terms of forgone production). Most economists either accept the law of comparative advantages or qualify it for reasons (e.g., game-theoretical models of retaliatory tariffs) that are vastly more opaque and limited in scope than the protectionist arguments that we find in the political arena. Notice that a country C may possess a comparative advantage over country C^* in producing a good without having an absolute advantage over C^* in producing that good – that is, without producing it at a lower cost than C^*. Moreover, every nation has a comparative advantage in something – namely, that product for which it forgoes least value relative to the rest of the world.

on the other hand, produces individual winners and losers, yet what winners win is more than what losers lose.[4]

2) The effect of trade liberalization on employment depends in great part on the degree to which a country is labor-intensive. This is so by virtue of the Hecksher-Olin theorem.[5] The claim that "free trade causes loss of jobs" is ambiguous. We must distinguish between several issues (recall that these questions are asked against the undisputed background of national and global gains from free trade):

a) Does free trade lower the *rate of employment* in a country? The answer is generally negative because consumers as a whole improve, and the corresponding rise in demand will create new jobs in the more efficient industries. The consensus is that in the long run the rate of employment *increases* with trade.[6]

b) Does free trade lower the *real wages* in a country, while leaving unaffected the unemployment rate? Generally speaking, the

---

[4] The literature is extensive. See Lori G. Kletzer, *Import, Export, and Jobs: What Does Trade Mean for Employment and Job Loss?* (Kalamazoo, Mich.: Upjohn Institute for Employment Research, 2002), pp. 144–5 (increased imports cause job losses and the *resulting* increased exports cause job gains, but "the employment-enhancing effect of expanding exports is significantly greater than the employment-reducing effects of increasing imports"); Hian Teck Hoon, *Trade, Jobs, and Wages* (Cheltenham, UK: Edward Elgar Publishing, 2002), pp. 184–90.

[5] For a statement of the Hecksher-Olin theorem, see Thomas A. Pugel and Peter H. Lindert, *International Economics* (Boston: Irwin–McGraw Hill, 11th ed., 2000), pp. 61–72. To understand the Hecksher-Olin effect, imagine two countries, Ruralia and Textilia, and two products, cloth and wheat. In a situation of autarky – that is, without trade – each country produces both products. Cloth requires more labor and less land; wheat requires more land and less labor. However, Textilia has a lot of labor available, while Ruralia has less labor and more and better land. When trade is opened, the theory of comparative advantages predicts that Ruralia will specialize in wheat while Textilia will specialize in cloth. Ruralia will buy all the cloth it needs from Textilia, and Textilia will buy all the wheat it needs from Ruralia. There will be a net gain for both countries in the long run. However, former cloth workers in Ruralia will see their wages go down, because they now have to work in the wheat fields, where demand for labor, and hence wages, is lower. Land rents, on the other hand, will go up in Ruralia. Notice, however, how unrealistic the model is: Land is, of course, finite; you can't "produce" more land. In any realistic situation where industries can expand by using more labor, the Hecksher-Olin effect will be less significant. But it is still true that if, say, the industries in which country *C* is relatively efficient require less labor than the industries in which *C* is relatively inefficient, those workers (usually unskilled) will suffer (will have to accept jobs at lower wages). Still, that will not affect the employment rate, and it will certainly be the case that the gains by other workers and by consumers at large will offset those losses. (The example is adapted from Pugel and Lindert, op. cit., p. 64.)

[6] See Steven Matusz, "International Trade, the Division of Labor, and Unemployment," *International Economic Review*, Vol. 37, no. 1, February 1996, pp. 71–83.

answer is no, because the real value of wages will rise by workers' having better-priced imports available. Cheaper imports in turn liberate purchasing power – something that will benefit other industries. More generally – and this is the main point of the law of comparative advantages – specialization in trade will result in the creation of *new* industries with the consequent beneficial effect on employment and wages. As a cautionary note, "the level of employment is a macroeconomic issue, depending in the short run on aggregate demand and . . . in the long run on the natural rate of unemployment, with microeconomic policies like tariffs having little net effect."[7]

c) Does free trade increase the *wage gap* between unskilled and skilled workers? The issue is controversial, but it seems that, at least in the United States, freer trade can widen the wage differential between skilled and unskilled workers.[8]

3) Even in cases where, because of the effect indicated in 2-c (which is a special case of the Hecksher-Olin theorem) or of high costs of labor adjustment, unskilled workers suffer, protectionism is *never* the optimal way to help them.[9] To the demonstrable losses already mentioned, one has to add the resources divested toward rent-seeking activities (lobbying, bribery, and other strategies to secure protection).[10]

In summary, the protectionist argument from job loss has minimal plausibility in one situation only: when, because of the Hecksher-Olin effect, the gains from trade go disproportionately to one factor of production – say, the landowners – or when trade increases wage differentials

---

[7] Paul Krugman, "What Do Undergraduates Need to Know About Trade?," *American Economic Review*, Vol. 83, 1993, pp. 23–6, at p. 25.

[8] See Elias Dinopoulos and Paul Segerstrom, "A Schumpeterian Model of Protection and Relative Wages," *American Economic Review*, Vol. 89, no. 3, June 1999, pp. 450–72.

[9] See Dinopoulos and Segerstrom, op. cit., who, after suggesting that unskilled workers may be worsened by opening trade, write: "We are anxious to point out that our analysis does not advocate protection as a way to raise the living standards of unskilled workers." Addressing the same issue, Jeffrey Sachs and Howard Shatz warn that "even if trade is an important factor in the recent widening of wage inequality, this does not suggest a case for increased trade protection. Theory and evidence both suggest that open trade is likely to be beneficial for the vast majority of the U.S. population." Jeffrey D. Sachs and Howard J. Shatz, "U.S. Trade with Developing Countries and Wage Inequality," *American Economic Review*. Vol. 86, no. 2, May 1996, p. 239.

[10] For a full analysis of the dynamics of protectionist rent seeking, see Gene Grossman and Elhanan Helpman, "Protection for Sale," *American Economic Review*, Vol. 84, no. 4, September 1994, pp. 833–50.

between unskilled and skilled workers (these are two applications of the same effect). But even in these cases, the consensus is that protectionism is a bad remedy. All one can say is a trivial truth: that if the government wants to protect *particular* workers from competition, then it can achieve that by protecting the industry. But trade barriers do not "protect" the national employment rate, nor do they "protect" the real value of wages – they positively harm consumers, and they almost always reduce general welfare. Particularly hidden are the harmful effects of protection in *other* sectors of the economy, including *reduced job creation* in those other sectors (holders of jobs not yet created do not have lobbyists).[11]

Despite these findings, the protectionist argument based on job loss remains alive and well in politics.[12] Moreover, in the public arena protectionists never pay due attention to economic theory. Their views usually rest on pre-Ricardian mercantilist notions that were refuted two hundred years ago. They never try to show, say, that the protectionist measures they propose meet the stringent conditions laid down by the Hecksher-Olin

[11] The literature recognizes another special case in which resorting to trade barriers may be beneficial: when they deter protectionist moves in a trade partner. In this case, a government that wishes to liberalize trade given protectionist pressures in a trade partner may have to make a credible threat to protect as a reprisal. This allows the government of the trade partner to resist internal protectionist pressures. This mechanism requires roughly equal trading partners, such as the United States and the European Union, because weak countries cannot credibly threaten strong ones. Also, even when it operates, the threat of retaliation does not enhance welfare and employment as much as free trade does. Finally, the threat of reprisals works only when trade partners yield to the threat. If they instead call one another's bluff, a trade war erupts, with national and global welfare losses and more unemployment. For a general discussion, see Kishore Gawande and Wendy L. Hansen, "Retaliation, Bargaining, and the Pursuit of 'Free and Fair' Trade," *International Organization*, Vol. 53, no. 1 (Winter 1999), pp. 117–59.

[12] In an *Investor's Weekly* poll, only 24 percent of those asked thought that free trade created jobs in the United States, while 45 percent thought that free trade destroyed them; 61 percent thought that restrictions to protect American jobs were justified. Most revealingly, a Pew Research poll found that 78 percent thought the top priority of trade policy should be "to protect American workers," while 74 percent *of the same pool* thought that the top priority should be "to keep [the] American economy growing." If mainstream economics is to be believed, these views are incoherent. Moreover, the way the question is asked, people cannot see the distinction between protecting *particular* American jobs (those that are lost to foreign competition) and expanding *the job market*. In a recent *Newsweek* poll, people were asked whether free-trade agreements such as NAFTA were good or bad for the United States. The answers: good, 28 percent; bad, 35 percent; mixed, 11 percent; don't know, 26 percent. Asked if they agreed with a government official who said that the "outsourcing" of service jobs was good for the United States, 23 percent did agree; 68 percent disagreed; and 9 percent didn't know. These and other opinion polls about international trade can be found at www.pollingreport. com/trade.htm.

theorem. And they invariably omit mentioning that, even if protectionist measures were effective to preserve jobs in the protected industries, they would frustrate the attainment of valuable goals, such as increasing the availability of cheaper goods and creating jobs in other industries. In the United States, politicians who mention how free trade "transfers our jobs to foreigners" enjoy a rhetorical advantage. Why is there such a profound divide between the views on trade of the public at large and those of professional economists – and this, in one of the most advanced, open, and stable democracies in the world, and nowadays the leader in economic research?

2.2. Discourse Failure

Deliberative pathologies, such as that illustrated by the trade example, are the result of a phenomenon we call *discourse failure*. Let us explain.

One would think that the gap between reliable social science[13] and public opinion exemplified by the trade debate would be bridged by robust public deliberation. For many writers, citizens who deliberate have a better chance of getting things right.[14] On this view, democracy is not about majority rule alone, or even about majority rule constrained by certain rights. It is a forum wherein citizens submit their views to the scrutiny that deliberation alone furnishes. Deliberation enhances the quality of political decision making. John Stuart Mill famously defended free speech on the grounds that the unhindered exchange of views improves citizens' understanding of things political. Present-day deliberativists urge citizens to use their right to free speech in a deliberative manner to advance their understanding of what is politically good.[15] Many questions are left open, of course. Good for whom? For each citizen? For the polity? How is the citizen supposed to identify his, or the polity's, good? What exactly is deliberation? How does it differ from the bargaining that characterizes market transactions? The questions multiply, but epistemic defenses of deliberative democracy face a preliminary difficulty.

---

[13] We discuss the notion of reliable social science in section 4.1.

[14] See relevant literature in note 1 of the previous chapter.

[15] Thus, Carlos Nino writes: "the value of democracy is of an epistemic nature with regard to social morality . . . [I]f certain strictures are met, democracy is the most reliable procedure for obtaining access to the knowledge of moral principles." *The Constitution of Deliberative Democracy*, p. 107. According to Goodin, "democracy has great epistemic merits, in any of its forms." See Goodin, *Reflective Democracy*, p. 108. See also Christiano, *The Rule of the Many*, op. cit., pp. 116–18.

The difficulty is this: As Anthony Downs has argued, a rational citizen will remain ignorant about politics because each individual vote is for all practical purposes nondecisive, and reliable political information is usually quite costly to the individual citizen.[16] In particular, citizens will not invest much time in careful deliberation. Moreover, for the average citizen, deliberating *in the manner recommended by deliberativists* is particularly onerous and thus unlikely to occur. The average citizen will not ordinarily consider all reasonable opposing political views offered in the deliberative forum, nor will he make sure, in most cases, that his proposals give equal consideration to everyone's interests.[17] Unfortunately, citizens who do not make the effort of acquiring accurate political information or of deliberating in an appropriate manner will often be mistaken. Actual deliberation, then, just moves the rational ignorance problem one step further.[18] Theories of deliberative democracy are utopian, if only because they assume that citizens have, or will acquire, the information that, we believe, it would not be reasonable for them to acquire.[19]

---

[16] See Anthony Downs, *An Economic Theory of Democracy* (New York: Harper, 1957), especially part III, pp. 207–76. We postpone until section 3.1 a discussion of the instrumental view of rationality presupposed by Downs's analysis, and how it connects with epistemic rationality. Psychological research has suggested that individuals, experts included, are often prone to invalid forms of inference. See the discussion and survey of relevant literature in Gerald Gaus, *Justificatory Liberalism* (New York: Oxford University Press, 1996), pp. 54–9. (We discuss the findings of cognitive psychology in section 2.3.) This innate propensity to err suggests that the task of becoming well informed is even more daunting than is implied by Downs's formulation of the rational ignorance effect. For a recent study of the level of political ignorance among U.S. citizens, see Stephen Earl Bennett, "Is the Public's Ignorance of Politics Trivial?," *Critical Review*, Vol. 15, no. 3–4 (2003). For indications about the extensive empirical literature showing the public's ignorance, see note 23 in this chapter.

[17] Defenses of such constraints on deliberation can be found in Gutmann and Thompson, *Democracy and Disagreement*, op. cit., pp. 126–7, and Nino, *The Constitution of Deliberative Democracy*, op. cit., p. 122. Rawls's idea of public reason can also be interpreted as imposing constraints on the kinds of reasons that citizens should offer. See John Rawls, "The Idea of Public Reason Revisited," in *The Law of Peoples* (Cambridge, Mass.: Harvard University Press, 1999), pp. 129–80.

[18] Ideal deliberation may take place in highly structured expert settings. But theories of deliberative *democracy* cannot rest on this possibility. It is no reply to say (as Christiano does in *The Rule of the Many*, op. cit., pp. 122–3) that institutions ought to be designed so that expert deliberators somehow represent the public at large. This, as Ilya Somin shows, moves the rational ignorance problem only one step further, because citizens would have to bear high informational costs in ascertaining who the experts are and whom to believe if these disagree. See Ilya Somin, "Citizens' Ignorance and the Democratic Ideal," *Critical Review* 12 (1998), pp. 424–6. See also note 12 in Chapter 4, and accompanying text.

[19] In the same vein, Russell Hardin observes that "if individuals have no reason to participate, because they cannot affect outcomes, then they would have no reason to know enough to participate wisely if they did participate." See *Liberalism, Constitutionalism, and*

Yet the claim that political deliberation brings us closer to the truth depends on the claim that citizens are able to acquire accurate information about the way society works. For deliberation to fulfill that epistemic role, citizens must be able to educate themselves about the workings of society, its economy, political processes, and likely social consequences of alternative policies. Unfortunately, the rational ignorance effect blocks this outcome, and as a result serious pathologies pervade deliberative politics. As we said, each voter knows that her vote will be, for all practical purposes, nondecisive on the outcome of an election – the chances that her vote will break a tie are negligible.[20] This is a major reason why she will remain ignorant about politics.

The citizens' rational ignorance is compounded by the rhetoric of those who stand to gain from it. Knowing that citizens will remain ignorant, politicians, lobbyists, and others will spread political "information" and theories that voters find easy to believe. Indeed, as we will see, politicians and lobbyists have an incentive to feed false, distorted, or misleading information and theories. Because citizens in modern democracies misunderstand how society works, they will systematically misdiagnose social problems and offer spurious arguments in their deliberative exchanges. As a result, they (and the politicians who seek their support) will often recommend inept policies to address those problems. Deliberative practices in modern democracies have an unfavorable impact on knowledge, understood as true belief, as contrasted with error and ignorance.[21] As

---

Democracy (New York: Oxford University Press, 1999), p. 166. Deliberativists have seldom addressed the problem of citizens' ignorance. Two exceptions are Thomas Christiano and James S. Fishkin. In *The Rule of the Many*, op. cit., chapters 3 and 4, Christiano presents the rational ignorance critique, but unfortunately he nowhere replies to it. See note 17 in Chapter 6, and accompanying text. Fishkin sees the problem raised by rational ignorance for the participatory and deliberative ideals, and he advances a solution (deliberative polls) that we criticize in section 4.2. See James S. Fishkin, *The Voice of the People: Public Opinion and Democracy* (New Haven, Conn.: Yale University Press, 1995), pp. 22–3. More recently, Ackerman and Fishkin seem to accept the rational ignorance postulate but immediately add that they "do not endorse the cynical conception of instrumental rationality that often motivates the expositors of the theory of 'rational ignorance.'" Bruce Ackerman and James Fishkin, *Deliberation Day* (New Haven, Conn.: Yale University Press, 2004), p. 8. We suggest a unified account of instrumental and epistemic rationality in section 3.1. A recent example of utopian requirements for deliberation is Goodin, *Reflective Democracy*, op. cit., pp. 15, 17, and 127 (claiming that citizens must not only heed to the opinions of others but also update their beliefs accordingly through Bayesian procedures); see section 4.7.

[20] See reference to Downs in note 16, this section.

[21] We are borrowing here the terminology of Alvin I. Goldman, *Knowledge in a Social World* (Oxford: Clarendon Press, 1999), p. 5. Unless otherwise specified, in our critique of the epistemic argument for deliberation we adopt a notion of "knowledge" that does not

we will argue in section 3.1, however, all actors in this process are both instrumentally and epistemically rational.

Political scientists have focused on the ignorance of citizens about various political facts, such as the number of senators representing their state, the identity of even a single representative in Congress, whether the Soviet Union was a member of NATO, or the basics of government's workings.[22] Indeed, the widespread ignorance of the public about the most elementary facts and actors of political life is "one of the best documented facts in all of the social sciences."[23]

We carry the rational ignorance hypothesis one step further. The same incentives that motivate citizens to ignore elementary political information lead them to a much deeper form of ignorance: They will systematically adopt and publicly endorse unreliable *theories* about society. So even if they knew who the relevant political actors were and what policies they favored, they would misconstrue social phenomena, including the consequences of those policies. Thus, the main problem with public deliberation about trade policy is not that the citizen does not know who the candidates are or even what their views on trade are. The deeper problem is that he typically holds pre-Ricardian views ("We need to protect our jobs," "Exports are good, imports are bad"). This theoretical error makes him vote for protectionist candidates and thus frustrate his likely goals (e.g., to enhance general welfare or reduce unemployment). The public's mistakes about theory are often deeper and more pervasive than the public's factual mistakes and ignorance found in the literature. The public frequently errs about whether the *policies* they endorse will bring about the *outcomes* they prefer.[24]

---

require that true beliefs be justified. We will show that deliberative practices often fall short of this weaker ideal. The foregoing work of Goldman's is a recent example of social epistemology targeted to the weaker notion of knowledge.

[22] We take the examples from Goldman, pp. 317–18. See also next note.

[23] Richard Lau and David Redlawsk, "Advantages and Disadvantages of Cognitive Heuristics in Political Decision-Making," *American Journal of Political Science*, Vol. 45, no. 4 (October 2001), p. 951. See the classical study by Philip Converse, "The Nature of Belief Systems in Mass Politics," in D. E. Apter, ed., *Ideology and Discontent* (Glencoe, N.Y.: Free Press, 1964). A modern study of political knowledge and ignorance is Michael Delli Carpini and Scott Keater, *What Americans Know About Politics and Why It Matters* (New Haven, Conn.: Yale University Press, 1996). The view that the public is politically illiterate has been challenged by Page and Shapiro, *The Rational Public*, op. cit., who argue that the *collective* preferences of the public over time are rational, stable, and sensible. We discuss their views in section 3.4.

[24] Alvin Goldman sees the relevance of the distinction between policies and outcomes for an inquiry about voters' knowledge. However, he focuses on formal and conceptual

We use *discourse failure* as a generic term denoting the public display of political positions that are traceable to truth-insensitive processes. For stylistic convenience, we sometimes use that term to refer to those processes themselves or the beliefs that result from them.[25] A truth-insensitive process is one that disregards the best available reasons, understood as those that define the *status quaestionis* in the relevant reliable scholarly disciplines.[26] Truth-insensitive processes will normally lead to false beliefs about society. However, someone may be right and yet reach the truth through a truth-insensitive process; to that extent, he engages in discourse failure (think about someone who formulates a correct prediction about the effects of free trade after having consulted a psychic). Conversely, not all false beliefs about society can be characterized as discourse failure, because people may err notwithstanding the fact that the process by which they reached the false view was truth-sensitive (think about trial and error in science). A political position evinces discourse failure when it is held for reasons other than the best available reasons in the sense indicated. Notice that the best *available* reasons may be bad reasons, because during any truth-sensitive investigation people may provisionally endorse reasons that are later defeated by better ones.[27]

We should distinguish, then, three possibilities. Someone may say things that are consistent with reliable social science (as defined in section 4.1) by chance or by consulting an unreliable source. We will say that this person engages in discourse failure: His utterance is the outcome of a truth-insensitive process. Someone may instead say things that are consistent with reliable social science, and *because* they are consistent with reliable social science, but without actually stating the reasons offered by reliable social science. This person does not engage in discourse failure: his utterance results from a truth-sensitive process. Finally, someone may argue for a position by offering reasons found in reliable social science. A fortiori, this person does not engage in discourse failure.

issues concerning the selection of the candidates most likely to bring about the voters' preferred outcomes. He offers no account of how citizens' mistakes about the causal relationships between policies and outcomes affect the epistemic value of democracy. See Goldman, *Knowledge in a Social World*, op. cit., pp. 320–48, esp. 347–8.

[25] Thus, we sometimes use the term "discourse failure" to refer to people's truth-insensitive motivations or to the "cognitive dissonances" from which they may suffer. See section 2.3.

[26] We propose an operational definition of "reliable social science" in section 4.1.

[27] We postpone until section 3.1 a fuller discussion of the notion of discourse failure and its relationships with instrumental and epistemic rationality.

We see discourse failure as an essentially *social* phenomenon. It results from the structures of incentives that various political actors face in the political arena. More specifically, discourse failure results from the combination of three factors:

1) The high cost that citizens face to become acquainted with reliable social science – the public's rational ignorance.
2) The tendency by politicians to take advantage of the public's ignorance for political and personal gain – the politicians' posturing.
3) The existence of wide redistributive state powers governed chiefly (though not exclusively) by majority rule. The more redistributive powers government has, the stronger the incentives to use it to further one's goals. The incentives to posture (that is, to exploit widespread ignorance) are directly related to the extent of redistributive powers. We shall expand on this point in sections 7.3 and 8.3, and in Chapter 9.

To the extent that citizens suffer from *ingrained* cognitive failures (that is, psychological quirks that are not the result of political communication), we treat such failures as increasing the cost for citizens of acquiring accurate information about the workings of society.[28]

Discourse failure, then, results from the combination of the incentive of politicians and lobbyists to spread inaccurate views, the high cost for members of the public to check the credentials of easily available views, and the possibility for politicians to access the redistributive apparatus of the modern state. One obvious such incentive is self-interest, broadly understood. Human beings have an inborn psychological tendency to argue in self-serving ways in all areas of social life, and they do this in more or less conscious ways. Market transactions are obvious instances of this disposition: Sellers tend to over-praise their products. Politics is a particularly insidious terrain for this kind of behavior because the relevant actors are expected to offer public-spirited arguments, and so, unlike what happens in market transactions, the self-interested nature of their statements is not always transparent. It is not just that, say, campaigning politicians and rent seekers will furnish pieces of information and theories that fit their lust for power or wealth, but also that others – for example, intellectuals who seek social esteem – will likewise argue self-servingly in ways we will later diagnose.

---

[28] Discussed in section 2.3.

Another crucial truth-insensitive incentive that affects political deliberation stems from the rational ignorance effect, already mentioned. The fact that citizens' investment in political information will fall short of the requirements for reliable political beliefs will not lead them to suspend political judgment. They will have those political beliefs that they can form at low cost to themselves. For example, in order to form an opinion on the current economic situation, citizens are more likely to look for debates on television, newspapers editorials, or magazine stories rather than undertake lengthy and costly studies of economics. In doing this, they err, but they act rationally. While the consciously self-serving deliberator does not necessarily believe what he says, the rationally mistaken citizen believes what he says but his beliefs stem from an unreliable cognitive process.[29] Of course, these motives will often interact in practice. Rent seekers and politicians will often appeal to those theories and "facts" that will most effectively persuade sincere but misinformed citizens.

On the epistemic model of democracy, deliberation ideally aims at reaching the best social policies by spawning public awareness of the best available normative and empirical views. Yet, if the incentives of all the relevant political actors run in the opposite direction, deliberators will predictably offer and endorse unsound arguments. Political discourse, then, fails when judged by the standards set by the epistemic model. Rational ignorance is compounded by rational error, and rent seekers and politicians will typically fuel citizens' error by making easily available to them those theories and "facts" that would command rational belief given their previous beliefs.[30] Goldman's terminology helps us see the extent of the discursive pathology involved here. A citizen C can be in one of three possible epistemic states regarding a true proposition P: C may either believe P, or withhold judgment on P, or reject P. In order to assess the amount of *social* knowledge, we can assign the following values to each of those states. If C believes P, the value is 1.0. If C withholds judgment on P, the value is 0.5. If C rejects P, the value is 0.[31] If, as we suggest, most poorly informed people will not suspend judgment on many political issues, the amount of social knowledge will not be as high as if those same people did suspend judgment. This is because the mistaken

---

[29] We further discuss the sense in which citizens' ignorance and error are rational in section 3.1.

[30] Again, we defer full discussion of the epistemic and instrumental aspects of rationality involved in this proposition until section 3.1.

[31] Goldman, *Knowledge in a Social World*, op. cit., p. 89.

yet convinced citizen will contribute 0 to social knowledge of political issues. Interestingly, discursive pathologies are less common in the public's attitudes toward the hard sciences. This may strike us as odd, but it is just a consequence of the fact that people who are uninformed about the hard sciences usually do suspend judgment. So, using Goldman's framework, we suggest that social knowledge of the hard sciences increases at a rate of 0.5 per each uninformed citizen – a higher rate than the one expected for the social sciences. There is here, then, a noticeable difference between the social and the hard sciences: The truth is that dabbling in physics is not socially acceptable, whereas dabbling in economics is. People err about the social world because they have ingrained theories about how society works. In contrast, in the modern world at least, people generally do not have similarly unreliable ingrained views about the physical world, if only because they have no views at all on many areas of physics.

In the past, people did have ingrained views about the physical world that we now find highly unreliable. Even well-educated people believed for centuries that the sun rotated around the Earth. After all, this view seemed to be borne out by massive and easily available observations. We now have, however, socially accepted educational processes that undermine the geocentric theory that was supposed to best explain those observations. Most people get rid of the mistake when the schoolteacher tells them that the Earth rotates around the sun.[32] There is no analogous process in many of the areas subject to political deliberation. Even respectable venues, such as prestigious newspapers, spread views about trade that, as we saw (section 2.1), would be summarily dismissed by serious economists (say, the view that free trade will in general increase unemployment). Notice, by the way, that no society teaches its children the basic propositions of reliable trade theory; that study is largely reserved to economists and a few other specialists. In an important sense captured by the foregoing notion of amount of social knowledge, political illiteracy is more widespread than hard-science illiteracy.

---

[32] The reader trained in the philosophy of science might point out that our description of the change from the geocentric to the heliocentric view relies on controversial "realistic" views of science. It might be said, for example, that a gain in simplicity (but not in descriptive accuracy or predictive power) motivated the adoption of the heliocentric view. However, these possibilities do not affect our main point: Massive evidence led everyone (and leads young children today) to believe that the geocentric theory was (is) true, and the view accepted by scientists today (whether on grounds of simplicity, descriptive accuracy, or predictive power) is *more difficult to understand.*

It is not surprising that elementary schools make significant contributions to citizens' literacy on the natural sciences, whereas they remain largely silent on many social theories that are relevant to understanding political issues. Imagine what would happen if politicians and school boards included the fundamentals of trade theory in the school curriculum, appropriately simplified in much the same way as other complex social or historical subjects (such as history or government) are now simplified. If we are correct, this curricular innovation would likely meet with bitter resistance from groups that benefit from subsidies, tariffs, and other trade barriers. These groups would employ a rhetoric (e.g., the need to protect domestic industries and jobs) that is more persuasive to ordinary citizens than the relatively complex arguments that the proponents of the curricular reform will use to substantiate the curricular change. Because educational authorities are sensitive to the electoral impact of vivid rhetoric, they will not include trade theory in the curriculum. If pressed for an explanation, they might say that trade theory is too controversial to form part of elementary teaching subjects. But this can mean only that groups affected by trade liberalization will get angry, not that serious economists contest trade theory. The ambiguity of the concept of "a controversial issue" allows politicians and others to appear as making a social-epistemological point (trade theory is contested among experts), when in reality they are making a political point (affected groups will strongly oppose those proposals). We further discuss education as an antidote to discourse failure in section 3.2.

2.3. Patterns of Political Belief

One would think that the diversity of views contained in readily available sources of information, such as newspapers and television shows, would be reflected in a diverse public opinion. The alternation in power between political parties seems to reflect such diversity. We will not pursue empirical questions about the specific political beliefs held by various categories of people. We argue, instead, that some underlying *patterns* of political belief will tend to prevail, whatever political differences people may have at a more superficial level (e.g., Democrats vs. Republicans, conservatives vs. liberals, environmentalists vs. industrialists, and so forth). Political views that people can apprehend at low cost to themselves share some structural features. Some examples may help.

Compare two possible explanations of interest rates that the public perceives as high. On one explanation, high rates are caused by greedy lenders. On the other, they are caused by the convergence of supply and demand of present control of resources.[33] The former is an explanation in terms of usury, the latter in terms of prices. The usury explanation is easier to understand than the explanation in terms of prices. Usury explanations appeal to human design (the greed of lenders). They are visible-hand explanations, in a sense that we will shortly explicate. Also, they conform to a zero-sum model of social interaction[34]: They portray lenders as exploiting borrowers. By contrast, the explanation in terms of prices appeals to the impersonal workings of the market – an invisible hand. It also relies on a positive-sum model of social interaction wherein borrowers, lenders, and (at least in a competitive economy) the public at large will benefit from interest rates largely determined by the free market. How much the market should determine interest rates (as opposed to, say, so-called "open market" operations, used by central banks to control the money supply) is a controversial issue among economists. But, revealingly, many people who call for legislative action against "excessive" interest rates rarely invoke the monetary theories that underlie open market operations and sometimes even appeal to usury and like concepts (abuse, greed) that divert public attention from the factors that cause "excessive" interest rates.

Now consider this other example. The government justifies a subsidy to farmers by extolling the values and lifestyle of farming.[35] Each taxpayer thinks that the benefits to farmers offset the negligible cost to him *qua* taxpayer. So people will generally tend to see the subsidy as a positive-sum game, rather than as what it really is – redistribution. In the eyes of the public, farmers, and somehow society at large, will benefit well in excess of the social cost. However, this view ignores the costs of rent seeking and the deadweight losses of artificial changes in relative prices.[36] When

---

[33] See Paul Heyne, "Interest," in *The Concise Encyclopedia of Economics*, available at http://www.econlib.org/library/Enc/Interest.html.

[34] Game theory defines a zero-sum game as an interaction in which one party gains if and only if the other party loses: The sum total of payoffs is zero. A positive-sum game is one in which some parties gain while no one loses. A negative-sum game is one in which both parties lose.

[35] For the arguments given by U.S. President George W. Bush in 2002 for the $190 billion farm subsidies enacted that year, see "Cringe for Mr. Bush," *The Washington Post*, May 14, 2002, Editorial, p. A20.

[36] A deadweight loss is the net social loss caused by a tax, including protectionist measures such as tariffs or subsidies – that is, a loss that no one recoups. For a general analysis of the economic inefficiencies caused by government subsidies, see K. Obeng, A. H. M. Golam Azan, and R. Sakano, *Modeling Economic Inefficiency Caused by Public Transit Subsidies* (Westport, Conn.: Praeger, 1997), pp. 31–9. For a demonstration that long-term

such drawbacks are properly taken into account, it is at least plausible to maintain that the farm subsidy program is a negative-sum game.[37]

The usury and subsidy examples illustrate a general phenomenon in political discourse: People are more likely to believe *vivid* theories of society. Vivid theories are easy to believe, in the sense that they trade on readily available "evidence" that fits into our unreflective theoretical mindset. But when is a theory vivid?

Facts that we directly perceive are vivid, especially if they are recent. We tend to assign disproportional importance to these vivid facts, and the theories of society that we hold will accordingly reflect that importance.[38] Psychologists define vivid information as that which is "(a) emotionally interesting, (b) concrete and imagery-provoking, and (c) proximate in a sensory, temporal, or spatial way."[39] For example, we will feel more indignant about a heinous crime if we watch the gory details on the evening news.[40] If the newscaster also tells us that the suspect was out of prison on a "technicality," we will overstate the relevance of the crime as confirmatory evidence for the theory that heinous crimes are due to the leniency of the justice system.[41]

losses of subsidies exceed short-term gains, see Jérôme Adda and Russell Cooper, "Balladourette and Juppette: A Discrete Analysis of Scrapping Subsidies," *Journal of Political Economy*, Vol. 108, no. 4 (August 2002), pp. 778–806. For a formal analysis of special-interest protection, see Gene Grossman and Elhanan Helpman, "Protection for Sale," op. cit.

[37] For a graphic demonstration, see, for example, Thomas Pugel and Peter Lindert, *International Economics* (Boston: Irwin–McGraw Hill, 11th edition, 2002), pp. 130–2.

[38] This was noted forty years ago by Philip Converse in his seminal essay on public opinion: "Where potential political objects are concerned [the public's processing of information] tends to [go from] abstract 'ideological' principles to the more obviously recognizable social groupings or charismatic leaders and finally to such objects of immediate experience as family, job, and immediate associates." Philip E. Converse, "The Nature of Belief Systems in Mass Politics," op. cit., p. 213.

[39] Richard Nisbett and Lee Ross, *Human Inferences: Strategies and Shortcomings of Social Judgment* (Englewood Cliffs, N.J.: Prentice-Hall, 1980), p. 45. See also Michel Tuan Pham, Tom Meyvis, and Rongrong Zhou, "Beyond the Obvious: Chronic Vividness of Imagery and the Use of Information in Decision Making," *Organizational Behavior and Human Decision Processes*, Vol. 84, no. 2, March 2001, p. 228. For further discussion of cognitive psychology, see below in this section.

[40] See Tuan Pham, Meyvis, and Zhou, "Beyond the Obvious: Chronic Vividness of Imagery and the Use of Information in Decision Making," op. cit., p. 228.

[41] As Nisbett and Ross point out, the degree of concreteness (i.e., the degree of detail about actors, actions, and situational context) enhances the emotional impact of the information. See *Human Inferences*, op. cit., p. 47. See also the discussion of the relevance of this attitude for the theory of deliberative democracy in Philip Pettit, "Depoliticizing Democracy," *Ratio Juris*, Vol. 17, no. 1, March 2004, p. 52.

Simple causal chains are vivid as well, although in many cases the two types of vividness (perceptual/temporal and causal) are intertwined. Consider first social theories that treat aggregate outcomes as the product of human actions having disparate aims. Adam Smith's famous passage on the benefits bestowed on society by self-interested agents interacting in free markets nicely exemplifies this kind of explanation:

> It is not from the benevolence of the butcher, the brewer, or the baker that we expect our dinner, but from their regard to their own interest. We address ourselves, not to their humanity but to their self-love, and never talk to them of our own necessities but of their own advantages ... [The individual] neither intends to promote the public interest, nor knows how much he is promoting it ... he intends only his own gain and he is in this, as in many other cases, led by an invisible hand to promote an end which was no part of his intention.[42]

Invisible-hand explanations are opaque, counterintuitive. For example, Smith explains prosperity in terms of myriad actions aimed at local outcomes dictated by self-interest. Similarly, the theory of comparative advantages discussed in section 2.1 is highly counterintuitive. By contrast, visible-hand explanations are vivid because they appeal to human design – typically, an easily identifiable agent intending to bring about the outcome we want to explain. Many people tend to view general prosperity as the result of someone (citizens, the government) pursuing it, rather than as the result of each one pursuing their narrow self-interest. On this view, general prosperity stems from widespread altruism or patriotism (everybody's disposition to "unite and pull in the same direction," everybody's disposition to "do his or her share" for the sake of general prosperity, etc.) or from political leaders' charisma, public-spiritedness, or vision. These visible-hand explanations trade on short-term effects of policies. When government seeks to alleviate poverty by handing out goods to the poor, it is natural to relate the recipients' immediate improvement to governmental action, *and to believe that this improvement exhausts the impact of those policies, including their impact on the poor.* This reasoning frequently overlooks more serious losses by those same recipients or other poor people in the long term, because of disincentives to productive activities. Such disincentives are hidden to the public because they involve complex causal mechanisms, like increased unemployment as a result of stronger fiscal pressure on productive activities,

---

[42] Adam Smith, *An Inquiry into the Nature and the Causes of the Wealth of Nations*, Book I, Chapter 2 and Book V, Chapter 2.

bureaucratic waste, disincentives to work, and restrictions on poor immigrants.[43]

There are other examples of invisible-hand explanations. Let us go back to the example of prices in competitive markets. The price of a product results from the convergence of supply and demand: It is the aggregate outcome of many individual actions aimed at different, local objectives. In a sufficiently competitive market, no individual seller or buyer can set the price of a product; nor is the price the result of collusive behavior by sellers. Likewise, consider the explanation of the success of moderate positions in electoral competitions. Politicians seek to win elections by appealing to the voter located at the median of a political spectrum, because addressing other voters would put them at risk of being outflanked by their opponents.[44] Although each politician seeks to maximize the votes she receives and might not be particularly interested in advancing moderate political views, the aggregate effect of electoral strategies is the victory of a moderate platform. Here again, politicians have not colluded to advance moderate positions. Indeed, we need not even assume that they genuinely endorse moderate positions.

Invisible-hand mechanisms are not the only source of opaque explanations. When a social phenomenon is the consequence of political decisions taken long ago, explanations that refer to those decisions tend to be opaque as well. Thus, current high interest rates, which discourage investment and raise unemployment, may reflect borrowing incurred by governments long ago to raise money for immediate, perceptible spending to the benefit of various groups. Similarly, current low retirement payments may be caused by former uses of retirement funds for various perceptible governmental programs. The general point is that long-term effects of current political decisions are typically harder to understand than short-term streams of costs and benefits. This epistemic shortcoming explains the public's support for present policies that predictably will cause economic hardship in, say, ten years. Arguably, such policies would not enjoy so much support had citizens anticipated the bad consequences. The fact that they do support those policies reflects discourse failure on the part of citizens and fosters discourse failure on

---

[43] See Tyler Cowen, "Does the Welfare State Help the Poor?," *Social Philosophy and Policy*, Vol. 19, no. 1, Winter 2002, pp. 36–54.

[44] The proposition in the text is a rough formulation of the median voter theorem. See Dennis Mueller, *Public Choice* (Cambridge: Cambridge University Press, 1979), pp. 98–111.

the part of politicians and other groups that benefit from policies biased toward the present.

One might object that citizens who discount distant effects in their current decisions are not erring. They reason as borrowers do. Borrowers are willing to return a sum of money greater than the loan they enjoy now – a disposition that is reflected in the interest rate they pay. But surely, the objection goes, no one claims that markets for money fail for this reason. Just as there is no market failure[45] when the borrower discounts the future, so citizens are not victims of discourse failure when they discount the future.

To be sure, both the borrower and the citizen are biased toward the present, in the sense that they discount future effects in making current decisions. Yet, the citizen and the borrower are different in one crucial respect. The borrower has full knowledge of the discount rate – he knows how much interest he will have to pay for the loan he takes. Interest rates are transparent. The citizen, on the other hand, is unaware of personal and social costs of current policies, especially if those costs will be borne in the long run. While both the borrower and the citizen are biased toward the present, only the citizen is *shortsighted*.[46] The borrower discounts the future streams of costs and benefits of the alternatives open to her – that is, to invest the amount borrowed and later repay the loan plus the interest rate, and to go on with less investment and less financial burden. She has obvious incentives to get things right because the total benefits and costs of his decision whether to borrow money will fall entirely on her. Moreover, she can calculate easily because she can use available information about interest rates and other prices. In contrast, the rational citizen, being sensitive to the personal costs of acquiring accurate information, is *mistaken* about future streams of politically generated costs and benefits. Typically, then, politicians will succeed in hiding from citizens the long-term costs of current policies. The citizen faces an epistemic barrier that is attributable to her lack of incentives to acquire political information. Unlike the borrower, the citizen cannot easily identify the reliable sources of information about future streams of costs of alternative policies.

Consider now explanations where either gains or losses are concentrated, and for that reason noticeable – for example, the view that poverty is the result of extraordinary gains by the rich. This explanation is vivid

---

[45] We define market failure shortly.
[46] See Mueller, *Public Choice*, op. cit., pp. 150–6.

because it appeals to elementary arithmetic. A given output is held constant, and any group of people can in principle be made better off by transferring wealth from another group. The metaphor of "slicing a pie" is here quite appropriate. One person's affluence is seen as the cause of another person's poverty.[47] This analysis asks no questions about the effects of redistributions on the size of the output – the pie. Indeed, many popular conceptions of justice focus on the allocation of resources and not on their production, although, as we will see in section 2.5, discourse failure often affects appeals to productive efforts as bases of desert too.

Such views invoke a zero-sum mechanism: Some gain if and only if others lose. Zero-sum mechanisms usually provide vivid explanations because of their arithmetic simplicity. Positive-sum explanations, on the other hand, tend to be harder to apprehend because they run counter to the ingrained intuition that resources remain constant, at least in the foreseeable future. However, sometimes a positive-sum explanation is easier to grasp. Consider the foregoing example of farmer subsidies. The public sees them as a positive-sum game, even though, as we saw, providing farmer subsidies is arguably a zero-sum or negative-sum game. Because the costs of the subsidy are dispersed, people are easily led to believe that no one loses. This public perception reflects the fact that costs are dispersed and (as a result) individually low, and benefits are concentrated on individuals seen as deserving (farmers convey an image of hard and honest work). It may be important for this perception that benefits not be *too* concentrated: Most likely, people receiving such benefits will not be seen as deserving.[48] Viewing farmer subsidies as a positive-sum game leads people to believe that the government awards those subsidies to benefit some without thereby harming anyone. This appearance is more salient if the tax system provides the taxpayer with no simple means to track a subsidy to his tax burden. Accordingly, we should expect that beneficiaries of subsidies will resist moves to simplify the tax system, especially if they make each taxpayer's share in the subsidy transparent. Widespread beliefs about the distribution of costs and benefits explain why positive-sum views have sometimes rhetorical advantages over their negative-sum (and more plausible) rival.

---

[47] There is just a short step to concluding that the rich person is responsible for the plight of the poor person.

[48] The fact that farmer subsidies in the United States benefit thousands of households might partially explain why those subsidies enjoy wide popular support.

Vivid explanations get additional credibility in the eyes of the ordinary citizen because he possesses massive confirmatory evidence. After all, we constantly see around us people gaining at the expense of others: We lose things that others find and keep, we read in the newspapers about robberies and other forms of plunder, our child is keenly aware of the connection between our giving a slice of the pie to his brother and the size of the slice he receives, a governor opens a new public school to benefit students in this neighborhood and with no losers in sight. It seems natural to generalize from this evidence in order to explain all gains and losses in society. Our everyday experience, then, seems to call for explanations that belong to one or more of the categories we already mentioned: visible-hand, zero-sum with concentrated benefits or costs, and positive-sum with dispersed costs. Moreover, in each of these categories the vividness of an explanation has a positive correlation with the simplicity of the causal route that gains and losses are supposed to take – this is why short-term causality in general adds to vividness. Given the rational ignorance effect, vivid theories enjoy rhetorical advantages in political deliberation.

There is no obvious way to overcome the opacity that often charac-terizes reliable social explanations. Suppose that most people, through education, learn the law of supply and demand. Still, the average citi-zen will have difficulty extending the law to domains other than those discussed in usual introductory illustrations. They see how supply and demand govern the behavior of sellers and buyers of wheat, apples, cars, and the other goods commonly used in textbook illustrations. They also see, let us assume, that should the government set the price of apples below the price resulting from the convergence of supply and demand, there would be a shortage of apples. Many people, however, have trou-ble connecting a *minimum* price of *wages* with *overabundance* of labor (or, to put it differently, unemployment). As a consequence, they will likely oppose price control for apples but support minimum wage laws, notwithstanding the fact that the same law of supply and demand that predicts a shortage of apples also predicts unemployment.[49] To be sure, minimum wage laws are sometimes defended on moral grounds. Some-one may claim that certain transactions, such as the exchange of labor for what he views as a meager salary, are inherently objectionable. We shall

---

[49] Or, more accurately: notwithstanding the fact that the same logic that led them to predict a shortage of apples should lead them to predict unemployment, unless they can indicate where other things are not equal in relevant respects. We briefly describe the *status quaestionis* on the minimum wage in section 6.9.

examine this line of argument in section 6.4. However, the argument sometimes takes a different form: Some argue that the economic laws which govern the exchange of apples *cannot possibly* govern the exchange of labor. People (including academics outside economics) often claim that the observation that minimum wages create unemployment evinces an "unduly economic" or "efficiency-driven" approach to the issue of labor. By this, they presumably mean that the economic approach misses something important: "Economics doesn't explain everything." It is hard to pinpoint exactly what the objection is here. Perhaps the objector means that an efficient solution to a social problem may nonetheless be objectionable on moral grounds. This position may be tenable, on condition that it is adequately supported by moral premises and passes what we will call "The Display Test" in section 6.2. The point here is that, notwithstanding its ostensible hostility to economics, this is not a challenge to any predictive use of economics but simply the familiar point that sometimes efficiency is trumped by moral (e.g., distributional) considerations.

But this rhetorical strategy ("Economics doesn't explain everything") has a less savory function, explained by the theory of discourse failure. Those who benefit from the rhetorical advantages of opacity have an obvious incentive to use rhetorical devices to block transparency-enhancing approaches to social and political issues. Thus, if I, an artist, want the government to benefit me by granting me a subsidy, I will enjoy rhetorical advantages if I succeed in concealing from the public the opportunity cost of the art subsidy – the value of forgone alternatives. More generally, special interests will score a decisive rhetorical victory if they can strike a preemptive blow against economics – the most powerful intellectual tool for identifying the full costs, including the less visible ones, of political proposals. Thus, appeals to the alleged specificity of human affairs that supposedly render them intractable by the tools of economics, or more generally rational choice theory, are all to be expected from those who stand to lose from the role of economics in rendering costs transparent.

This brings us to yet another form of discourse failure. Often, people hostile to the use of economics will appeal to notions that are vague or obscure. For example, many Latin Americans objected in the 1990s to economic arguments showing that state enterprises were wasteful and offered low-quality services. The idea was that state enterprises are required by the ideals of nation, sovereignty, or community and that economic analysis cannot help us achieve those ideals. That this rhetoric is notoriously vague and obscure is not to its detriment. Quite to the contrary, it has a stirring effect in the public, in part because many people have a vague belief that what benefits the nation benefits each of us. But it may also be that evolutionary pressures operated on humans to develop those beliefs. Tribal attachments seem to have played an adaptive role in stages of human evolution where endorsing strong notions of strict group liability and communal property had survival value. After millennia of human interaction where economies of subsistence and nomadism made no room for the opaque idea of mutual gains from trade, individuals who developed vivid worldviews may have had adaptive advantages. Perhaps individuals with collectivistic dispositions had adaptive advantages over less collectivistic individuals, and tribes thus composed had in turn advantages over less collectivistic ones in the struggle for scarce resources.[50] Arguably, the evolutionary pressures toward the elimination of those psychological traits operate at a slower pace than the change in the technological conditions that made those traits adaptive at the tribal stage.[51] Evolution made those views so ingrained in us that replacing them with the opaque findings of reliable social science may

[50] See F. A. Hayek, *Law, Legislation, and Liberty* (Chicago: University of Chicago Press, 1976), Vol. 2, pp. 133–52. After surveying the literature on the evolutionary forces that have instilled certain patterns of behavior in animals, Robert Nozick speculates that "intelligent organisms capable of conscious thought, planning, control of impulses, etc. are similarly advantaged... Our higher capacities have been selected for because of the benefits they bring." See Robert Nozick, *Invariances: The Structure of the Objective World* (Cambridge, Mass.: Harvard University Press, 2001), p. 243.

[51] Harold Demsetz argues that technological changes alter relative prices and hence make private appropriation of some communal things profitable. See Harold Demsetz, "Toward a Theory of Property Rights," *American Economic Review* 57, 1967, pp. 347–9. For interesting speculation that evolutionary pressures have not had time to adapt the patterns of reasoning prevailing in the hunter-gatherer days to the circumstances created by the introduction of property, writing, and modern technology, and that this disharmony explains the findings of cognitive psychology that we shall shortly discuss, see Richard A. Epstein, *Skepticism and Freedom* (Chicago: University of Chicago Press, 2003), pp. 199–200. See also Owen D. Jones, "Time-Shifted Rationality and the Law of Law's Leverage: Behavioral Economics Meets Behavioral Biology," *Northwestern University Law Review*, Vol. 95, p. 1141 (2001). The convergence toward animistic, normative interpretive frameworks (as opposed to mechanistic, causal ones) everywhere in tribal cultures is not only evidence of evolutionary pressures over extended periods of time. It also helps explain the resilience of visible-hand explanations today. For a detailed anthropological and philosophical study of the interpretive mindset of tribal cultures, with illuminating hypotheses about the transformation of the primitive notion of design into the scientific notion of causation, see Hans Kelsen, *Society and Nature: A Sociological Inquiry* (London: Kegan Paul, 1946).

be quite costly. The fact that some of those beliefs are obscure has not prevented them from having had adaptive value in the past, provided that they generated the behavioral patterns conducive to inclusive fitness. Theoretical beliefs ingrained in us by evolution should be added, then, to those resulting from inductive generalizations from easily available evidence to the list of beliefs that people come to hold effortlessly, without deliberate investment in information and analysis. We will say that these two types of beliefs are held *by default*.[52]

It is hard to overestimate the role played by default beliefs in the spread of discourse failure. Here we want to point to a particularly insidious mechanism. When we hold someone morally responsible, we rely on causal beliefs. We tend to hold responsible those who caused an outcome, or those who, contrary to our expectations, failed to interrupt (by initiating causal processes of their own) causal processes leading to that outcome.[53] Politicians who would be hurt should the public realize they have caused an unpalatable outcome tend accordingly to deceive the public by manipulating the causal explanations of those outcomes. The politician's hope is that the public will locate certain causal explanations within default theories that in turn exonerate the politician. Here is an example: In those countries where the state owns public utilities or heavily regulates them, governments have populist reasons to set below-market utility rates. There might be circumstances, however, where rate increases

---

[52] Default beliefs need not be *unjustified,* even if those who hold them may have unreflectively obtained them. As Kent Bach writes, "[p]erceptual judgment, recall, recognition, and understanding utterances are all clear cases of generally reliable jumping to conclusions." Kent Bach, "A Rationale for Reliabilism," in Sven Bernecker and Fred Dretske, eds., *Knowledge: Readings in Contemporary Epistemology* (Oxford: Oxford University Press, 2000), pp. 199–213, at pp. 211–12. According to Bach, such a jumping leads to *justified beliefs* (though the *cognizer is not justified* in holding them) because the cognizer follows (though not explicitly) the following principle:

   Its appearing to one that *p* justifies directly inferring that *p* provided that

   (a) it does not occur to one that the situation might be out of the ordinary, and
   (b) if the situation were out of the ordinary, it probably would occur to one that the situation might be out of the ordinary. (Quoted from op. cit., p. 212.)

Following terminology used in artificial intelligence, Bach defends a "default conception of reasoning" that partially overlaps with our notion of "beliefs held by default" (op. cit., pp. 207–10). Yet his focus is different from ours, because he is mainly concerned with defending reliabilism (see section 3.1) rather than with showing that in some domains (what we would call) default beliefs are systematically false.

[53] See H. L. A. Hart and Tony Honoré, *Causation in the Law,* 2nd ed. (Oxford: Clarendon Press, 1985), pp. 62–83.

are unavoidable because of rising costs (imagine that the government has decreed a huge devaluation, forced by its own wasteful policies, and that the utilities companies import most of their equipment). Suppose further that, in the absence of rate increases, electricity supply will collapse – something that will be politically costly to the government. Incumbent politicians will then be well advised to increase rates while diverting their responsibility onto third parties. They may therefore authorize utility companies to charge higher electricity rates to big businesses only, and not to households. Such businesses will then be forced to raise the prices for the goods they market, thereby attracting the public's condemnation of their "greed." In this way, incumbent politicians would have successfully exploited default, visible-hand price theories based on big business's greed. They would have led the public to believe that big business is primarily responsible for the general price increase.[54] In general, then, governments will bring about their preferred outcomes through those causal routes that effectively take advantage of citizens' default theories and the ascriptions of responsibility stemming from them.

Sometimes a political deliberator eager to convince an audience of the validity of a theory *T* needs only to point to a single fact, on the assumption that that fact, processed in the light of the audience's default theories, will be taken to confirm *T*. Here is a telling example: In the late 1990s in Argentina, media opposed to free-market ("neoliberal") policies allotted considerable time in the news to showing images of "poor people grilling cats for food in Rosario," the second largest Argentine city.[55] Public opinion was thus exposed to further evidence of the evils brought about by "neoliberal" policies, which were by that time vastly unpopular. The sheer fact of cat eating triggered, through default theories, the theoretical belief that "neoliberal" policies were causing poverty. Notice that our main point would remain even if the television images were bogus: Default theories make it politically profitable to allege certain types of bogus "facts."[56] Or consider a less dramatic example: the

---

[54] For a current illustration, taken from Argentina's politics, see "Desde enero, aumentan luz a empresas (no a hogares)," *Ámbito Financiero*, Buenos Aires, December 8, 2004.

[55] See Ricardo Luque, "En una villa comen animales domésticos para sobrevivir," *La Nación*, Buenos Aires, May 8, 1996, available at http://www.lanacion.com.ar/172344.

[56] To the best of our knowledge, no cat-eating or similarly vivid manifestations of destitution were reported by the media since a new administration, more in line with anti–free-market views, took office in January 2001, even though the huge financial crisis of 2001–2 brought about far more serious unemployment and poverty.

images, shown in American television with some frequency, of farmers forced to foreclose on their farms. Here the sheer fact of foreclosure, through default theories, is taken as evidence that free trade in agricultural products cannot possibly benefit "America."

A noteworthy case of this form of discourse failure is political art. Many people regard works of art as legitimate vehicles for political views. Indeed, many have insisted that artists *ought* to be politically committed.[57] The aesthetic experience may raise people's awareness about political and social problems. And, if one believes in certain moral-political truths, it seems natural to recommend that artists convey those truths in a way people can readily understand. Thanks to the emotional power of beauty, art can, at least sometimes, help noble ideals reach the general public. The tradition of political art is old and venerable; it comprises many of the most sublime works ever created – examples are Aristophanes' satires, Pablo Picasso's *Guernica*, Aldous Huxley's *Brave New World*, and Serguei Eisenstein's *Potemkin*. Yet not all political art is high art, accessible mostly to connoisseurs. Popular culture harbors songs of protest and political movies addressed to massive audiences.[58]

Many of these works have great artistic value, and some of them have surely contributed to worthy causes. However, from the point of view of a theory of discourse failure, political art is a refined version of the rhetorical mechanisms that we saw at work in the "cats as food" example. Art is a type of concrete imagery, and as such it evokes a "fact" that may activate default theories in the audience. Those willing to challenge the political stances generated by this process confront the increased cost of overcoming the suggestive power of the beauty inherent in the artistic imagery. Here is an example: A painting shows two impoverished Mexican peasant women with a partially clothed child standing between them. To the left are the bodies of two slain peasants, bleeding from their mouths. On the top of the scene is a portrait of the American banker J. P. Morgan. Close by, the observer can identify the then–Mexican president, Plutarco Elías Calles, dressed as an armed bandit with money bags at his feet.

---

57 In the opening paragraph of his entry on aesthetic judgment, Nick Zangwill observes that "to suggest, in the recent climate, that an artwork might be pleasurable, as opposed to cognitively, morally or politically beneficial, is to court derision." Nick Zangwill, "Aesthetic Judgment," *The Stanford Encyclopedia of Philosophy* (Fall 2003 Edition), Edward N. Zalta, ed., URL http://plato.stanford.edu/archives/fall2003/entries/aesthetic-judgment/.

58 Most political art is from the left, though there is, of course, conservative or patriotic art – Toby Keith's country songs, for example. Why most artists are left-wing we explain, *mutatis mutandi*, in section 2.7.

Finally, at the opposite end of the painting we see a communist soldier bearing a rifle.[59] Given the default theories held by an average viewer, this painting will have, we submit, the following effects on the viewer: It will induce the belief that capitalism, imperialism, poverty, and death are interconnected in a way that leaves radical change as the only remedy. Or, if the viewer already believes that, the painting will move her to political action of a sort. The causal connections suggested by the painting fit nicely into the patterns of discourse failure that, for the reasons already indicated, permeate theories that people hold by default: Visible-hand and zero-sum mechanisms are particularly salient here (poverty and death are caused by a regime subservient to powerful foreign economic interests).[60]

Concreteness is a feature shared by documentaries (as in the "cats as food" example) and political art. In both cases the author avoids arguing for a political position; instead, she depicts a concrete fact in the hope that it will activate the theories that the audience holds by default. They differ in one interesting respect, however. Documentaries show a poignant *fact* (hungry people grilling cats), whereas political artists are freer to imagine situations with various degrees of descriptive accuracy, including none at all. This does not prevent works of political art from being as effective as political documentaries, because they trade realism for beauty. The emotional effect of the documentary's poignant realism is matched by the uplifting aesthetic experience sparked by the work of art. Both usurp reasoned political argument.

Political satire is an interesting case. One reason it is particularly effective is that it generates an additional cost for those willing to challenge its purported message, for in that case the challenger becomes the "party pooper" who spoils the fun by taking the satire seriously. So comedians not only ridicule political figures or views. Whether intentionally or not, they also preempt objections to the intended political message ("Give me a break! Where is your sense of humor?").[61]

---

[59] We have just described the mural by the celebrated Mexican artist David Alfaro Siqueiros, *Portrait of Mexico Today*, 1932 (Museum of Santa Barbara, California). The crudeness of the discourse failure in this particular example does not exclude that Siqueiros's political views could be supported by sound argument.

[60] We do not pass judgment on whether the political message is inherently present in the work of art, independently intended by the artist, or placed in the work of art by the audience.

[61] The rhetorical strategy involved here conforms to what we will call "bootstrap arguments." See section 4.3.

Many people see political art as a healthy form of social criticism. For them, consuming and appreciating political art epitomizes the critical attitude. If we are correct, however, political art *hinders* critical *thinking*. It reinforces people's *fundamental* default beliefs, and sometimes it does so by questioning their *superficial* beliefs. Thus, a novel may convince someone that his prior belief in the kindness of the police is wrong, and that in reality the police are henchmen of the ruling class. No doubt this reader may regard this novel as having transformed his beliefs on the matter, and in that sense political art may be seen as challenging his beliefs. At a deeper level, however, the novel may well have appealed to the reader's default theories, for example by showing the role of the police in making some people rich at the poor's expense – a zero-sum explanation that, for the reasons already expounded, is inferior to explanations derived from reliable social science.

The theory of discourse failure is about the *structural features* of the views and theories that, we submit, will predominate in political deliberation. It is *not primarily* about the kinds of *policies* that a liberal democracy is likely to implement. Thus, world trade has been increasingly liberalized over recent decades, in spite of the fact that, as we saw, trade theory (which shows the advantages of liberalization) is noticeably opaque. This fact does not affect our theory of discourse failure, however. First, the theory can be undermined only by evidence that the predominant patterns of political discourse are not the ones it indicates. Second, what makes a politician win an election (discourse failure) is often not what makes him remain in power. Protectionist rhetoric may help a politician win labor votes, yet once in power he may realize that free-trade policies will help him remain in power. His advisors, for example, may tell him that free-trade policies will boost the economy – something that, for the reasons we indicated, would have been suicidal for him to argue publicly. This example shows that, to the extent that the theory of discourse failure is used to explain or predict public policy, it sometimes does so through indirect or seemingly paradoxical mechanisms.

Politicians have an incentive to spread vivid explanations, for the public will believe them given their default views. But this is not the only reason why politicians favor vivid explanations. Vivid explanations suggest that social problems are under someone's control (as opposed to their being the result of impersonal forces). Responsibility, not causation, is here the central concept. It seems a short step from this to conclude that the state (hence, politicians) should be summoned to make persons discharge such responsibilities in acceptable ways. By offering a vivid explanation, a speaker naturally leads the audience both to ascribe responsibilities for good or bad social outcomes and to acquiesce in increased governmental power.[62]

It might seem that the theory of discourse failure cannot explain the success of some opaque arguments. For example, many people support environmental protection. One standard argument in favor of environmental regulation relies on the notion of market failure, which is opaque. Economists define market failure as, roughly put, those situations in which unhampered markets would not reach outcomes that everyone would prefer to the status quo. Thus, free markets will not produce public goods such as national defense. Public goods are those commodities that possess these two features: (i) *nonrivalrous consumption* (consumption of the good by one person does not leave less for others), and (ii) *nonexcludability* (it is too expensive to exclude nonpaying consumers of the good). Consumers of a public good have an incentive to be *free riders* – that is, to rely for free on the productive efforts of others. For this reason, public goods will be underproduced unless the state provides the appropriate inducements to potential consumers, typically through taxation or regulations. The environmentalist version of the public goods argument maintains that we would all prefer to have certain environmental conditions (e.g., cleaner air), even sharing the costs of it, yet we free ride on the efforts of others to produce such conditions (reduce pollution). This is an invisible-hand, long-term argument, and as such opaque. The theory of market failure is invisible-hand because it explains an aggregate outcome in terms of individual behaviors having disparate aims. Each of us wants to drive cars to some extent, whatever the others do, and in doing so we reach a result (polluted air) that in terms of our preference rankings is inferior to an alternative cooperative result (cleaner air and driving to a lesser extent). Some environmentalist arguments appeal also to long-term effects – they recommend present sacrifices for the sake of benefits that will accrue to future generations. Yet, the objection concludes, the public does not seem to have difficulty grasping

---

[62] This is not always so. People's causal and normative beliefs might lead them to support a redistributive policy even without ascribing responsibility. Someone may recommend a redistributive policy for reasons of justice, even if he also believes no one is at fault. Someone might believe, for example, that distributive justice mandates incomes in proportion to effort. If he also believes that society is a zero-sum game, he might feel entitled to use coercion to redistribute resources in order to satisfy his standard of distributive justice. Someone may endorse a vivid theory of society without ascribing responsibility to particular individuals or groups.

this opaque environmentalist argument, as shown by the growing public support for environmental policies.

However, most people offer vivid reasons, rather than the public goods argument, in support of environmental measures. Environmentalist activism is more vocal when environmental damage is imminent and visible or when the polluters can be easily identified and blamed. We see everyday demonstrations against oil spillages, whale hunting, contamination of rivers, and the like. On the other hand, few protest against people's using spray containers or firms that produce them, even though, according to many scientific reports, the long-term effects of such products on the ozone layer may be devastating. Or take global warming caused by automobile fumes. While most people have perhaps realized that global warming is or may be a problem, few people understand its causes and impact.[63] Furthermore, no one seems to be protesting against drivers or automakers for this reason, even though, here again, the eventual harm may be great.[64] These facts suggest that environmentalist activists are more likely to condemn pursuits from which a few people benefit at the expense of environmental features valued by many others. Both in the cases of car fumes and whale hunting we easily identify the polluters (drivers, whale hunters). But only in the case of car fumes do we appreciate the total benefits of the activity: After all, most of us are polluters as a side effect of activities that benefit us. In contrast, the total benefits of whale hunting are hard to see because they result from complex causal processes. To be sure, many people can see that whale hunters will supply whale-derived products. But few people will attribute the reduction in prices in, say, vegetable oils to the availability of whale-derived oils.[65] The upshot is that few people have actually in mind market failure when they

---

[63] See K. R. Stamm, F. Clark, and P. R. Eblacas, "Mass communication and public understanding of environmental problems: The case of global warming," *Public Understanding of Science*, July 2000, Vol. 9, no. 3, p. 219 (people are aware of the problem in a general sense, but understanding of causes and impact is more limited); and Julia B. Corbett, Jessica L. Durfee, Roger D. Gunn, K. Maja Krakowjak, and Jeffrey T. Nellermoe, "Testing Public (Un)Certainty of Science: Media Representations of Global Warming," Paper presented to the 7th International Conference on Public Communication of Science and Technology, December 5, 2002, Cape Town, South Africa, available at www.hum.utah.edu/communication/classes/fa02/1600-1/africa.pdf (deficient media presentation of the issue influences the public's support for environmental measures).

[64] People do demonstrate against automakers in the case of defective cars that harm people. Notice that the perpetrator, the victim, and the harm are easily identifiable here.

[65] We are not suggesting here that, all things considered, legal restrictions on whale hunting are not a good thing. We are merely pointing to the opaqueness of the possible beneficial effects of whale hunting.

support environmental protection. Rather, most people seem to react to pollution when they see it as a zero- (if not negative-) sum game where the losses, though dispersed (lower environmental quality for all), are the result of visible deterioration of the environment.[66] We conclude, then, that, in general, the public's support for environmental policies does not rely on opaque (and reliable) explanations of environmental damage (although they may grasp in a vague sense a danger of future environmental damage). On the contrary, the public seems to support environmental regulation on vivid grounds.[67]

Significantly for our purposes, most vocal environmentalists advocate sweeping bans on polluting activities to protect the environment. Relatively few of them endorse incentive-based regulations, such as tradeable rights to pollute within efficiency constraints.[68] We do not take sides on which of these two approaches is preferable. Rather, our theory of discourse failure explains why virtually all nonspecialists favor the absolute ban.[69] People can easily grasp both "the problem" (say, extinction of whales) and its "solution" (government's halting indiscriminate hunting). Both ideas are vivid. Induced by vividness, people disproportionately support strong bans, as opposed to incentive-based schemes, such as some form of privatization of commons-like resources. The opaque market failure argument, and its nuanced implications for public policy, plays little if any role in the anti-industrialist rhetoric that informs much environmentalist activism.

---

[66] The *visibility* of losses is then the independent variable in this analysis of environmentalist discourse failure, *concentration* of losses (e.g., in some cases of river pollution) being instrumental to visibility. Whale hunting visibly affects whales (and so the environment), and this is enough to activate the environmentalist concern. Interestingly, people's psychological harms due to whale hunting are dispersed, which might make mobilization less likely. But here the decisive fact is the vividness of the defenseless cetaceans killed by harpoons.

[67] One example: The Sierra Club advocates a clean energy policy on the grounds that it would create jobs. See "Sierra Club Blasts Energy Policy Act," October 12, 2004, available at http://www.sierraclub.org/globalwarming/bluegreen.asp. Our point is not that this claim is false. Rather, it is that in order to motivate citizens to act politically, the Sierra Club appeals to vivid arguments that the public can relate to and not to the complicated opaque arguments that consider all the tradeoffs implicated in a sound scientific analysis of environmental policy.

[68] Some writers have suggested combining incentive-based recipes with environmental regulation. See, for example, Richard L. Revesz, "Rehabilitating Inter-State Competition: Rethinking the 'Race-to-the-Bottom' Rationale for Federal Environmental Regulation," *New York University Law Review*, Vol. 67 (1992), p. 1210.

[69] The closer students of the environment are to scholarly work, and so the further they are from political activism, the more likely they will seriously address incentive-based regulation. We discuss, however, academic discourse failure in section 2.6.

Interestingly, discourse failure is sometimes about discourse failure. Consider again some usual arguments for protectionism. In many developing countries, protectionists claim that free trade allows the powerful to prey on the weak. Thus, in Argentina politicians and politically connected domestic manufacturers have long persuaded the public that *el pez grande se come al pez chico* (big fish eats small fish). They usually supplement this mistaken view of trade with a conspiracy theory: The economic interests that manipulate American trade policy will spread free-trade views. Because these ideas are vivid and appeal to zero-sum processes, they enjoy a rhetorical advantage over standard international economics, which predicts various kinds of mutual benefits from free trade, even for poor people in both trade partners.[70] Now this rhetoric would be undermined were the public to learn that many *American firms* (and as we saw, the American public generally) oppose free trade: Indeed, if the Argentine conspiracy theory were true, American business interests would uniformly champion free trade. But, of course, this is not the case. To be sure, there are powerful pro–free-trade lobbies in the United States. Yet not only do many people support protectionist measures in the United States,[71] but they also use the exact opposite rhetoric: "Cheap labor" and "deficient environmental protection" overseas amount to "unfair trade practices." In short, *el pez chico se come al pez grande* (small fish eats big fish). Notwithstanding their superficial differences, both parties complain about the other's illegitimate competitive advantages. It is important for Argentine politicians and other political actors to supplement their discourse failure about trade with concealment of the discourse failure involved in the protectionist rhetoric used by their American counterparts. Not only that: In Argentina the same people who believe that American imports are instances of abuse by the powerful argue that imports from, say, Indonesia are objectionable because "they are made on the backs of the poor" – that is, by people subjected to deplorable working conditions. Notice two features in the trade example. First, political actors use mutually inconsistent trade theories in different deliberative settings, one for American imports and another for imports from developing countries. Second, political actors who promote a zero-sum theory of trade have an incentive to conceal the discourse failure that affects the prevailing rhetoric used by the trading partner. Discourse failure is effective here by concealing the discourse failure that affects the actual rhetoric of the supposed exclusive beneficiaries of free trade.

[70] See section 2.1.
[71] See notes 1 and 12 (section 2.1) and accompanying texts.

2.4. Discourse Failure and Cognitive Psychology

Our claim that the public holds vivid theories by default is supported by findings in cognitive psychology. Daniel Kahneman and Amos Tversky, among others, have experimentally shown that individuals tend to err in a variety of situations.[72] This literature embodies two central suggestions. First, thoughts differ in accessibility: Some thoughts are easier to access than others. Second, our cognitive apparatus has three layers, or levels of apprehension: the perceptual, the intuitive (which together form "System 1"), and the rational ("System 2"). Intuitive judgments occupy a position "between the automatic operations of perception and the deliberate operations of reasoning."[73] Individuals make a number of mistakes at the intuitive level, mistakes that cannot be easily corrected by the more deliberate system of reasoning. The idea of *accessibility*, that is, "the ease – or effort – with which particular mental contents come to mind,"[74] is key here. A number of factors, such as high emotion and motivation, influence and often impair accessibility. Likewise, the relevant experiments show that ways in which choices are framed can significantly affect the choices made – the "framing effect." In particular, people assess risk differently: If the risky choice is framed in terms of potential future losses, people are more risk seeking, whereas if the same choice is framed in terms of potential future gains, people become more risk averse.[75] The

---

[72] The research (by Kahneman-Tversky and others, spanning more than thirty years) is summarized in Daniel Kahneman, "A Perspective on Judgment and Choice: Mapping Bounded Rationality," *American Psychologist*, Vol. 58, p. 697 (2003) (hereinafter "A Perspective on Judgment"). The literature is voluminous. See especially the seminal article by Daniel Kahneman and Amos Tversky, "Prospect Theory: An Analysis of Decisions Under Risk," *Econometrica*, Vol. 47, pp. 263–91 (1979), and the essays collected in D. Kahneman and A. Tversky, eds., *Choices, Values, and Frames* (Cambridge: Cambridge University Press, 2000) and in T. Gilovich, D. Griffin, and D. Kahneman, eds., *Heuristic and Biases: The Psychology of Intuitive Judgment* (New York: Cambridge University Press, 2002); and D. Kahneman, A. Tversky, and P. Slovic, *Judgment Under Uncertainty: Heuristic and Biases* (New York: Cambridge University Press, 1982).

[73] Kahneman, "A Perspective on Judgment," p. 697.

[74] Kahneman, "A Perspective on Judgment," p. 699.

[75] That is to say: People will *risk more* to *avoid* losses than they would to make gains. Suppose we know that traffic accidents will kill 50,000 people next year. Two programs are proposed. If Program A is adopted, 30,000 people will be saved. If Program B is adopted, there is a one-third possibility that all 50,000 will be saved and a two-thirds possibility that no people will be saved. Experiments show that, naturally, most people are risk averse and choose to save 30,000 by adopting Program A. Now consider this different way of presenting the options on the same facts: If Program C is adopted, 20,000 will *die*. If Program D is adopted, there is a one-third probability that nobody will die and a two-thirds probability that all 50,000 will die. It is easy to see that options C and D are

upshot is that people will ordinarily reach judgments and form opinions that seem at variance both with straight classical rationality (i.e., with choice grounded on expected utility) and with dispassionate, reasoned examination of theory and evidence.

A subclass of cognitive errors is particularly important for our purposes: those caused by motivational and social factors. Consider the bias in favor of confirmatory evidence (and, correspondingly, *against* falsifying evidence). Thomas Gilovich writes:

> Our motivations... influence our beliefs through the subtle ways we choose a comforting pattern from the fabric of evidence. One of the simplest yet most powerful ways we do so lies in how we frame the very question we ask of the evidence. When we prefer to believe something, we may approach the relevant evidence by asking ourselves, "what evidence is there to support this belief?" If we prefer to believe that a political assassination was not the work of a lone gunman, we may ask ourselves about the evidence that supports a conspiracy theory. Note that this question is not unbiased: It directs our attention to supporting evidence and away from information that might contradict the desired conclusion. Because it is almost always possible to uncover *some* supportive evidence, the asymmetrical way we frame the question makes us overly likely to become convinced of what we hope to be true.[76]

If citizens' search for evidence is biased in this way, the theories they hold by default will be reinforced. The evidence that people seek, even with the conscious intentions of checking their already-held beliefs, will not have the function of falsifying those beliefs – just the opposite.

These cognitive dissonances increase for citizens the cost of becoming properly informed. These costs should be added to the costs of overcoming the opacity of the more reliable theories. To say that individuals tend to err in certain ways – in particular, that they form mistaken judgments when they are presented with certain vivid facts and their emotions and motivations are engaged – is to say that it is *costly* for them to activate their reasoning faculties ("System 2" in Kahneman's terminology),

---

undistinguishable from options A and B, respectively, in terms of expected utility, yet experiments show that most respondents chose D – that is, that they are risk seeking when the choices are framed negatively. This hypothetical is adapted from the famous Asian disease hypothetical by Kahneman and Tversky. See Daniel Kahneman and Amos Tversky, "Choices, Values, and Frames," in Kahneman and Tversky, eds., *Choices, Values, and Frames*, op. cit., p. 1. For an application to political decisions such as choosing political candidates and voting on referenda, see George A. Quattrone and Amos Tversky, "Contrasting Rational and Political Analyses of Political Choice," in *Choices, Values, and Frames* (D. Kahneman and A. Tversky, eds.) op. cit., p. 451.

[76] See Thomas Gilovich, *How We Know What Isn't So* (New York: Free Press, 1991), p. 81.

which could check the credentials of those judgments. In politics, the way in which individuals are affected by the cognitive quirks that this research identifies is this: Citizens will tend to believe intuitively the *theories* about society that best fit their vivid beliefs, defined in turn as those that their intuitive cognitive system (affected by bias, emotion, motivation, framing, asymmetrical risk evaluation, and so on) will favor. Most significantly, the research shows that these vivid beliefs (and, we add, the social theories that support them) stubbornly resist scrutiny by our reasoning cognitive apparatus,[77] a tendency that is surely aggravated by our limited *introspective* access to higher cognitive processes – that is, our relative inability to report accurately what beliefs caused us to act as we did.[78]

The language of cost can also account for the social and motivational causes of error. Consider the three categories discussed by Gilovich: bias toward confirmatory evidence, exaggerated value attached to hearsay, and appeal to (imaginary) social consensus.[79] It is cheaper for people to view every piece of evidence as confirming something they have already come to believe. If people approached the evidence impartially, in a scientific spirit, they would try to *test* their beliefs, not merely confirm them. While confirmation usually requires mere consistency with the facts,[80] testing involves more complex logical and experimental operations (think of Mill's methods). Similarly, speakers often attach too much value to second-hand information because they derive a *benefit* – namely, to chat pleasantly, to tell a "good" (i.e., entertaining) story. They value

---

[77] Work on belief acquisition further supports the point in the text and is thus congruent with our treatment of vividness. Daniel Gilbert has suggested that when we *understand* an idea we simultaneously *believe* it, and that therefore a further effort is needed to *reject* that idea. Acceptance and rejection are not symmetrical. See Daniel T. Gilbert, "How Mental Systems Believe," *American Psychologist*, Vol. 46, p. 107 (1991).

[78] See Richard E. Nisbett and Timothy DeCamp Wilson, "Telling More Than We Know: Verbal Reports On Mental Processes," *Psychological Review*, Vol. 84, no. 3 (May 1977), pp. 231–59. These authors drew three main conclusions from their research: (1) "People cannot report accurately on the effects of particular stimuli on higher order, inference-based responses"; (2) "When reporting on the effects of the stimuli, people may not interrogate a memory of the cognitive processes that operated on the stimuli; instead, they may base their reports *on implicit, a priori theories about the causal connection between stimulus and response*" (our emphasis; this suggests that people may have mistaken default theories about the causes of *their own* behavior); and (3) "Subjective reports about higher mental processes are sometimes correct, but even [these instances] are not due to direct introspective awareness [but to] incidentally correct employment of a priori causal theories." Id., p. 233.

[79] Gilovich, op. cit., pp. 88–122.

[80] Or, more accurately, people's *default theories of confirmation* (themselves cheaper to believe) require, in many contexts, just consistency with the facts.

the act of chatting, as it were.[81] And finally, it is less costly for us to convert others to our cause if we can invoke social consensus for it.[82] This is so, we suggest, because people believe by default that widespread political views are by and large correct or worthy of respect. Such default theories involve a mix of Bayesian intuitions (see section 4.7) about the epistemic credentials of consensus and normative views about the prima facie respectability of consensus. Moreover, people want to appear on the right side of a sensitive political issue (we extensively illustrate this phenomenon in the case of intellectuals in section 2.6).

There are two fatal problems with such appeals to consensus. First, to invoke social consensus in support of a theory is, in most cases, to commit the fallacy known as *argumentum ad populum*. A proposition is not made true by showing that many people believe it, especially in contexts plagued by discourse failure.[83] Second, if psychologists are right, we suffer from "a systematic defect in our ability to estimate the attitudes and beliefs of others,"[84] which in turn leads us to overestimate the degree of social support for our views. Indeed, it is quite common to hear political actors "spinning" statistics and opinion polls. They are, of course, insincerely trying to persuade – they know that their invocation of social consensus is bogus. The point here is that even a sincere citizen will usually accept the argument *ad populum* in favor of a belief if she is already inclined toward that belief. Citing agreement of others is, in short, a particularly vivid (and often fallacious) way to argue in politics.

Of course, this research is relevant to one source of discourse failure: the rational ignorance effect, because (but for the "spinning" politician just mentioned) the subjects in those experiments *believed* what they said. We can generalize and say that rational ignorance – that is, the ignorance that results from high information costs – encompasses the relative difficulty that citizens have in scrutinizing the intuitive vivid beliefs they routinely form (for example, by checking those beliefs against reliable social science). We can say, in our terminology, that ingrained tendencies to err reinforce discourse failure.[85]

---

[81] See Gilovich, *How We Know What Isn't So*, op. cit., pp. 90–3.

[82] We shall have occasion in section 3.1 to discuss the presuppositions about rationality that underlie the notion of cost in this analysis.

[83] We further discuss the epistemic credentials of consensus in section 4.7.

[84] Gilovich, op. cit., pp. 112–13.

[85] The fact that people suffer from ingrained cognitive failures (or other epistemic failures, for that matter) does not undermine the rational choice approach we adopt in this book. We discuss the issue extensively in section 3.1. For a criticism of the use of this research in law and public policy, see Gregory Mitchell, "Taking Behaviorism Too Seriously? The

Discourse failure as a societal phenomenon results, as we have said, from the mutually reinforcing interaction of rational ignorance and posturing against the background of redistributive politics. Political actors who stand to gain from spreading certain kinds of information will be helped by citizens who are willing to do their share, as it were, in the acquisition of confirmatory evidence of their default vivid beliefs. In other words, the cost of supplying convenient information is reduced by ingrained cognitive errors, and, correspondingly, those who want to change public opinion in the direction of opaque theories will face higher costs. Not only will they have to argue against vivid views that the public holds by default; they will also have to counter the psychological biases just discussed.

2.5. Persuasive Definitions

Certain forms of discourse failure involve persuasive definitions. It is well known that some words prompt emotional reactions to the actions, objects, or events they denote. Speakers can manipulate the attitudes of the audience by changing the descriptive meaning of words.[86] Various definitions of "democracy" are classical examples of this rhetorical technique. "Democracy" has positive connotations for most people, so political activists have an obvious interest in making it designate the political arrangement they favor (communism, the welfare state, limited government, etc.).

Persuasive definitions are rhetorically effective because they exempt deliberators from complex causal and normative analysis. Persons who are told that arrangement *A* is genuinely democratic will favor *A*, because they hold by default a theory of meaning ("essentialism," in one of the senses of this term) according to which each term invariably denotes a certain fact. (They have massive evidence for this theory.[87]) In politics,

Unwarranted Pessimism of the New Behavioral Analysis of the Law," *William and Mary Law Review*, Vol. 43, no. 5 (April 2002).

[86] See the seminal treatment in Charles L. Stevenson, *Ethics and Language* (New Haven, Conn.: Yale University Press, 1944), pp. 210–17. Cf. Simon Blackburn, *Ruling Passions: A Theory of Practical Reasoning* (Oxford: Clarendon Press, 1998), pp. 101–4.

[87] We speculate that there is a positive correlation between higher levels of education and acceptance of conventionalist (as opposed to essentialist) theories of language. This might explain why many college students, for example, have relativist moral views. They have acquired sufficient argumentative skills to abandon essentialism, but perhaps not enough to anticipate the standard objections to moral relativism. It is also interesting that no average citizen with default essentialist views would support them with the kinds

the typical facts are institutional arrangements (e.g., capitalism, communism) or policies (e.g., affirmative action, the "drug war"). If one convinces others that "democracy" denotes communist institutions, one raises the argumentative costs of critics of communism. Persuading those who accepted this definition that communism is nondemocratic is, given their belief in essentialism, quite costly – surely, they want to avoid the *contradictio in terminis* involved in saying that communism is nondemocratic. Those costs should be added to the costs of showing that communism thwarts cherished goals or rights. To show this, one has to appeal to complex theories and facts. These combined costs explain why a usual way to counter essentialism is to propose an alternative *essentialist definition* (say, democracy *is* majority rule, political pluralism, and civil liberties), rather than address the complex reasons for and against the *institutions, policies, or regimes* denoted by each definition.[88] On our account, then, the rhetorical success of persuasive definitions is not merely tied to the mysterious emotive force of words. Rather, it ultimately rests on the costs of apprehending and spreading an essentialist conception of meaning, relative to the costs of apprehending and spreading reliable social theories.

Transformations in the legal concept of property provide another interesting illustration of this kind of discourse failure. Consider rent-control laws. Robert Nozick observes that these laws typically forbid subletting, despite the fact that both the principal tenant and the secondary tenant benefit and the landlord is not made worse off. Why, then, do rent-control laws forbid subletting? Nozick's answer is that allowing subletting "makes explicit the partial expropriation of the owner."[89] A possible explanation of the hostility to subletting may be, then, that defenders of rent-control laws do not want to appear as condoning expropriation, so they make it appear as if the landlord retains the title over the property. As Nozick perceptively observes, allowing subletting would make transparent a taking of private property. If Nozick's speculation is accurate, one mechanism of discourse failure (here: cognitive processes insensitive to the truth about what the constitutional protection of private property means) is at work. Legislators and special interests do not want to defy the entrenched popular belief that a just and prosperous society

---

of complex arguments given by, say, Saul Kripke in "Identitiy and Necessity," in Stephen Schwartz, ed., *Naming, Necessity, and Natural Kinds* (Ithaca, N.Y.: Cornell University Press, 1977), p. 66.

[88] This, in addition to showing that the merits of communism cannot be established by definitional maneuvers.

[89] See Robert Nozick, *Anarchy, State, and Utopia* (New York: Basic Books, 1974), pp. 270–1.

must countenance a *core* of property rights. Predictably, then, legislative rhetoric will strive to make legislation consistent with the "objective" meaning of the Constitution. And judicial redefinitions of property rights and related constitutional concepts (such as the taking and commerce clauses of the U.S. Constitution) are the predictable outcome.[90] Legislators will be pleased, of course, if that "objective" meaning affords them as much discretionary powers as possible. In our example, the prohibition of subletting allows users of legal discourse to say that the landlord retains title over the property, and so that rent-control laws pose no threat to constitutional guarantees to private property. (Of course, this speculation is neutral on the wisdom or otherwise of having rent-control laws.)[91]

The subletting example suggests that, while free-market theories, being opaque, are generally disfavored in the deliberative forum, the public's built-in beliefs include acceptance of a modicum of private property. People believe that we should have some control over external things. Legislators and others do not want to be seen as supporting legislation (such as rent-control laws with subletting provisions) that makes expropriation transparent. The strength of beliefs in private property will diminish as the opacity of whatever net social benefits ensue from a regime of private property increases. Thus, people will be more distrustful about inherited property than about the products of labor.[92]

Indeed, it is hard to imagine any justification of the ban on subletting that does not involve discourse failure. Consider this one: The tenant should not sublet because rent-control laws implement a desirable pattern of distributive justice. Subletting would upset this pattern, which involves a just rent, defined as a ceiling over which the rental contract would be exploitative or otherwise objectionable. The problem with this is that the belief that price controls can be effective – that government can decree "just" prices without creating scarcity or black markets – is

---

[90] For a valuable recent discussion of the transformation in the concept of property used by the U.S. Supreme Court, see Leif Wenar, "The Concept of Property and the Takings Clause," *Columbia Law Review*, Vol. 97, no. 6 (1997), pp. 1923–46.

[91] For opposing views, see Margaret Jane Radin, "Residential Rent Control," *Philosophy and Public Affairs*, Vol. 15, no. 4 (Autumn 1986), pp. 350–80; Timothy J. Brennan, "Rights, Market Failure, and Rent Control: A Comment on Radin," *Philosophy and Public Affairs*, Vol. 17, no. 1 (Winter 1988), pp. 66–79; Margaret Jane Radin, "Rent Control and Incomplete Commodification: A Rejoinder," *Philosophy and Public Affairs*, Vol. 17, no. 1 (Winter 1988), pp. 80–3.

[92] For a brief indication of the complexities involved in estimating the social costs and benefits of bequests and inheritances, see Robert Cooter and Thomas Ulen, *Law and Economics*, 3rd ed. (New York: Addison Wesley Longman, 2000), pp. 145–7.

discredited today by reliable economics. This belief, however, still enjoys some popularity because it is vivid at two levels. On the one hand, the public sees the visible hand of government setting the just rent. On the other hand, the public can easily see tenants, here and now, being rescued from eviction. Yet they will rarely notice that rent-control laws will aggravate the homelessness problem or reduce the quality of housing,[93] because the social mechanisms by which this occurs are opaque.

The rent-control example illustrates a general tendency to describe one and the same legal or institutional structure in different ways, as political needs dictate. Consider the view, common among civil law scholars, that private property is a relation between a thing and its owner: The owner exclusively controls the thing. In common-law countries, writers talk, less misleadingly, about property as a "bundle of rights."[94] As against these views, the Austrian legal philosopher Hans Kelsen argues instead that private property is best analyzed in terms of the notion of an *erga omnes* obligation – that is, the obligations that all others have not to interfere with the owner's use of her property. Kelsen perceptively observes that traditional doctrine used the owner-related-to-thing notion for ideological reasons – namely, to stress the connection between private property and personal autonomy, manifested in the owner's ability to control things, thus concealing the fact that non-owners are excluded from use.[95] Kelsen diagnoses here a case of what this book calls discourse failure: Supporters of capitalism might want to conceal the fact that private property, as any other system of property, is just one way of demarcating spheres of freedom and unfreedom to use resources.[96]

Or consider this other example: In communist Cuba today, work is mandatory and the government largely decides who and when will produce what, and at which salary.[97] The regime and its apologists boast

---

[93] Writers as diverse as Richard Posner and Cass Sunstein agree that rent-control laws harm the very people they are supposed to help. See Richard A. Posner, *Economic Analysis of Law* (Boston: Little, Brown, 1st ed., 1972), pp. 167–72; Cass R. Sunstein, *Free Markets and Social Justice* (New York: Oxford University Press, 1997), pp. 282–3.

[94] See Jesse Dukeminier and James Krier, *Property* (New York: Aspen Law & Business, 4th edition, 1998), p. 80.

[95] See Hans Kelsen, *Pure Theory of Law*, trans. Max Knight from the Second, Revised and Enlarged, German edition, 1960 (Berkeley: University of California Press, 1967), pp. 130–2.

[96] For a conceptual analysis of the relationships between property rights and freedom, see G. A. Cohen, "The Structure of Proletarian Unfreedom," *Philosophy and Public Affairs*, Vol. 12, no. 2, Spring 1983, pp. 3–33.

[97] See the section "Labor Rights in Cuba," in the "Summary and Recommendations" of the 2005 Human Rights Watch report on Cuba, available at hrw.org/english/docs/

about zero unemployment. Now the legal consequences attached to labor relations in Cuba largely overlap with those that we find abhorrent in paradigmatic instances of slavery: Some people (the government, slave owners) have the legal power to tell others what to do and when to do it. They also unilaterally determine the form and amount of compensation, and punishment for disobedience. Restricting the use of the term "slavery" to, say, the kind of situation that existed in the antebellum American South, while refusing to apply it to social realities in Castro's Cuba is symptomatic of discourse failure. People often wish to induce different attitudes toward political regimes even if they are relevantly similar.

Somebody may object that there is an important distinction between living under a tyranny and being a slave: Slavery, but not tyranny, typically involves the possibility of legalized transfer of ownership. However, the feature that makes slavery objectionable is not primarily that people are bought and sold. In modern democracies we have after all markets for athletes, professors, and executives, who, in one natural sense, are bought and sold. Yet we do not think we live in a slave society. Slavery is objectionable mainly because the master (the government) has the power to make slaves (the people) work at the master's will, and punish them for deviation – a feature that is present both in Cuba and in the antebellum South. The same holds against someone who claims that present-day Cubans are much better treated than slaves were in the antebellum South. The crucially immoral feature of slavery is the absolute coercive powers that the master has over the slave. This feature is enough to condemn slavery, even in cases where slaves are relatively well treated. The plantation owners who treated their slaves "well" were still participating in an objectionable institutional practice.[98]

Those who think Cubans do not live in a slave society face, then, a dilemma. If they believe that Cuban citizens are relatively well treated (and that this is the only thing that matters), they would have to concede that sometimes slavery is good. This position commits them to approving some instances of American slavery (e.g., those where the masters treated their slaves well). If, on the other hand, they think that master/slave relationships are never justified, then they will have to withdraw their support for the Cuban regime, unless they challenge what we said about labor relations in Cuba. In particular, they have to deny that the Cuban

2005/03/10/cuba10306.htm; and the report on Cuba in *Freedom in the World 2004*, published by Freedom House, available at www.freedomhouse.org/research/freedomintheworld/2004/countryratings/cuba.

[98] We do not mean to pass judgment on how well the average Cuban is treated vis-à-vis the antebellum slave.

government possesses the wide discretionary powers over people's lives that characterize master/slave relationships. This position would lead them to, among other things, regard the 250,000 Cuban troops sent to fight for the "liberation" of Angola between 1975 and 1989 as substantially different from slaves. This example shows, by the way, that the same kind of discourse failure occurs when someone who does not want to soil the credentials of a democratic society refuses to use the term "slavery" to refer to military conscription.

But perhaps we are being unfair. Someone may insist that the two situations (antebellum United States and present-day Cuba) are different. He might give an argument structurally analogous to the one that is sometimes offered to defend the military draft in democratic societies. He might say that better health care, literacy, and equality are public goods that, in Cuba, can be achieved only by a labor system such as the one currently in place. Let us grant these facts, for the sake of argument. Just as national defense is sometimes treated as a public good that justifies the draft, so equality and those other achievements are public goods that mandatory labor alone can adequately supply. The objector may then restrict the use of the term "slavery" to instances of mandatory labor that are *not* instrumental to the production of public goods. He may support his terminology by saying that people are willing to bear the cost of producing public goods. That is, they would rather have the good produced at a personal cost than incur no cost but lack the good – this follows from the definition of "public good" (see previous section). It just happens that barriers to collective action, such as the incentive to free ride, prevent them from satisfying that preference. There is a sense, then, in which the draft, but not slavery, is voluntary: Arguably, only the former produces an identifiable public good. This position assumes a stronger concept of slavery, one that requires not only institutional arrangements akin to those that existed in the antebellum South but also the inability of those arrangements to produce public goods. Given his factual beliefs, this objector then applies the strong concept of slavery to the antebellum United States but not to present-day Cuba.

In order for this argument to work, even conceding the dubious premise that Cuban labor conditions produce public goods,[99] our objector must be able to say, without embarrassment, that (i) the regime in the antebellum American South would have been justified had it been

---

[99] Indeed, to be persuasive the argument needs to assume that the public goods presumably produced by the Cuban system are worth their cost (in terms of, for example, personal freedom or better standards of living).

able to produce public goods, and (ii) in that case that regime would not have instantiated slavery. It is hard to imagine, however, anyone's saying either (i) or (ii) without embarrassment. Hardly anyone, that is, wants public goods at the price of slave labor. What is objectionable about slavery is surely the fact that the master dominates the slave at will. We do not easily switch from condemnation to approval of such forms of domination when informed that they produce public goods. It is interesting to note that in standard debates about the production of public goods, national defense is the only example cited that can plausibly justify serious governmental coercion. Even here, however, it is unclear whether the draft (which some might want to equate to slavery), rather than a voluntary army financed through taxes, would best provide an optimal amount of national defense, in addition to being more congenial to individual autonomy.[100] In general, part of what makes the public goods argument plausible is the use of taxation, not forced labor, to produce the good.[101] Moreover, should the objector acknowledge the similarities between slavery and the Cuban regime, he would be guilty of a blatant inconsistency with the egalitarian ideals in the name of which he defends the regime. Slavery is as inimical to equality as any institution can be.[102] Here as elsewhere, ignorance of relevant facts and theories combines with essentialism to make the use of persuasive definitions politically attractive.[103]

2.6. Discourse Failure and Desert

The types of discourse failure we have diagnosed so far have competitive advantages in the political arena. But they are not all equally successful.

---

[100] See Harold Demsetz, "Toward a Theory of Property Rights," op. cit.

[101] But see Robert Nozick, *Anarchy, State, and Utopia*, op. cit., p. 169, who argues that "taxation of earnings from labor is on a par with forced labor." Our remark about taxation in the text assumes that taxation lacks a crucial ingredient underlying our disapproval of slavery – that is, the state's ability to direct at will the work of others and punish at discretion their deviations. We do not take sides on Nozick's point.

[102] It is a symptom of discourse failure that, although slavery is prohibited in the strongest terms by most international human rights treaties, it apparently did not occur to governments or to most human rights advocates to denounce the Soviet Union, or now Cuba or North Korea, as violators of those treaties. The sources of discourse failure are abundant here. Two come to mind. First, the interests of diplomats and governments in maintaining commercial relations with those states, or gaining their votes in international organizations. Second, the well-known sympathies for "socialist" regimes in intellectual circles. See section 2.6.

[103] In the slavery example, other sources of discourse failure are likely to be present as well, such as the desire to send convenient political signals, discussed in section 2.6.

Thus, public attitudes toward redistributive measures will often depend on whether or not winners and losers are perceived as deserving their fate. Typically, the public will like redistribution if they see the beneficiaries as deserving, and, conversely, they will decry gains by persons or groups they regard as undeserving. Consider, for example, why so many people see farmers, physicians, and schoolteachers as more meritorious than bankers. First, these groups appear to bestow tangible benefits on society. Farmers turn uncultivated land into a harvest; physicians make the infirm healthy again; teachers transform illiterate into literate children. Second, the *processes* by which these transformations occur are highly vivid as well. The public conjures up the images of the farmer's working from dawn to dusk; of the physician's saving a life in the operating room; and of the schoolteacher's laboriously trying to keep pupils focused on the blackboard. A related perception is that these persons have true vocations. The public does not see them as economic agents interested in exchanging a good or service *for a price* but rather as valuing the activity in itself. Most people (and indeed the members of those groups) believe that the remunerations perceived by those workers should not come below a certain floor compatible with the dignity and social value of the services they render. The popular view about these professions is that their members are typically motivated by a commitment to lofty values; earning money is a side effect of the pursuit of such values. Sometimes people even describe these activities as higher callings where the agents do not simply have a vocation but also sacrifice themselves for the good of society (the terms "profession" and "service" are suggestive in this context).[104]

Such ascriptions of intent create an aura of nobility to these professions. Many people take at face value public teachers' lobbying for pay raises in the name of education, or "the future of our children." In the case of physicians, the aura of nobility neutralizes a negative factor in the public eye – their high earnings, which in turn stem from anti-competitive regulations of the medical profession.[105] Farmers are an interesting case:

---

[104] The observation in the text is not meant to suggest that people should assess the social or moral value of an activity exclusively by its market price. We merely note the mechanisms (vivid beliefs) that often inform judgments of desert in public discussions.

[105] Lawyers' and physicians' official organizations use public-interest grounds to justify regulations of their activities that keep fees high and set barriers to entry even to those services that can effectively be provided by persons who have not completed formal medical or legal studies. A classic locus for the argument for deregulation of the professions is Milton Friedman, *Capitalism and Freedom* (Chicago: University of Chicago Press, 1962), pp. 137–60.

The public sees them more clearly as working for money but on the other hand values them as symbols of the ethic of toil and frugality.[106]

Bankers do not benefit from any of these vivid characterizations. The public thinks bankers simply lend money and wait for the financial returns. They do not seem to be "working" in any sense that the public can readily grasp. More important, the notion that there is a market for money is considerably opaque. Most of us find it hard to replace our vivid theories about bankers with the economics of banking, which tells us that the banker is selling something for a price, just like any other agent in the market (including farmers, doctors, and schoolteachers). One might ask, then, why market opacity, here manifested in the public's failure to see the social benefits *and costs* of an activity, helps the foregoing professions but not bankers. This apparent anomaly vanishes when we wonder what exactly the opacity is about in each case. What people perceive as salient in the case of farmers, doctors, and schoolteachers is that they are giving to society more than they receive. This makes them, in the eyes of the public, especially deserving, because most people are assumed to exchange goods and services of approximately the same value. These ideas assume theories of just or fair prices, which need not coincide with market prices, coupled with the theory that political decisions *can* bring about such prices. Now the theory of just prices rests on mistakes disclosed by contemporary price theory, which is notoriously opaque. The idea that prices do not reflect values that are independent of people's preferences was opaque to various degrees to even the brightest economists until the late nineteenth century, when marginal analysis was introduced and has remained at the core of mainstream economics until today. Because the goods or services offered in the foregoing "noble" professions are salient, their practitioners seem an exception to the general rule that people exchange approximately equivalent values.

Compare this with popular views about bankers. People have a hard time seeing how bankers contribute to productive activities. The world of finance is often contrasted with the world of production, with the suggestion that finance does not really contribute to social output. Bankers seem to gain without "doing anything." Here, the remuneration (interest) is salient. While many people can perhaps understand the benefits of banking to the borrowers, they will not easily see how others (e.g., workers) may benefit by increased investment financed through credit. (Indeed, this view of bankers as undeserving gainers pervades a long history of moral

---

[106] See note 35, this chapter, for a reference to arguments used by the U.S. government to justify farm subsidies.

and religious condemnation of usury.) Again, people do not believe that anyone can have a vocation for banking. Whatever bankers do, they surely do it for money. While people believe a schoolteacher who says, "My students are my life," they would laugh at the banker who said, "My depositors and borrowers are my life." These differences make many people favor public subsidies to farmers and wage increases for schoolteachers (as opposed to incentive-based educational policies, such as school vouchers).[107] In contrast, the public regards with suspicion even unsubsidized gains by bankers.

2.7. The Cost of Dissent

One key source of discourse failure, already examined, is the mutually reinforcing interaction between the rational ignorance of voters and the posturing of politicians and other political actors. But political discourse may fail for another reason as well – namely, the benefits that accrue from siding with mainstream views, and the costs of dissenting.[108] Take the following puzzle: It is well documented that for decades communist regimes around the globe ruthlessly oppressed and killed millions of individuals. Yet during that extended period many prominent intellectuals of the West purportedly concerned with human rights and poverty focused their strictures on liberal democracies without ever mentioning the massive assaults on human rights and the terrible famines brought about by communist regimes.[109] Some even praised the supposed achievements

---

[107] The case of physicians is complicated by arguments in favor of regulation that do not rely on the intrinsic worth or value of medical practice but on the need to protect consumers. For a general discussion, see Timothy Jost, "Oversight of the Quality of Medical Care: Regulation, Management, or the Market?" *Arizona Law Review*, Vol. 37 (1995), p. 825.

[108] For an evolutionary account of the propensity to conform, see Jonathan Klick and Francesco Parisi, "Social Networks, Self Denial, and Median Preferences: Conformity as an Evolutionary Strategy" (September 2, 2004), Florida State University College of Law Public Law Research Paper No. 126; George Mason Law & Economics Research Paper No. 04-41, available at http://ssrn.com/abstract=589325.

[109] The point in the text is difficult to document because it is essentially the history of an omission. What is remarkable is not so much that a group of influential intellectuals *praised* these regimes at the time when they were perpetrating massive crimes (see references further in this note) but that many other intellectuals ostensibly concerned with human rights and poverty – the majority – simply remained silent. We surveyed the JSTOR database and found that scholars specialized in the Soviet Union wrote about the Soviet economy, or U.S.–Soviet relations, or the structure of the Soviet bureaucracy, or Soviet–Third World relations – sometimes, timidly, about prospects for democratization in the U.S.S.R. The authors apparently didn't feel any pressure to include a footnote denouncing human rights violations, even after episodes such as Stalin's Great

of those regimes.[110] Some equated, on a moral plane, those regimes with
Western liberal democracies.[111] At any rate, they kept silent about the

Purge (1936–8), with widely publicized show trials at which defendants invariably con-
fessed their "crimes against the State." The atrocities committed by communist regimes
are now well documented. See Stéphane Courtois, Nicolas Werth, Jean-Louis Panne,
Andrezj Paczowski, Karel Bartosek, and Jean-Louis Namolin, *The Black Book of Communism: Crimes, Terror, Repression* (Cambridge, Mass.: Harvard University Press, M. Kramer
and J. Murphy, trans., 1999). Communist regimes killed about 100 million people: 20
million in the U.S.S.R.; 65 million in China; 1 million in Vietnam; 2 million in North
Korea; 2 million in Cambodia; 1 million in Eastern Europe; 150,000 in Latin America;
1.7 million in Africa; 1.5 million in Afghanistan; and about 10,000 deaths caused by
the international communist movement and communist parties not in power. *The Black
Book*, p. 4. As Martin Malia notes in the foreword, communist regimes did not simply
commit criminal acts (all states do on occasion); "they were criminal enterprises in their
very essence: on principle, so to speak, they ruled lawlessly, by violence, and without
regard for human life." *The Black Book*, p. xvii. The reception of this book in the West is
suggestive. It caused a furor in France when it first appeared in 1997, and in the United
States, while it received favorable reviews in the *New York Times* and the *Wall Street Journal*
(see reviews at www.hup.harvard.edu/reviews), it was ignored by National Public Radio,
The New York Review of Books (a venue de rigueur for mainstream U.S. intellectuals) and
the major television networks. For a discussion of the favorable attitude of intellectuals toward communism throughout many decades, see Hilton Kramer, *The Twilight of
Intellectuals* (Chicago: Ivan Dee Pub., 2000). See also Paul Johnson, *Modern Times* (New
York: HarperCollins, rev. ed., 1991), esp. pp. 544–7. We cite Johnson's work to make a
point. When we mention his work to historians, we sometimes receive hushed replies
suggesting that, for some reason, he should not be cited. We were never able to elicit the
reason, except for vague dismissals of Johnson as a "right-winger" and a "conservative."
This may well be another instance of the sending-the-correct-signals form of discourse
failure that we will shortly diagnose in this section. It does not matter whether Johnson
is right in his claim that Western intellectuals condoned communist crimes: You just
don't cite him, and if you do, you are a "right-winger." We disagree with some themes of
Johnson's book (such as his praise for the contribution of religion to human freedom,
and his attempt to link British analytic philosophy to an alleged decline in British culture and values), but the reluctance by mainstream historians to address the facts he
reports about intellectuals and communism is certainly unwarranted. For a discussion
of the bias in favor of "socialist" regimes and against the West in the United Nations'
treatment of human rights, see Jack Donnelly, "Human Rights at the United Nations
1955–1985," *International Studies Quarterly*, Vol. 32, 1988, pp. 275–303.

[110] There are many examples of this. See, for example, Joel Eldestein, "The Future of
Democracy in Cuba," *Latin American Perspectives*, Vol. 22, no. 4, 1995, pp. 7–26. In
the acknowledgments he thanks the "people of Cuba, appreciating their struggle for
national dignity and independence and their revolutionary efforts to create a just, self-
governing society in which human solidarity is a cardinal virtue." Id., p. 7. Of course,
by the time Eldestein wrote this passage, human rights organizations such as Amnesty
International (widely cited, quite correctly, by most intellectuals ostensibly committed
to the cause of human rights to condemn noncommunist dictatorships) had published
worrying reports on violations of human rights in Castro's Cuba.

[111] Many Western intellectuals have consistently derided efforts to draw moral distinctions
between the West (especially the United States) and the Soviet Union, calling those
efforts "conservative" or "right-wing." See, for example, Michael Frisch, "American
History and the Structures of Collective Memory: A Modest Exercise in Empirical

true nature of those regimes in contexts where sincere preoccupation with human rights and fulfillment of basic needs made such references obligatory.[112] Most notably, few of these intellectuals recanted even after the massive evidence of gross human rights violations under communist rule became readily available.

How can this gross distortion be explained?[113] A well-known game-theoretical model may help. Consider the rational course of action for each driver in the absence of rules of the road. Initially, some of them will drive on the left while others will drive on the right. As soon as a driver perceives that a majority, however tiny it may be, of drivers is circulating on the left, she will do likewise in order to reduce the probability of her suffering an accident. Moreover, her joining the majority reinforces other drivers' reasons to drive on the left. After a while, virtually all drivers circulate on the left.[114]

We think the intellectuals we are discussing were playing an analogous game. It is well known that in many academic and intellectual circles it has become increasingly fashionable since the 1960s to flirt with Marxism and cognate anti-capitalist views. Even today, other things being equal, it is easier to get an academic position if one is a vocal critic of capitalism than if one is a vocal conservative or libertarian. For that reason, in many (not all) academic circles within the humanities and social sciences,[115] job candidates have an obvious disincentive to publicly take positions, such as anti-communism, that may make them less desirable, so they believe, in the eyes of academic employers. Someone seeking

---

Iconography," *The Journal of American History*, Vol. 75, no. 4, March 1989, p. 1153. This is another telling example of discourse failure in the form of signaling. Frisch identifies Jeane Kirkpatrick as holding the view that we should make moral distinctions between the West and the U.S.S.R. and then cites a *New York Times* reference in which the view is classified as conservative. The implication is, of course, that if someone as "right-wing" as Kirkpatrick holds that view, then anyone who criticizes the U.S.S.R. must be a right-winger too.

[112] Thus, the issue is not Left versus Right, or *laissez-faire* capitalism versus the welfare state or nontotalitarian forms of socialism. Indeed, a number of intellectuals from the Left, to their credit, denounced the crimes of communism. The analysis in the text is confined to a high proportion of *human rights* intellectuals who ignored those crimes.

[113] For a discussion of the cost of dissent in non-academic contexts, see Cass R. Sunstein, *Why Societies Need Dissent* (Cambridge, Mass.: Harvard University Press, 2003), pp. 39–73.

[114] This analysis assumes, for simplicity's sake, that no salient coordination points are available (e.g., steering wheels equidistant between the front doors). The basic point (that the cost of diverging from a convention rises disproportionately as the convention expands) remains if we drop that assumption. See Robert Sugden, *The Economics of Rights, Co-operation and Welfare* (Oxford: Basil Blackwell, 1986), pp. 34–54.

[115] In the remainder of this discussion, we assume this qualification on humanities and social sciences, except when the context requires otherwise.

an academic job who believes that most members of hiring committees are unsympathetic to conservatism or to free markets may fear that voicing anti-communist views will automatically link her, in the eyes of the committee, to positions generally shunned by the academic world. She risks being tagged as a McCarthyite; conservative; libertarian; supporter of Ronald Reagan, Margaret Thatcher, or George W. Bush; or of similar stances lumped together under the rubric "right-wing views." It is not that the candidate or the hiring committees would, if asked, condone the crimes of communism. Rather, the rational, self-interested candidate will send those signals that *set her views apart from* the disfavored ones. This is why she will not volunteer views that may be perceived as *major themes* within the disfavored positions. Thus, someone who denounces, say, oppression in Cuba is sending a message that *overlaps* with that of "right-wingers" and so faces a *competitive disadvantage* vis-à-vis candidates who provide hiring committees with no evidence of their being "on the wrong side" on other issues. This explains why both candidates and committees *would, if pressed,* condemn oppression in Cuba as well. They send the right signals (in terms of their own careers, or such perquisites as invitations to conferences and research grants) without incurring the cost of blatant inconsistency with mainstream liberal values: After all, they show their willingness to condemn communism (only under contextual pressures, in order to avoid the impression that their opposition to communism is part of a "right-wing" outlook). An exactly symmetrical matrix of payoffs explains the frequency of *spontaneous* anti-capitalist stances – that is, even in the absence of contextual pressures. Candidates, then, signal their ideological reliability by refraining from comments about communism and thus, by implication, reassuring their convergence toward the safe, left-of-center, dominant view. Signaling will be all the more effective if everyone converges on a readily available term to refer to *all* the positions disfavored in academia, especially if that term has negative connotations in that particular setting – in the present example, "conservatism" and "right-wing views" have served this purpose well. Of course, one consequence of these dynamics is to blur the differences between the various doctrines that are lumped together: Witness the distortion involved in assimilating libertarianism to conservatism.[116]

---

[116] The differences are big indeed. Consider how sharply libertarians and conservatives disagree, inter alia, on the following issues: adult drug use and traffic, the role of the state in promoting religion and communitarian values, barriers to immigration, trade policy, bans on pornography and prostitution, censorship on allegedly offensive speech.

This process is self-enforcing and independent, within a broad range, of the particular mix of ideological and merit-oriented motivations that each committee member may have. The candidate knows that, for whatever reason, the average committee leans to the left, and wants to maximize his chances of getting the job offer. Of course, the specific predictions of this analysis will turn on data about institutional structures. Thus, if hiring committees included nontenured members, we would expect the incidence of left-of-center votes, and correlatively of left-of-center candidates, to be higher. The incentive structure is reversed in those (predictably) few places where right-wingers have the upper hand. Moreover, the model allows for places where ideological considerations play *absolutely no* role in the appointment process. There may well be reliable signals of sheer academic competence that are ideologically neutral. We speculate, however, that those cases will be infrequent, given the foregoing convergence-toward-majority mechanisms and the difficulties in disentangling ideological from academic assessments.[117] We conjecture, in short, that the failure to comment on the crimes of communism in contexts where such reference would have been relevant is largely a response to the foregoing incentives.

But why do most academics endorse left-of-center positions *in the first place?* The answer is by no means self-evident. One reason, we conjecture, may well be internal to scientific inquiry – that is, the honest balance of reasons for and against various views. Thus, after World War II, Keynesian economics and the burgeoning theory of market failure were generally taken to support strong regulation of economic activity. Those views were at the time reliable social science, in the sense that we will explain in section 4.1. Now once the academy reached, *for these internal reasons,* a left-of-center coordination point, subsequent incentives to converge on that same point emerge, in accordance with the game-theoretical mechanisms outlined previously. To the extent that allegiance to the mainstream view weighs in the award of academic benefits, it is simply irrational to deviate.

The list should be expanded if, as is frequently the case, "conservatism" is another name for policies favored by Republicans in the United States; in this sense, conservatives, but not libertarians, favor many forms of regulation of markets.

[117] The formal theory of political coalitions demonstrates that the optimal strategy for the political careerist is sometimes to support relatively small minoritarian coalitions. For example, sometimes smaller minorities defeat larger minorities in the competition for political power. See Robert Cooter, *The Strategic Constitution* (Princeton, N.J.: Princeton University Press, 2000), pp. 73–7. *Mutatis mutandis*, the same is true for the academic careerist.

Our model also predicts, for the same reasons, that those who are publicly known as conservatives (perhaps because they held prominent positions in conservative administrations or think tanks) and decide to join mainstream academia will gradually drift toward the political center.[118]

Another reason is the effect on academia of the forms of discourse failure that pervade society at large. The most simplistic left-of-center views, those that tend to be aired in public, are usually affected by discourse failure, especially those critical of free markets. A main reason is that many of these simplistic anti-market positions rely on vivid assumptions that are discredited by serious economic theory. Many academics, in particular those not trained in economics (e.g., literature professors), tend to endorse those views. Of course, this charge does not extend to academics who defend left-of-center-views with respectable arguments. These scholars represent, however, only a fraction of the academic world. There are, of course, many bad right-wing arguments as well, but they are *not* picked up by the typical academic.

Interestingly, the most reliable anti-market argument, and also the least invoked *by non-economists*, rests on opaque invisible-hand theories, such as the theory of market failure (see section 2.3).[119] Social scientists are nowadays both more optimistic about market mechanisms for overcoming apparent instances of market failure and (as shown by public-choice theorizing about *government failure*) more skeptical about the ability of governments to cope with even clear instances of market failure.[120] Accordingly, our analysis also explains why anti-market views are less common today among economists and other social scientists specialized in the formulation and testing of invisible-hand theories – in short, among those familiar with theories that make transparent the costs of

---

[118] Of course, predictive accuracy can be achieved only by a full-fledged game-theoretical model. Such a model would have to assign payoffs to the *allegiance* and *originality* strategies pursued by scholars. Moreover, we find no a priori obstacle to treating such assignments endogenously, within a more comprehensive game-theoretic model (e.g., an evolutionary model wherein academic circles result from selection and self-selection pressures toward more or less bold styles of research).

[119] Again, we refer the reader to section 4.1 for the characterization of reliable social science. It is less clear how much discourse failure affects views sometimes classified as "left of center" in non-economic issues, such as abortion and capital punishment. All will depend on how the agent formulates the argument – that is, to what extent she passes The Display Test that we will introduce in section 6.2, with the caveat stated in section 6.8.

[120] For a nontechnical discussion of the extensive literature, see, for example, William C. Mitchell and Randy T. Simmons, *Beyond Politics: Markets, Welfare, and the Failure of Bureaucracy* (Boulder, Colo.: Westview, 1994).

political decisions. We should expect, then, the deviation to the left to be greater among, say, literature professors than among economists. The source of discourse failure we identify in this section (i.e., the cost of dissent) presupposes majoritarian academic coalitions formed in virtue of the general mechanisms of discourse failure percolating from society at large.

Finally, many people might have ended up in the academy because they had anti-capitalist views to begin with and perhaps regarded the academic world as a refuge from the capitalist or business world they so much despised. They might regard their choice as a way to remain true to their principles. Intellectually gifted libertarians or conservatives, on the other hand, would not have qualms about joining the capitalist workforce. This self-selection would explain the deviation of intellectuals to the left in the first place.[121] But once an initial imbalance toward the left is reached, our analysis explains its perpetuation. In other words, a comprehensive game-theoretical model of ideological shares in academia should make room not only for the cost of dissenting but also for self-selection mechanisms.[122]

Given our assumption that people are sensitive to the personal costs and benefits of their choices, it may seem puzzling that relatively few intellectuals pointed out flaws in communist regimes during times when a large segment of the citizenry had anti-communist sentiments. Indeed, typical intellectuals often succeeded in projecting themselves, even in the educated public's eye, as proud dissenters, especially during periods of conservative administrations, such as Ronald Reagan's and Margaret Thatcher's.[123]

---

[121] We are grateful to Lynn Roseberry for this idea.

[122] Self-selection mechanisms seem stronger now, when left-wing theories are available to prospective academics, so that they can easily fine-tune their scientific positions to the ideological signals they want to send. American academia lacked this scientific repertoire until the late nineteenth century. Up to that time, social scientists largely adopted *laissez-faire* views. That equilibrium was upset by the need to import Ph.D.'s from Germany, where academia was much more hostile to free markets, in order to get doctoral programs started in the United States. For an account of this episode in American intellectual history, see Daniel D. Rodgers, *Atlantic Crossings: Social Politics in a Progressive Age* (Cambridge, Mass.: The Belknap Press, 1998), pp. 76–111. These facts suggest the kinds of exogenous forces that may accelerate the game-theoretical process we indicate in the text. We thank Jeff Paul for drawing our attention to this point.

[123] Use of the rhetoric of dissent can be very misleading. Consider the grotesque example of Fidel Castro's portraying the Cuban people as *rebelling* against the might of American imperialism. This rhetoric is in tune with the regime's officially being named as *la Revolución* and Che Guevara's being portrayed as the symbol of rebellion and social

The coordination model outlined previously dissolves this puzzle. The electorate at large is not the intellectual careerist's constituency. Rather, it is composed of those who, primarily in the academic and related environments, hold the key to the intellectual's success. The model also explains why many of those intellectuals felt no pressure to revise their idyllic views about communism even after the disclosure of massive evidence of genocides. Although their failure to recant earned them the indictment of hypocrisy, sometimes leveled by conservative commentators with wide audiences, this was hardly a loss to them, given the matrix of payoffs to which they reacted. What mattered to them was that an openly anti-communist stance may have weakened the loyalty signal to the *relevant* constituencies. In particular, young left-of-center academics who privately may well abhor the crimes of communism nonetheless want to avoid an open anti-communist stance that may blur their differences with right-wing anti-communists and weaken their perceived commitment to a number of *other* left-of-center positions. In short, softness toward communism works as a package signal: It allows people to distance themselves from a number of causes and positions, loosely associated with anti-communism, that are unpopular among academics.

It may be useful to compare our explanation of why academics lean to the left with Nozick's.[124] Nozick claims that intellectuals in the humanities and the social sciences (he calls them "wordsmiths") have anti-capitalist views because they resent the fact that society does not fully reward their talents. He observes that those intellectuals were recognized and praised during their schooling, where they experienced a structured system of rewards for intellectual merit. But, of course, in a market society merit is not rewarded as such; rather, rewards are a function of how much others demand, for whatever reason, what we have to offer. According to Nozick, then, intellectuals become disgruntled with the market because, so they think, it fails to reward them in the way they have become accustomed to during their school years. When they leave school and join

---

criticism. This rhetoric pervades Castro's long speeches in Plaza de la Revolución, Havana, addressed to crowds who obediently clap when cued by "revolutionary guards," who also take attendance. All of this occurs while vocal *dissenters* are either shot, imprisoned, or exiled. So powerful is this rhetoric that many young people in liberal democracies wear T-shirts with the image of Che Guevara as a symbol of dissent. The payoffs matrix that we diagnose next in the text explains away this apparent anomaly, common to many dictatorships: The rhetoric of dissenting with outsiders ("anti-imperialism") serves to eradicate internal dissent ("traitors").

[124] See Robert Nozick, *Socratic Puzzles* (Cambridge, Mass.: Harvard University Press, 1997), pp. 280–95.

the work force, they experience a downward mobility in terms of social esteem. To make things worse, they see others succeed who they know are intellectually less deserving (because they did not do as well as they in school).

Nozick may be on to something here. It is not uncommon for intellectuals to sneer at rich people who are unable to chatter about intellectual, scientific, or artistic matters. We think, however, that our explanation improves on Nozick's for the following reasons. If Nozick were right, we would expect wordsmiths to be left-leaning uniformly across different disciplines, because all of them are similarly affected by the downward social mobility he describes. As we pointed out, however, there is less incidence of left-of-center views among, say, economists than among, say, experts in literature or cultural studies, and we saw how our model explains this: Those trained in identifying the hidden costs of laws or social policies are less likely to be affected by the discourse failure that characterizes many anti-capitalist positions. Moreover, Nozick explains the tendency to the left among intellectuals as the result of resentment: They perceive their downward mobility as undeserved and naturally regard egalitarian policies as the means of redressing such injustice. But this claim is somewhat farfetched: In modern societies, intellectuals have, after all, quite privileged positions, as Nozick concedes.[125] Our explanation does not rely on resentment or other emotions. It is tempting to point to those emotions to explain why people adopt egalitarian positions, but this move has an ad hoc flavor. We conjecture instead that many intellectuals stand to gain by leaning to the left, and we suggest testable implications of this hypothesis (in terms of, e.g., the higher incidence of ideologically disfavored positions among tenured and nontenured faculty). Our model explains the ostensible behavior of academics in terms of tangible gains and losses: positions, salaries, grants, and other academic perquisites that define the payoffs in the game that academic careerists are playing. How much envy and resentment pull in the same direction is a question we do not address.

As we have pointed out, our analysis does not exclude the possibility of a demand for academic products free of discourse failure. This need not be the result of agents primarily motivated by the attainment of knowledge. Some academics seek glory or recognition. In this case, what is instrumental to their ends is by its very nature truth-sensitive. But even people who seek positions outside the academic world may well be

---

[125] Ibid., pp. 280–1.

concerned with the truth. Consider someone who wants to engage in serious study of tax policy with the aim of landing a high-paying job in government. We can easily imagine that he would be of little use in that position unless he could help the government choose, among alternative tax policies, that which furthers its electoral goals. There is little room for discourse failure here: He needs to understand the opaque, highly complex consequences of those policies.[126]

Is this portrayal of the motivations behind academics' political leanings consistent with our claim that there is such a thing as reliable social science? Views free from discourse failure require concern with sound argument. Yet, it may be objected, our story about the ideological patterns observed in academia depicts academic careerists as people concerned with things other than the truth. It seems we cannot have it both ways.

The inconsistency is illusory, though. First, most, if not all, serious deliberation takes place in academic, elitist settings. This is consistent with many academics' *simultaneously* sending the ideological signals explained by the foregoing game-theoretical framework. These two activities are easily severable. One might imagine grotesque examples of this kind of behavior, such as a highly scholarly philosophical discussion of equality in which the author drops a passing reference to what he views as the hideous policies of George W. Bush, or someone involved in right-wing circles finding a place to criticize Bill Clinton amid a highly analytical discussion of Locke's theory of property rights. Our point here is that the theoretical discourse in these cases, subject to the critical scrutiny of peers and so free from discourse failure, is conceptually and pragmatically severable from the ideological signals that the author sends. Therefore, saying that academics lean to the political left is consistent with the existence of a demand for truth-sensitive academic products – that is, products non-incidentally free from discourse failure.

The objection also overlooks our previous remark that both discourse failure and truth-sensitive views are products supplied and demanded in various kinds of markets, including of course the academic market. Our analysis implies that the academic markets for discourse failure will be less extended in those fields – for example, economics – devoted

---

[126] For an illuminating analysis of why people may deliberately give *false* advice to others in order to maximize the chances of giving correct advice in the long run, see Stephen Morris, "Political Correctness," *Journal of Political Economy*, Vol. 109, no. 2 (April 2001), pp. 231–65.

to making transparent social costs that are seldom noticed by laypersons. Conversely, we will expect a higher incidence of discourse failure in fields where neither teachers nor students are expected to master the analytical framework that renders such costs visible, and this only when the speaker oversteps the boundaries of her specialty to enter the political domain. Of course, there is a negative correlation between the incidence of discourse failure and the reliability of the propositions accepted in a given circle. We should expect, then, a convergence between the results of our operational tests for reliable social science (see section 4.1) and the relative degree to which academic fields make social costs transparent.

Most fundamentally, nothing in our analysis rules out the possibility of a demand for *reliable social science* itself. In order to show that our appeals to reliable social science are consistent with the forms of discourse failure that we have diagnosed in academia, we simply insist that some people indeed value truth-sensitive cognitive methods in social science. A market-clearing supply of such methods is therefore to be expected (assuming free entry in academic markets).[127]

There are, of course, more obvious forms of discourse failure in academia. Legal academics, for example, frequently switch back and forth between academia and government. Thus, it is not uncommon for international-law professors to aspire to an appointment in an international organization or in the federal government. This is a favored practice in law schools. Yet whatever merits this practice may have, it begets discourse failure among legal academics.[128] Similar distortions occur when legal academics are seeking a judicial appointment, given that those appointments are made through the political process. Law professors thus motivated will shape their scholarly views in a manner calculated to please decisive political coalitions. It is apparent that such incentives should be taken into account, in addition to those described previously, in any detailed model of discourse failure in academia.

One last point: We have been loosely using in this section the words "right" and "left" because the cluster of positions denoted by these words is definite enough for our purposes in this section. It has repeatedly been observed, however, that this classification is quite confusing. At the very least, it involves the following equivocation. Sometimes the term

---

[127] See Guido Pincione, "Should Law Professors Teach Public Choice Theory?," *Chicago-Kent Law Review*, Vol. 79, no. 2, 2004, pp. 463–5.

[128] See Fernando R. Tesón, "International Law," in Peter Cane and Mark Tushnet, eds., *The Oxford Handbook of Legal Studies* (Oxford: Oxford University Press, 2003), pp. 941–7.

"left-wing" denotes a commitment to equality. Other times, however, that term denotes a commitment to various forms of governmental interference with market processes. In the former case, someone is a leftist if she endorses certain principles or values. In the latter, someone is a leftist if she endorses certain policies or institutions.[129] Two aspects of this equivocation are interesting from the point of view of a theory of discourse failure. The first one is this: Suppose David says that he cares about equality and that free markets will better serve equality than government intervention. In most contexts, David would not be classified as a leftist. Perhaps people think that free markets do not serve equality. One reason David is not considered a leftist may be that he is allegedly making a causal mistake: Free markets fail to promote equality. However, many people would find David's causal argument irrelevant: The mere advocacy of free markets suffices to exclude him from the leftist community. This suggests that endorsing government intervention is a necessary condition for membership in that community. To be a leftist, one has to defend government intervention on behalf of equality, but the connection between these two things need not be causal. Leftists may believe that supporting government intervention best *symbolizes* or otherwise *reflects* their commitment to equality. Suffice it to say here that these attempts to bypass causal analysis are symptomatic of discourse failure for the reasons we shall give in Chapters 5 and 6.

Second, the positive connotation of the word "left" is an epiphenomenon of the mechanisms of discourse failure we identified in academia. Few academics want to be pegged with the label "right-winger," whereas hardly anyone feels uncomfortable carrying the reputation of being a leftist. Given that academics tend to support government intervention on behalf of equality, the word "left," which designates such positions, will inherit favorable treatment.

---

[129] The word "right" is also used equivocally, as we indicated in note 115 (this chapter), but because we said that academics lean to the left, the points that follow in the text refer to left-wing positions.

3

The Rational Choice Framework

Conceptual and Moral Problems

3.1. Instrumental and Epistemic Rationality

The theorist of deliberative democracy may point out that we have wrongly assumed an instrumental conception of rationality. A proper epistemic defense of deliberative democracy requires instead, he might claim, a specifically deliberative conception of rationality.[1] Citizens who deliberate are not necessarily, or solely, attempting to pursue their self-interest in the sense presupposed by the instrumental view. Rather, deliberative rationality is an application in deliberative settings of rules of epistemic rationality. Thus, sincere people who have beliefs based on sensory perceptions under normal conditions and use valid rules of inference will assert those beliefs in deliberation, when relevant. The kind of deliberative rationality involved here is, according to the objection we are imagining, intractable in instrumental terms. Deliberative rationality is moored to epistemic rationality, which has an inner logic, or objectivity, that need not be aligned with our goals – think of unpalatable truths that we nevertheless believe. The suggested conclusion is that the instrumental model of rationality cannot capture behavior governed by the rules of epistemic rationality. Epistemic rules are irreducible to means–ends recipes or to cost–benefit analysis. Those rules best explain and

---

[1] An example of this general approach might be Joshua Cohen's view that a reasonable position in deliberation is whatever a reasonable person would accept. See Joshua Cohen, "Democracy and Liberty," in Jon Elster, ed., *Deliberative Democracy* (Cambridge: Cambridge University Press, 1998), p. 195. For a criticism, see Gerald Gaus, *Contemporary Theories of Liberalism*, op. cit., pp. 141–2. Similarly, Habermas's view of deliberative rationality is moral, not instrumental. See Jürgen Habermas, *Between Facts and Norms*, op. cit., pp. 3–4.

predict deliberative behavior, especially in well-designed deliberative settings, where the objective force of arguments holds sway.[2] On this view, then, we should abandon the rational choice assumption we've used so far to explain and predict discursive political behavior. To understand deliberative practices, we should instead use an epistemic conception of rationality. Persons believe things not because it is cheap to believe them but because they have *grounds* for believing them.

To answer this critique, we need to say more about instrumental rationality. Recall that, under the instrumental model, an action is rational if and only if it achieves the agent's subjective goals at his lowest cost, given his beliefs. This rough characterization of the instrumental conception of rationality[3] can be refined with the aid of decision theory. Decision theory assumes that preferences are transitive, complete, and independent. An agent's preferences are transitive if and only if, for all options x, y, and z, if the agent prefers x to y and y to z, then she prefers x to z. Her preferences are *complete* if and only if, for all options x and y, she either prefers x to y, or y to x, or is indifferent between x and y. The *independence* condition is defined for choices under risk and uncertainty, which occur when the agent knows each outcome's probability only, or when she has no knowledge of probabilities, respectively. In those cases, the theory sees actions as *lotteries* with outcomes as prizes.

---

[2] This is one of the various junctures at which the deliberativist may be tempted to extend some models of scientific deliberation to politics (for another example, see section 4.2). One articulation of the notion of the "inner logic" of arguments (a notion that, on some views, provides a better explanation of human action than a subjectivist "reenactment" of the agent's goals and beliefs) can be found in Karl R. Popper's idea of "world 3," developed in his later epistemology. See Karl R. Popper, *Objective Knowledge: An Evolutionary Approach* (Oxford: Clarendon Press, 1972). For a thoroughgoing discussion of Popper's views on this matter, see the essays by J. C. Eccles, J. W. N. Watkins, Donald T. Campbell, Eugene Freeman and Henryk Skolimowski, and Herbert Feigl and Paul E. Meehl in Paul Arthur Schilpp, ed., *The Philosophy of Karl Popper*, Vol. 2 (La Salle, Ill.: Open Court, 1974), pp. 349–559, and Popper's replies on pp. 1048–80. A classical presentation of the "re-enactment" view is R. G. Collingwood, *The Idea of History* (New York: Oxford University Press, 1956), pp. 282–302. For a defense, see Rex Martin, *Historical Explanation: Re-Enactment and Practical Inference* (Ithaca, N.Y.: Cornell University Press, 1977).

[3] Writers frequently associate the instrumental conception with David Hume's dictum that "reason is, and ought to be the slave of the passions, and can never pretend to any other office than to serve and obey them." *A Treatise on Human Nature*, ed. David Fate Norton and Mary Norton (Oxford: Oxford University Press, 2000, orig. pub. 1739), 2.3.3.4. However, a purely instrumental conception of reason, holding that reason presupposes a "moral sense" or "affections," had been extensively defended by Francis Hutchison a little earlier. See his *An Essay on the Nature and Conduct of the Passions and Affections, with Illustrations on the Moral Sense*, ed. and with an Introduction by Aaron Garrett (Indianapolis: Liberty Fund, 2002, orig. pub. 1728), pp. 137–60.

An agent's choice satisfies the independence condition if and only if, given two actions (lotteries) that differ only in one possible outcome (prize), the agent prefers the action that has her preferred possible outcome.[4]

When we know the agent's preference ranking, we can use decision theory to predict his choices. Thus, if (i) *A* prefers a pea to an apple and (ii) an apple to an orange, we can predict that (iii) *A* will prefer a pea when offered a choice between a pea and an orange. But suppose we find that *A* prefers the orange. This behavior in principle refutes a hypothesis *H* which asserts that, other things being equal, persons choosing in accordance with (i) and (ii) will choose in accordance with (iii), where *H* is an empirical interpretation of the transitivity axiom. We say that such behavior "in principle" refutes *H*, because the experiment may have failed to hold other things equal. *A* may abandon his initial intransitive ranking between a pea, an apple, and an orange as soon as he realizes that preserving that ranking would frustrate his goals. When *A* sees the consequences of his intransitive choices, he may decide to shift to a transitive ranking. For example, *A* may realize that the intransitive ranking will cost him money. To see this, imagine that *A* has an apple. Given that he prefers a pea to an apple, he would be willing to give his apple and some amount of money (say, $1) in exchange for a pea. *B* offers *A* this exchange, which *A* predictably accepts. *A* has now a pea that, by hypothesis, he is willing to exchange for an orange and some amount of money (say, $1 again). *B* offers *A* this exchange, which *A* predictably accepts too. *A* has now an orange. Because *A* prefers an apple to an orange, he is now willing to give up his orange and some money (say, $1 again) in exchange for an apple. *B* offers *A* this exchange, which *A* accepts again. So, after this round of exchanges, *A* ended up with exactly the same thing he initially had (an apple) and $3 less! Indeed, given *A*'s preferences, the exchanges can go on indefinitely until *A* has been pumped dry of every dollar. In short, *B* can easily exploit *A*'s intransitivity. Thus the *money-pump argument* for transitivity as a component of rationality: Because agents with intransitive preferences are vulnerable to exploitation, intransitive preferences are irrational.[5]

---

[4] Marginal analysis, which lies at the core of current economics, can be derived from the axioms of preference. See a seminal discussion in John von Neumann and Oskar Morgenstern, *Theory of Games and Economic Behavior* (Princeton, N.J.: Princeton University Press, 1953), pp. 15–31.

[5] See Daniel M. Hausman and Michael S. McPherson, *Economic Analysis and Moral Philosophy* (Cambridge: Cambridge University Press, 1996), pp. 27–8.

Generalizing from this example, we can predict that an agent *A* will conform to the axioms of decision theory *when A knows the consequences of not doing so in terms of his subjective goals. A* will choose transitively if intransitive choices are expensive. Thus, we can treat the instrumental account of rationality as a general empirical hypothesis: In the pursuit of their subjective goals, agents will *try to* conform to decision-theoretic axioms, given the personal costs of doing so (including the personal costs of obtaining the relevant information). And this is precisely what researchers have found in experimental situations. Agents with intransitive preferences switch to a transitive ranking as soon as they realize that they are vulnerable to money pumping.[6] We can now see how decision theory is related to instrumental rationality. Agents who violate the axioms of preference frustrate some of their goals – in the foregoing example, those they could have achieved with the money they lost. If they anticipate such losses, they no longer violate the axioms. Conformity to the axioms is *instrumental* to their goals.[7]

---

[6] See Yung-Peng Chu and Ruey-Ling Chu, "The Subsidence of Preference Reversals in Simplified and Marketlike Experimental Settings: A Note," *American Economic Review* 80, 1990, pp. 902–11; and J. Berg, J. Dickhaut, and J. O'Brien, "Preference Reversal and Arbitrage," in Vernon Smith, ed., *Research in Experimental Economics*, Vol. 3 (Greenwich, Conn.: JAI Press, 1985), pp. 31–72. Notice that these findings are relevant to test a *certain empirical* interpretation of decision theory. They do not address other questions concerning the relevance of money-pump arguments to the validity of *formal* decision theory. For example, it may be argued that money-pump arguments do not really show the absurdity of intransitivity because they operate with a temporal, or sequential, reading of transitivity, which does not follow from the transitivity axiom. For this and related problems, see Paul Anand, "The Philosophy of Intransitive Preferences," *The Economic Journal*, Vol. 103, no. 417, 1993, pp. 337–46, esp. pp. 341–3.

[7] We have been assuming that the agent ranks outcomes by the relation "brings more money than." Agents who hold intransitive preferences between *extensionally identified* outcomes (i.e., not outcomes-under-a-certain-description but rather as particular objects, or states of affairs) may not be pumped for different reasons. For example, an agent who holds intransitive preferences between outcomes that he sometimes sees as "more profitable than the other" and some other times as "fairer than the other" might not be pumped if he could not be made to shift from one description to the other as he is offered an exchange. See Frederic Schick, *Making Choices: A Recasting of Decision Theory* (Cambridge: Cambridge University Press, 1997), p. 146. Our assumption that the agent cares primarily about money allows us to illustrate why genuine intransitivities (i.e., intransitivities that cannot be attributed to shifting descriptions) are instrumentally irrational. Notice, also, that the axioms are formal in the sense that they belong to a formal deductive system. The theorems that welfare economists prove on the basis of such axioms and standard rules of inference cannot, of course, possibly be false if the premises are true – this is of the nature of valid deduction. They state how people *who conform to the axioms* will behave in all possible worlds. But *whether* actual people's behavior conforms to the axioms is an empirical matter.

The fact that instrumental agents will conform to (empirical interpretations of) preference theory[8] sheds light on a feature of rationality that is crucial to our argument in this book. An instrumentally rational agent does not necessarily act on the best reasons available, if by "the best reasons available" we mean beliefs consistent with reliable social science. For example, instrumentally rational agents will *in general* reason logically in the selection of means to their ends, because in most contexts it is easy to follow valid rules of inference. By definition, the agent has to follow those rules to form true beliefs from premises that he believes to be true. And, of course, if he has true beliefs he is more likely to reach his goals. Instrumentally rational people will deviate from logic when they cannot gauge their costs of doing so – that is, when those costs are opaque, as is the case in some experimental settings. They will return to logic when, as we saw in the foregoing discussion of transitivity, such costs are made transparent to them.[9] More generally, people are sensitive to their personal costs of abiding by rules of reasoning (including the rules of practical reasoning laid down in rational choice theory).

We characterize *instrumentally rational belief* as follows:

(IRB) Person *P* is instrumentally rational in believing *B* (a belief *B* is instrumentally rational) if and only if *P* came to believe *B* as a result of a personally cost-effective investment in information and reflection ("IIR," for short).

(IRB) defines "instrumentally rational belief," not "warranted" or "true" belief. (IRB) captures the idea that *having* a belief is an epiphenomenon of *making choices* governed by instrumental rationality – in this case, choices about how much IIR one is going to make. An agent *does* things (watches carefully, reads books, listens to experts, and so on) in order to *form* true beliefs.[10]

---

[8] We use "preference theory," "rational choice theory," "decision theory," and the respective family expressions interchangeably.

[9] See Epstein, *Skepticism and Freedom*, op. cit., pp. 152–6. See also note 6, this chapter, for literature. Sometimes people have beliefs that violate principles of logic, such as the principle of noncontradiction. See Steven A. Sloman, "Two Systems of Reasoning," in Thomas Gilovich, Dale Griffin, and Daniel Kahneman, eds., *Heuristics and Biases: The Psychology of Intuitive Judgment* (Cambridge: Cambridge University Press, 2002), p. 379, esp. pp. 384–9. We discussed those cognitive shortcomings in section 2.4.

[10] Most of the time most persons do not *decide* which beliefs they will have (a few persons occasionally manage to do this, e.g. by ingesting hallucinogens). For a classical discussion of self-induced beliefs, see William K. Clifford, *The Ethics of Belief*, in *The Ethics of Belief and Other Essays* (Amherst, N.Y.: Prometheus Books, 1999), originally published in *Contemporary Review*, 1877. For present purposes, we need not take sides on the nature of the relationship between, on the one hand, IIR, and, on the other, forming certain

When is an agent's IIR cost-effective? Our rational choice assumptions commit us to the following:

(CE) Performing a certain amount of IIR is cost-effective for A if and only if A's marginal benefit and marginal cost of doing so are equal, measured in terms of A's goals.

(CE) subjects the IIR to the standard marginalist approach. Indeed, (CE) is an application of the instrumental account of rationality: It says that an agent will invest in information and reflection up to the point at which further investment will frustrate his goals more than it furthers them, on a subjective measurement of goal fulfillment.

Suppose we read (IRB) in the light of (CE). It then becomes apparent that an instrumentally rational belief need not be true; indeed, it need not even be well grounded. Cost-effective IIR may occur at a point at which, given A's prior beliefs, A will form false beliefs, or beliefs that would look unwarranted to better-informed observers. At that point, A may be using unreliable theories (in the sense explained in section 4.1). Alternatively, A may be following invalid rules of inference. For example, A very much wants to watch a game on television, does his math homework in a hurry, and in his haste uses invalid rules of inference in his attempt to find the correct geometrical representation of an algebraic statement. The analysis could be extended to those cases in which A violates the standard logic of preference (imagine that, because of framing effects, A's vulnerability to money pumping is opaque to him).[11] On ordinary understandings of epistemic rationality, A is in such cases epistemically irrational. Still, A is, in our sense, instrumentally rational, because, by hypothesis, his beliefs resulted from a cost-effective amount of IIR, measured in terms of A's goals. Both when A violates valid rules of inference (including the logic of preference) and when he uses unreliable empirical theories, he engages in discourse failure if his utterances match his beliefs: The agent's incentives (his marginal benefits and costs) led him to form beliefs that are not warranted by reliable social science. His beliefs have been acquired through a truth-insensitive process that leads, as we argued in the previous chapter, to various patterns of political beliefs. A's cost-effective IIR induced him to form beliefs to which reliable social

---

beliefs. Maybe certain amounts of investment in certain kinds of information and reflection *cause* people to believe certain things; alternatively, there may be accounts of IIR that *logically entail* the possession of certain beliefs; and there may be still other connections between IIR and belief.

[11] We discussed framing in section 2.4. See also note 7, this chapter.

science lends no support.[12] (CE) offers an account of belief formation that guarantees that *even sincere citizens will frequently engage in discourse failure, for an agent's cost-effective amount of IIR will frequently be insufficient for her forming true beliefs.*

We extend, then, instrumental rationality to include belief formation. More generally, epistemic rationality can be accounted for in instrumental terms, in the following sense: Recall that if A is instrumentally rational, A holds a (true or false, reliable or unreliable) belief b if and only if A formed b through cost-effective means of achieving A's goals, given A's prior beliefs. A may not be trying to form true beliefs: *A* may be pursuing noncognitive goals, and *b* may be a by-product of that pursuit. For instance, during his journey to Los Angeles, *A* is likely to form many incidental beliefs. *A* likes sushi and may have come to believe (perhaps wrongly) that quite a few restaurants offer Mexican food along the Sonora desert. This belief is in turn a by-product of *A*'s intending to find out where sushi is offered along the highway. *Epistemic* rationality enters this instrumental picture in the following way: The usual standards of epistemic rationality (logical consistency, empirical support, disposition to address initially plausible objections, and so on) are instrumental to truth, and truth is in turn instrumental to *A*'s achieving most of her goals. For example, *A* must get the relevant causal connections right – otherwise, in most contexts she will not achieve her goals.[13]

One central claim of this book can therefore be formulated thus: The systematic divergence between the patterns of political beliefs that we have identified and the patterns of explanation and prediction advanced by reliable social science results from the fact that the cost-effective level of IIR lies below the amount needed to form beliefs consistent with reliable social science. Instrumental rationality tends to produce, on the one hand, unreliable political *beliefs*, and, on the other hand, the patterns of

---

[12] When the agent violates valid rules of inference, he fails to rely on the reasons provided by reliable social science even if those beliefs could be validly inferred from reliable social science. By definition, he would thereby engage in discourse failure (see section 2.2).

[13] To be sure, *A* may pursue goals for which self-deception is necessary. She may want to be brave enough to defeat an enemy and may also believe that, by taking a certain drug that makes her believe that the enemy is not as dangerous as he really is, she will be able to defeat him. But notice that *A*'s goal will not be reached unless *A*'s belief that the drug works in that way is *true*. To the extent that we may intelligibly say that *A*'s goal is to defeat that enemy, *A* must want her belief about the drug's relevant properties to be true. *Wanting our beliefs about the means–ends relationship to be true* is a conceptual prerequisite of our pursuing goals.

discourse failure that emanate from the mutually reinforcing interaction between such beliefs and the incentives to posture furnished by electoral politics and other truth-insensitive settings.

Instrumental and epistemic rationality are related, then, in a way that supports our approach, to the detriment of the deliberativist's. We argued that an *instrumentally* rational agent's beliefs may have resulted from unreliable cognitive processes. We now want to challenge the *epistemological* view known as *reliabilism,* according to which a belief is epistemically rational if it was caused by a cognitive process that maximizes the individual's chances of forming true beliefs. On this view, an epistemically rational individual A will believe only those propositions filtered by plausible rules of critical thinking. Thus, if A believes the proposition "if P, then Q" and also believes "P," A will not reject "Q." The weakness of reliabilism can be seen by a mental experiment imagined by Richard Foley. He asks us to imagine that person X is unwittingly transported to a world w^* that *looks* to X exactly like the actual world w, including X's experiences, recollections, and reflective abilities and practices, because an evil demon induced on X systematically false experiences, recollections, and so on. Foley points out that our judgment that X holds in w *epistemically* rational beliefs is not undermined at all by X's using unreliable cognitive processes. That X does use such processes in w is shown by the fact that w and w^* are indistinguishable from X's viewpoint. Foley concludes that epistemic rationality does not presuppose reliable cognitive processes – that is, processes that make it more likely for us to form true beliefs than to form false beliefs.[14] Evil-demon arguments show that our beliefs may be epistemically rational despite the fact that they arose from unreliable cognitive processes. However, such arguments do not state the necessary and sufficient conditions for a belief to be epistemically rational. Evil-demon arguments play a purely negative role: They tell us what epistemic rationality is not. They leave unanswered the question of what epistemic rationality would look like. Yet we need that positive characterization to determine how epistemic rationality relates to instrumental rationality. We will next show that the two types of rationality are related in a way that allows us to dispose of the deliberativist's objection to our instrumental account of deliberation.

[14] See Richard Foley, "What's wrong with reliabilism?" in Sven Bernecker and Fred Dretske, eds., *Knowledge: Readings in Contemporary Epistemology* (Oxford: Oxford University Press, 2000), pp. 166–77, esp. pp. 166–72 (orig. published in *The Monist* 68, 1985, pp. 188–202). Foley's views are now collected in two books: *The Theory of Epistemic Rationality* (Cambridge, Mass.: Harvard University Press, 1987) and *Intellectual Trust in Oneself and Others* (Cambridge: Cambridge University Press, 2001).

Clearly, (IRB) does not call for reliable beliefs. The following is perfectly possible: The agent believes *B*, his believing *B* is rational under (IRB), and yet *B* was not formed through a cognitive process that yields mostly true beliefs. This is so because, as we have seen, the agent's cost-effective IIR may well not be reliable. We would be extremely fortunate if, given our time pressures in the pursuit of many (frequently noncognitive) goals, our cost-effective IIRs were located exactly[15] at the point at which we end up believing the propositions supported by reliable social science, whose opacity frequently demands careful and lengthy study. On the other hand, the instrumentally rational agent has an obvious interest in getting things right, for otherwise he cannot achieve her goals, cognitive or otherwise.[16]

The use of epistemically rational procedures is here *relativized to the cost-effective IIR*. This allows us to make room, within our instrumental account, not merely for Downsian rational ignorance – that is, the ignorance displayed whenever marginal costs and benefits of looking for information are equal – but also for a more general epistemic shortcoming. As we saw, at his optimal IIR the agent may rely on (in addition to insufficient or distorted information) invalid *rules of inference*. For example, *A* may be in such a hurry that she relies on her "feeling" concerning what the "facts" show, rather than on correct inductive rules. Our very judgments about the *validity* of rules of inference are instrumentally rational in the present sense: We formed such (more or less conscious) judgments through a cost-effective IIR. Ideal rules of epistemic rationality are no exception: We teach them in our logic courses given our optimal IIR, and our students will be likely to internalize them, given their

[15] More IIR may in certain contexts take us away from truth. For example, a nonbiased sample will turn into a biased sample if we add certain types of (true) information, and so we will be more likely to err if we generalize on the basis of the latter sample.

[16] It might be tempting to reduce this epistemic component ("getting things right") to instrumental concepts as follows:

(WB) Person *X*'s IIR is cost-effective for *X* if and only if *X* made such investment in light of warranted beliefs about the amount of information and reflection that further *X*'s goals or values.

However, this will not do as a way of fleshing out (IRB), because WB uses the notion of warranted beliefs. WB yields an account of belief formation that is parasitic upon an account of epistemic rationality, which is precisely what (IRB) intended to avoid. This means that, when fleshed out by WB, (IRB) would not have succeeded in providing an *independent, instrumental* model of belief. (IRB) is intended to provide a notion of belief relativized to the agent's goals and prior beliefs (warranted or not). WB relies instead on an objective notion of rationality – a notion of epistemically rational, or warranted, belief.

cost-effective IIRs (given, that is, their prior beliefs and their goals, such as passing our courses). Because of their incentives to teach and learn well, teachers' and students' cost-effective IIRs tend to be higher than in most contexts outside the classroom.

The deliberativist might welcome the fact that, on our account, an agent's A instrumental rationality is consistent with A's forming systematically false or unreliable beliefs. This possibility is left open by (CE), because an agent's cost-effective IIR may occur at a point at which A has not formed true beliefs. This is good news for the deliberativist, because it sets the stage for his account of civic virtue. He might say that civic deliberation will be epistemically valuable on condition that citizens embrace a variety of civic virtues (e.g., a disposition to participate in politics, or to see others' allegations in their best light) that presuppose the abandonment of purely instrumental (and usually selfish) attitudes.[17] A related suggestion, mentioned at the beginning of this section, is that an instrumental model of rationality will misrepresent the behavior of persons committed to epistemic rationality. Construing *epistemic* rationality in instrumental terms is hopeless because it involves a category mistake. The inner logic of political deliberation, this deliberativist concludes, cannot be reduced to cost–benefit analysis.

However, this divide between instrumental and epistemic rationality cannot be formulated in a way that undermines our analysis in this book. Our aims are explanatory and predictive, not justificatory. The instrumental model at work in our discussion of patterns of political belief was intended to serve such aims. The category mistake is apparent only because the *fact* that a cognizer is epistemically rational can be *explained* on instrumental grounds. Although the *rules* of epistemic rationality differ from the *rules* of instrumental rationality, the fact that someone follows the former rules may be explained on instrumental grounds.

We can now offer a *positive* characterization of rationality. Recall that the foregoing refutation of reliabilism (which we accepted) was essentially negative: It told us that epistemically rational belief does not presuppose reliable methods of cognition. The person systematically misled by the evil demon is epistemically rational, because, by construction, his cost-effective IIR and that of his real-world counterpart are equal. Because, from the point of view of the cognizer, the two worlds are indistinguishable, the systematically misled cognizer cannot possibly have more reason (evidence) to change her mind than her real-world counterpart has.

---

[17] We discuss civic-virtue arguments in another context in sections 6.1 and 7.5.

Evil-demon examples not only show that epistemic rationality does not presuppose reliability. They also point to the practical significance of having a belief, whether true or false: According to (IRB), the IIR that led A to a certain belief helps A achieve her goals in the least costly way. Because A's achieving her goals will in general turn on A's having true beliefs about the relevant means–ends relationships,[18] instrumental rationality pulls toward epistemic rationality – toward, that is, adopting truth-sensitive cognitive processes, given that these in general help A achieve her goals. However, it is always possible (as in the evil-demon situation) for the agent's cost-effective IIR to be systematically below the amount necessary to form true beliefs, including beliefs about the most reliable cognitive processes. Just as a court may fail, *despite making an optimal IIR*, to select the most reliable witness, an agent may err in deferring to a certain cognitive process. Persons who search for the truth may not merely form false beliefs about *the world* – they may misidentify *the most reliable source of beliefs about the world*. Instrumentally rational agents will take care to avoid such meta-errors, because they need to correctly identify the means to their particular goals; but they will avoid those errors at their lowest personal cost in terms of their total set of goals. We submit, then, that the epistemic rationality we discern in both the evil-demon's victim and his real-world counterpart is nothing but their instrumentally rational, and so truth-sensitive, adoption of a (possibly unreliable) cognitive process.

An objector may say that in w^*, the world where X falls prey to the evil demon's tricks, X is not really as successful in attaining X's goals as X is in w, the actual world – X's rate of success in w^* just *looks* the same from X's perspective. X cannot be instrumentally rational to the same degree, so this objector concludes, in both worlds. It would seem, then, that the fact that X is epistemically rational in both worlds cannot be explicated in terms of X's instrumental rationality.

This objection rests on a mischaracterization of instrumental rationality. As we have already seen, the instrumentally rational person pursues her goals in cost-effective ways, given her beliefs. Now these include *beliefs about the authenticity of her achievements*. For the purposes of explaining, or predicting, X's behavior in w^*, we must infer X's goals and beliefs from X's observed behavior. We would proceed in a similar fashion if we were interested in explaining, or predicting, the behavior of people on whom we induced, by means of hallucinogens, certain experiences. Of

---

[18] See note 13.

course, *actually* achieving certain goals will normally be highly ranked in an agent's hierarchy of goals. This explains why X would, in all likelihood, feel disappointed should she realize that her great achievements were illusory. To the extent that agents value authenticity, they will adjust their behavior and beliefs to their (meta-) beliefs about what counts as a genuine achievement. And, by construction, X will do this as successfully as her real-world counterpart: In w^*, X has by hypothesis no way of learning that her achievements are fictitious. It follows that both are instrumentally rational to the same degree.

In the evil-demon refutation of reliabilism, epistemically rational agents form beliefs through a second-order process that tries to identify the most reliable first-order cognitive process. In doing so, they are governed by rational choice postulates as they invest in information and reflection. For the reasons already given, this behavior is truth-sensitive. However, there is no guarantee that agents will pick the most reliable first-order (cognitive) process: It all depends on whether their cost-effective IIR leads them to adopt such a process.[19]

This account underpins our theory of discourse failure. Deception – whether by evil demons, politicians, or others – does not preclude

---

[19] Foley comes close to characterizing epistemic rationality in terms of instrumental rationality. He writes: "[W]hat it is rational for a person to believe is a function of what it is appropriate for him to believe given his perspective. More exactly, it is a function of what it is appropriate for him to believe given his perspective and insofar as his goal is to believe truths and not to believe falsehoods." Op. cit., p. 171. Foley is writing here about what it is *rational to believe* for a person who has truth as his *goal*. This is slightly confusing, because pursuing goals consists in *doing* things, whereas, as we have noted, a person just *has* beliefs. Our account clarifies the idea that it is instrumentally rational for a person to *do* certain things to *form* true beliefs at his lowest cost in terms of his total set of goals. Epistemically rational belief is here instrumental in the sense that (i) it is belief formed by an instrumentally rational agent, and (ii) instrumentally rational agents pursue the truth, either as an end or as a means to noncognitive goals. Even when, as is often the case, instrumentally rational agents pursue noncognitive goals, they must form true beliefs about the least costly means to achieve those goals. Foley observes, and we agree, that a *rational* belief may well be *false*. Op. cit., pp. 169–72. Our instrumental, or rational choice, account of what it is rational to *do* given the aim of forming true beliefs is context-dependent and accommodates Foley's claim. It depends on how the agent ranks that aim within his total set of goals, and on his prior beliefs, including beliefs about what he can correctly infer from his prior beliefs. Kent Bach draws a distinction "between a person being justified in holding a belief and the belief itself being justified" (i.e., being the result of a reliable cognitive process) in order to clarify the dispute between reliabilists (sometimes called "externalists") and anti-reliabilists ("internalists"). He argues that some "internalist" arguments lose plausibility when viewed as analyses of justified belief. Kent Bach, op. cit., at 205–7 (originally published in *The Monist* 68 [1985], pp. 246–63).

epistemic rationality.[20] And epistemic rationality has a place, in the ways just explicated, in instrumental rationality. The epistemically rational agent follows the appropriate rules for the attainment of truth, given his goals (whether cognitive or not) and prior beliefs, including beliefs about what time he is to devote to discerning and applying such rules. He may be not merely ignorant vis-à-vis the total amount of available information relevant to his decision but also inaccurate at discerning or applying valid rules of inference. Both kinds of epistemic shortcomings result from his cost-effective IIR, given his prior, empirical and logical, beliefs. Epistemic rationality enters this picture insofar as true beliefs (including beliefs about rules of logic, broadly understood) are instrumental to most goals.

Let us summarize. In this section, we suggested how an instrumental account of rationality can accommodate the notion of belief formation, whether those beliefs are true or false. On an instrumental account, persons pursue their goals in cost-effective ways, given their beliefs. Such beliefs are in turn epiphenomena of instrumentally rational actions performed in the pursuit of their goals, whether epistemic or not. Goals, even noncognitive ones (e.g., losing weight, rescuing a drowning person) necessitate true beliefs about cost-effective means (e.g., cognitive intermediate goals, such as finding out the phone number of a good nutritionist, or where the closest life buoy is). The IIR aimed at forming such intermediate beliefs must itself be cost-effective, and as a result it may pick an unreliable source of belief (e.g., visual perception amidst a dense fog). Instrumental rationality pulls toward epistemic rationality without guaranteeing reliability, let alone truth.

Recall now the objection with which we started this section: Given the objectivity or inner logic of reason, citizens will be led to positions that no instrumental account can explain or predict. We now see that our instrumental account of belief-formation questions neither the objectivity of reason nor its motivational force, nor the possibility, discussed in section 2.4, that people suffer from cognitive dissonances. On our account, belief is instrumental in the sense that the actions leading to it (seeing, listening, thinking, and the other activities embodied in the agent's IIR) fit rational choice assumptions. We certainly do not claim that the *truth*

---

[20] Foley argues that evil-demon, brain-in-the-vat, and like examples disprove the more general claim that "the mere fact that we do have, or have had, or will have, or would have false beliefs, implies that we cannot be epistemically rational." Op. cit., pp. 168–71, at p. 170.

or *falsity* of a belief can be given an instrumental interpretation – that claim may well be a category mistake. But we hope we have shown in this section that the idea of an instrumental account of *belief formation* is plausible. Indeed, we can state one central thesis of this book by saying that, at least in a typical liberal democracy, instrumentally *and* epistemically rational agents will display certain patterns of political error. They are instrumentally rational because their investments in information and reflection are cost-effective. And they are epistemically rational because, given the informational constraints under which they act, it is rational for them to believe what they believe.

3.2. Rational Choice and Morality

So far we have analyzed political discourse with the tools of rational choice theory. A common objection to this approach is that it overlooks moral behavior. Surely, many people overcome the temptation to behave immorally. We all know people who act on principle at great personal cost. Rational choice theory, so the objection continues, can accommodate moral behavior only by circular maneuvers. Thus, it would be circular to invoke the very fact that someone stands to gain by legislation to infer that he was advocating such piece of legislation out of self-interest. Other hypotheses (e.g., ones that ascribe public-spirited goals to the agent) are consistent with the facts as well. Moreover, the possibility that people act in principled ways suggests remedies to discourse failure. For example, educational campaigns may enhance civic awareness so that citizens will be disposed to inform themselves suitably and participate in the political forum. Such campaigns would significantly reduce discourse failure.

We have three replies. Consider, first, the objection that rational choice explanations of political behavior are circular. It would be indeed circular to point *merely* to the fact that Joe supported legislation that benefits him in order to defend the proposition that Joe's self-interest caused him to support that piece of legislation. But, as Nozick observes, "it is *not* a uniform circle to say that event A caused event B, and that our reason for thinking event A occurred is that event B occurred."[21] Here, "'causes' goes in one direction, and 'is a reason for thinking' goes in the other direction."[22] Thus, to use Nozick's example, we may believe that the cause that a bridge collapsed was that it had a structural defect, where our reason for such belief is the collapse itself. This is not circular

---

[21] Nozick, *Invariances*, op. cit., p. 50.
[22] Ibid.

if we possess independently tested theories about why that type of structural defect often causes bridges to collapse. Similarly, it is not circular to say both that Joe's self-interest *caused* him to support legislation that benefited him and that our *reason for thinking* that he supported the legislation was that he was self-interested. We may believe this, not *just because* he supported legislation that benefited him (this would be circular) but because we have reliable, independently tested theories telling us that most people in Joe's situation who support legislation that benefits them are self-interested. Thus, the contention that most lobbyists in the political arena are narrowly self-interested rests on independently testable hypotheses. Of course, empirical evidence may force us to abandon a specific attribution of self-interest in a particular case. In many other cases we might need more information. Suppose Helen is a human rights activist lobbying for the ratification of human rights treaties. If we find out that she does this at great personal cost, we will hypothesize that she is acting altruistically. But if she ends up at a high-profile, highly paid post in an international organization or in government, we need additional evidence to decide whether or not we should abandon the original hypothesis. It is not too farfetched to assume that the *best explanation* of a politician's success should appeal to some version of the self-interest postulate (in terms of, say, maximization of a mix of power, glory, and money), as opposed to his pursuing lofty goals, but this is of course a rebuttable presumption.[23]

Second, our account of discourse failure suggests that many people are morally motivated but mistaken. People's widespread endorsement of vivid explanations leads them to make (perhaps questionable) moral judgments. We saw, for example, that the public will hold successful groups morally responsible for the plight of unsuccessful groups (thus, anti-globalization protesters blame big business for the plight of sectors disadvantaged by free-trade policies). When such ascriptions of moral responsibility are not instances of posturing but a reflection of genuine moral indignation, they stem from causal mistakes. Obviously, a citizen who is trying to act morally will advance policies that are mistaken in terms of his own values if he gets the relevant facts wrong. To these causal pathologies we should add the specifically moral mistakes that we will discuss in section 6.6.

Third, the claim that educational campaigns can make citizens more altruistic and so more inclined to participate in politics is open to doubt. Perhaps *some* educational process could make citizens more altruistic and

---

[23] See also our remarks on ad hoc hypotheses in section 5.4.

participative. Our point is, however, that no feasible majoritarian deliberative mechanism will implement *that type of* educational process. (In
section 2.2, we illustrated this phenomenon with the teaching of trade
theory.) Educational campaigns will reflect the very pathologies that
helped create the political majorities and elect the officials in charge
of implementing those campaigns. Thus, educators will typically teach
people *vivid* ways to be altruistic; for example, they will tell them to help
others either privately or through the state (by voting for tangible subsidies, for example). If our analysis is correct, this approach has advantages
in the political competition over educational campaigns that teach people
opaque ways to be altruistic (for example, by voting for trade liberalization
as a way to help the poor, given the findings in section 2.1). Moreover,
there is evidence that philanthropic attitudes flourished more in times
when the prevailing ethos embraced individual self-reliance under free-
market rules than nowadays, when an ethos of collective responsibility
discharged through the state is much stronger.[24] In light of this, it may
well be the case that an educational campaign aimed at promoting solidarity should teach not only the virtues of private charity but also the
role of private markets in fostering such virtues. These teachings are,
of course, considerably more opaque than statist messages. As a result,
the educational campaign that voters are likely to implement will spawn,
rather than counteract, discourse failure. Moreover, it is far from clear
that teaching concern for others goes hand in hand with defending the
redistributive role of the state. The assumption that the state (or rather,
the politicians who ultimately constitute it) is willing and able to redistribute resources in accordance with justice underlies the educational
policies favored by many citizens. However, there is reason to doubt this
assumption, in light of informational[25] and motivational[26] shortcomings

[24] See, for example, David Schmidtz, "Taking Responsibility," in David Schmidtz and Robert
Goodin, *Social Welfare and Individual Responsibility* (Cambridge: Cambridge University
Press, 1998), pp. 63–9.
[25] See the classical statement of the informational superiority of markets over government
in meeting human needs in Friedrich A. Hayek, "The Use of Knowledge in Society," in
Richard M. Ebeling, ed., *Austrian Economics* (Hillsdale, Mich.: Hillsdale College Press,
1991), pp. 247–63. For a critical survey of the epistemic argument for markets, see John
Gray, "The Moral Foundations of Market Institutions," in *Beyond the New Right: Markets,
Government, and the Common Environment* (London: Routledge, 1993). See also, for a well-
documented theoretical and empirical case for epistemic skepticism about the effects of
public policies, Gerald F. Gaus, "Social Complexity and Moral Radicalism," unpublished.
[26] The rational choice scholarship about perverse incentives in political decision making
is sometimes known as "public-choice theory." For examples of relevant literature, see
note 24, Chapter 7.

that afflict government. To entrust the state with the function of redis-tributing resources while avoiding the issue of government's informa-tional and motivational shortcomings is itself symptomatic of discourse failure: It trades on the vivid notion that the visible hand of the state will do a better job than the opaque workings of the market.

Finally, even were such campaigns to succeed, it is hard to see why altru-istic citizens, if rational, will participate in politics to the extent hoped by deliberativists. The altruistic citizen knows that her marginal contribu-tion to deliberative politics is significantly lower than many other things she could do to help others. That contribution crucially depends both on the citizen's becoming adequately informed about the policies that are most effective in helping others and on her ability to persuade others to vote accordingly. But she surely has more effective ways of helping oth-ers, here and now, than becoming involved in political deliberation. She might, for example, channel her altruism through individual charity.[27]

Why not, then, directly instill *participatory* attitudes in citizens, and not just altruistic impulses? Educational campaigns would commend the virtue of intense participation, of shedding one's political apathy and acquiring the taste and passion for politics. One interpretation of this view can be summarily dismissed: If the aim is to reduce discourse failure, surely increasing the level of passion will be ineffectual, if not counterpro-ductive. If we are correct about the roots of discourse failure, educational campaigns should motivate citizens to dispassionately and carefully study reliable social theories and facts. The view can be reformulated to include the duty to become properly informed: The educational campaign would recommend properly informed participation. We believe, though, that this view is both utopian and morally questionable. It is utopian because, given the rational ignorance effect, it stretches credulity to suppose that education will make people undertake lengthy and difficult studies at great personal cost. Moreover, there is little hope that educational short-cuts will bridge the gap between citizens' ignorance and the threshold political literacy required to overcome discourse failure.[28] The view is also

---

[27] Even in societies entirely composed of altruists, certain forms of beneficence will be underprovided, either because they are public goods for those altruists or because each altruist lacks assurance that a sufficient number of others will contribute. In both cases, free riding in the collective effort and engaging in private (by hypothesis, less effective) charity is the rational course of action. See Allen Buchanan, *Ethics, Efficiency, and the Market* (Totowa, N.J.: Rowman & Allanheld, 1985), pp. 71–5.

[28] We further discuss the practical import of utopias in sections 4.6 and 9.5. See also our discussion of simplified versions of social theory in section 4.1.

morally questionable because the duty to become properly informed to the point of overcoming error requires people to forgo many personal projects and activities they may legitimately pursue. The alleged duty to become so politically informed does not seem to be part of any but the harshest moralities.

A final reflection on the relationships between rational choice analysis and morality is in order. Far from rejecting morality, rational choice analysis enables us to do a better job of judging actions and persons. We routinely make our moral judgments depend on the incentives faced by the agents whose behavior we evaluate. We excuse otherwise objectionable behavior if it was coerced; we admire those who help others at great personal cost. Rational choice analysis helps us see incentive structures and in doing so facilitates our moral evaluation. Discourse failure ultimately arises from the mutually reinforcing interaction between rational error and posturing. There is a short step from this diagnosis to passing moral judgment on the discursive behavior of key political actors. Thus, we should expect certain roles or positions, such as those of successful politicians, to be disproportionately filled by individuals whose discursive behavior is morally objectionable. By the same token, rational choice theory may help us identify morally worthy political behavior: It may help us see the background of incentives against which it makes sense to say that behavior is self-denying (e.g., it places a candidate at a political disadvantage) for the sake of principle.[29]

3.3. Why Our Argument Is Not Ad Hominem

Does our analysis of discourse failure commit the ad hominem fallacy – that is, the rhetorical technique of criticizing a position not by addressing its merits but by pointing to characteristics of the person who holds it? Suppose Joan gives an argument in favor of environmental regulation and Peter rejects it on the grounds that Joan is on a short list for head of the Environmental Protection Agency under a pro-environment administration. Peter's response is arguably fallacious because it points to a fact (the speaker's having been short listed) that, though possibly relevant to assessing Joan's sincerity, is irrelevant to assessing the *soundness* of her argument. An argument is sound if and only if its premises are true and

---

[29] For a more detailed defense of the idea that rational choice theory helps us understand moral motivation, see Guido Pincione, "Should Law Professors Teach Public Choice Theory?" op. cit., pp. 451–70, esp. pp. 455–65.

bear the appropriate (deductive or inductive) relations with its conclusion. Adducing the fact that the speaker aspires to a government job targets neither of these conditions for the soundness of her argument. In this book we argue that people engage in various patterns of political discourse (such as visible-hand explanations) because they have incentives to do so. More specifically, we argue that citizens in a typical liberal democracy will find it costly to acquire the information that would enable them to get rid of unreliable default theories, and that in turn politicians and other politically connected actors will benefit from spreading information and views that conform to those theories. We may accordingly be accused of committing an ad hominem fallacy because we refuse to address the merits of the public positions in question and instead dismiss them on account of the structure of incentives faced by the speaker. Just as it is irrelevant, in response to an environmentalist argument, to cite the speaker's job ambitions, so it is irrelevant to remark that the speaker faces a certain structure of incentives. The idea is that, in either case, the respondent should assess the argument on its merits.

We do not need to discuss when and why an ad hominem argument is really fallacious,[30] because our argument is not ad hominem. We do not claim that a public position is mistaken *because of* some characteristic of the speaker, including the structure of incentives he may be facing. We instead defer to reliable social science.[31] In other words, to determine whether a public position is mistaken, we resort to evidence that is independent of the circumstances surrounding the speaker. We appeal to such circumstances to explain the patterns of political beliefs we observe, but not to determine the truth-value of those beliefs. Given that popular opinions clash with reliable social science, we claim that many people are mistaken about the way society works. The theory of discourse failure explains that pathology.

3.4. A Note on Empirical Testing

The theory developed in this book can be subject to empirical tests. For example, the kinds of beliefs that people have about society can be determined by polls and other methods of empirical research that are well developed in political science, sociology, psychology, history, and economics. In this book, however, we do not undertake the empirical

---

[30] Goldman discusses the issue in *Knowledge in a Social World*, op. cit., pp. 152–3.
[31] For discussion of reliable social science, see section 4.1.

research that would be needed to test many of the consequences of our theory. We leave that task to scholars better equipped for it than we. We intend to contribute to the tradition of speculative social theory – that is, a conceptual framework that predicts human behavior by identifying the structure of incentives under which people operate. We show what the discursive behavior of citizens, politicians, rent seekers, and other political actors in modern democratic societies would look like if the relevant actors' behaviors conformed to usual rational choice assumptions. On these grounds, we predict that the public positions endorsed by political actors will be generally at odds with reliable social science, and that this disharmony will conform to definite patterns. Applications of price theory to rent control, which predict shortages and lower quality in housing under the assumption that landlords and tenants are wealth maximizers, illustrate this methodological tradition.

Of course, empirical testing of speculative social theories is vital. Our theory is methodologically incomplete in the same sense in which the economics of rent control or labor economics are incomplete: Many of their predictions require empirical confirmation. Having said this, we should note that some of the most obvious and pervasive empirical consequences of our model are already borne out by massive evidence available in the public domain.[32] Thus, our model predicts that people will be more likely to support tax cuts if they are told that "they get to take a hundred dollars home" than if they are told the cuts will directly benefit the rich as a means to increase production, employment, and general prosperity.[33] A related prediction is that politicians will tend to use the former rather than the latter argument. To a great extent, our argument proposes to reinterpret well-known social phenomena in a new light.

While we do not address empirical testing generally, we conclude this chapter by considering a possible challenge to our assumption that the public errs in politics. Benjamin Page and Robert Shapiro have claimed that, at least in the United States, the public's collective preferences are

---

[32] For a recent example, see Michael J. Boskin, "Economic Illiteracy on the Campaign Trail," *The Economists' Voice*, Vol. 1, issue 2, 2004, Article 8, available at http://www.bepress.com/ev/vol1/iss2/art8/.

[33] Consider this: Many writers find it uncontroversial that utilitarians are committed to redistributive taxation. The idea is that, given diminishing marginal utility of wealth, redistributing from rich to poor increases overall utility. But this is far from obvious. See the argument that David Schmidtz advances against it in *Elements of Justice* (New York: Cambridge University Press, forthcoming 2006), Part 5, Chapter 5.5.

stable (as opposed to capricious and fickle) over time; and that public opinion, considered collectively, is rational in that it is able to make distinctions, organized in coherent patterns, reasonable (i.e., based on the best available information), and adaptive to new information and changed circumstances.[34]

These claims have been challenged,[35] but even if they are correct, they do not undermine our thesis in this book. Our claim is not that public opinion is unstable. On the contrary, we identify systematic patterns of political belief. The public has views about society that are at odds with reliable social science, those views assume specific patterns, and in turn politicians and others encourage those views for self-interested reasons. In fact, the problem is *precisely* that public policy tends to track the citizens' preferences for various types of *policies* – or, in less charitable terms, that politicians reinforce the public's mistakes about *how* to satisfy their preferences for *outcomes*. Similarly, our views are consistent with Page and Shapiro's findings that the public's voting behavior changes with new information. We just claim that a subset of that information (social explanations) is often wrong. Page and Shapiro concede the rational ignorance hypothesis,[36] and the empirical data they use does not speak to the epistemic credentials of public opinion. For example, they claim that the public is rational because it reacts to *the best available* information. That is precisely our point: that the public acts rationally, both epistemically and instrumentally, when they ignore reliable social science, given the information they receive.[37] We add that the theoretical and factual information that the media feeds to the public (i) is deficient when contrasted with reliable social science and (ii) fits vivid theories that the public holds by default. That entire process conditions, in truth-insensitive ways, their public political positions. Finally, Page and Shapiro's optimistic view of deliberation does not seem to follow from their general theses about the public's preferences. They claim that after scientists debate in academic

---

[34] *The Rational Public,* op. cit., p. 14. See also p. xi (opinion changes are "sensible" adjustments to new information and circumstances).

[35] See Delli Carpini and Keater, *What Americans Know About Politics and Why It Matters,* op. cit., pp. 43–4 (Page and Shapiro's "collective rationality" poses serious problems of representativeness); Norman R. Luttbeg, review of *The Rational Public,* op. cit., *The Journal of Politics,* Vol. 55, no. 2, 1993, pp. 518–19 (the public's stability of opinion over time can be explained with equal ease by largely random responses); W. Lawrence Neuman, review of *The Rational Public* cit., *The Journal of Sociology,* Vol. 98, no. 5 (March 1993), pp. 1174–5 (criticizing Page and Shapiro's quick leap from data to broad generalization).

[36] *The Rational Public,* op. cit., p. 14.

[37] See section 3.1.

journals, the media capture the essential points and transmit them to the public.[38] This claim is highly implausible, at least with regard to social science, for the reasons we have suggested. As a preliminary matter, the media will often fail to identify reliable social science, if only because they seek high ratings, not truths, and high ratings will of course be sensitive to a public opinion already affected by discourse failure. And even if the media accurately broadcast reliable science, they will oversimplify the issues in order to grab the public's attention. Politicians will deal truth the *coup de grâce* by spinning the information for electoral gain. The public will lack effective shortcuts for weeding out junk social science (see section 4.4).

[38] Id., pp. 362–6.

4

The Resilience of Discourse Failure

4.1. Reliable Social Science and Opacity

We have seen why ordinary citizens will hold political views at variance with the findings of reliable social theories. People believe vivid explanations of how society works, whereas many reliable social theories provide opaque explanations. Most citizens are doomed to ignorance and error by the dynamics of political discourse. Politicians and rent seekers will take advantage of this, in turn fueling discourse failure. This situation is fatal to theories of deliberative democracy.

When is a social theory *reliable?* While the conditions for theoretical reliability are much debated in the philosophy of science, for our purposes it suffices to say that a theory is reliable when the relevant research community generally accepts it. Identifying the relevant research community in terms of the methodology used can nevertheless be tricky. For example, writers differ about the scientific status of psychoanalysis, or about the features that make astronomy a science – in contrast to astrology, for example. Many such controversies turn on views about the proper methods of scientific inquiry.[1] Of course, were we to probe into such questions we would run the risk of reintroducing the very problem

---

[1] One major topic in the literature on the philosophy of science is the demarcation between science and pseudo science. Two particularly influential, and opposing, positions are Karl R. Popper, *The Logic of Scientific Discovery* (New York: Harper & Row, 1968, first ed. In German 1934), and Thomas S. Kuhn, *The Structure of Scientific Revolutions* (Chicago: University of Chicago Press, 1996, first ed. 1962). See also the essays in Imre Lakatos and Alan Musgrave, eds., *Criticism and Growth of Knowledge* (Cambridge: Cambridge University Press, 1970).

that we hope to avoid – how to persuade skeptics that some branches of scholarship are more reliable than others.

We bypass these problems by proposing a series of operational tests. Reliable social science (and philosophy, where applicable) is the corpus of propositions that meet the following conditions:

1) They are the most widely accepted, at least as an initially plausible target of critique, in the top fifteen journals in the relevant discipline (political science, economics, sociology, law, philosophy, and so forth). To identify the top fifteen journals in the relevant discipline, we propose a further operational test: They are the journals that would be voted as the best ones by the majority of faculty in the top thirty departments of the disciplines in English-speaking universities. An operational definition may also identify the top thirty departments using reliable (as defined, in turn, through further operational tests) publicly available rankings.

2) They should not appear in journals that are vulnerable to the kind of parody illustrated by the famous "Sokal affair."[2]

3) Even if conditions (1) and (2) are met, propositions about society that are *taken for granted* in published articles, thus ignoring their treatment by the relevant disciplines, do not count as such as reliable social science. For example, imagine an article in a Latin American studies journal that discusses whether or not the film *María Full of Grace* is a statement against globalization, where the author assumes or implies without argument that globalization is bad. Whatever its merits as film criticism, the article cannot be part of the evidence against globalization. (The same exclusion would apply, of course, should the ideological message be reversed; however, for reasons we indicated in section 2.6., that situation is less likely to occur.)

A few clarifications about these operational tests are in order. For example, someone may challenge our deference in condition (1) to English-speaking journals. We certainly believe that English-speaking universities are leaders in social science and philosophy, but our operational test is intended to convince those who deny this. Thus, to someone who questions the choice of English-speaking academia we respond that the

---

[2] Alan Sokal, a professor of physics, submitted an article to the journal *Social Text* in which he parodied deconstructionist and postmodernist writing style. The journal published the article in all seriousness. For a full account, see Alan Sokal and Jean Bricmont, *Intellectual Impostures* (London: Profile Books, 1998).

journals that English-speaking departments would choose are those that practice the most rigorous scrutiny of the materials submitted for publication. We would invite those who in turn deny *this* to conduct further operational tests. For example, we may introduce a definition of "rigorous scrutiny" in terms of minimum number of words used in a double-blind review that rejects a manuscript. Also, we choose departments from the English-speaking world for a pragmatic reason: The most comprehensive rankings of academic performance primarily survey those universities.[3] We surmise that at some point most disputants will accept the verdict of operational tests to determine what counts as reliable social science. Thus, one could compare the length and thoroughness of reviews by referees of different journals. We presume that all parties to the dispute will agree that journals which rarely produce blind reviews should not weigh as heavily as those that do.[4] Of course, our test does not exclude the possibility that journals off the list publish valuable material. We adopt the test described as operationally accurate to identify *reliable propositions* in the social sciences or philosophy. Good social science will sooner or later reach the journals mentioned previously, even if it initially saw the light of day elsewhere.

The second condition privileges *arguments* – not gibberish, "narratives," or free association. However, we want to stick to operational tests, thus avoiding as much as possible substantive judgments about which areas of scholarship, or orientations, are inherently more or less valuable.

Finally, the third condition is necessary to exclude *segmentations* in academic markets that enable many academics to perpetrate discourse failure with impunity. Manifestations of such segmentation are departments

---

[3] Thus, the Leiter rankings may be used for philosophy departments and law schools, but any reliable ranking will do. For rankings of philosophy departments, see www.philosophicalgourmet.com; of law schools, www.utexas.edu/law/faculty/bleiter/rankings02; of economics departments, www.economics.utoronto.ca/ranking.html; of political science departments, www.usnews.com/usnews/edu/grad/rankings/phdhum/phdhumindex_brief.php. A refined version of our test should include operational indicators for high-quality books.

[4] The one exception we make to this requirement is the practice of American law reviews, which have a unique, non–peer-review system that nonetheless tends to select the leading research in law. This system has its critics. See Richard A. Posner, "Against the Law Reviews," *Legal Affairs*, November–December 2004, available at www.legalaffairs.org. Perhaps the most prestigious law journals could be vindicated to various degrees by looking at the number of citations they receive in the journals that directly pass our operational tests. A related suggestion is that we use *weighted sums* along various dimensions (average number of words used in double-blind rejections of manuscripts, number of citations in journals that meet the former requirement, etc.). Operational tests conducted in this way will yield comparative, rather than absolute, judgments of reliability.

and journals that feel entitled to advance positions at odds with reliable social science without bothering to show why (what we would call) reliable social science is mistaken – this was precisely the point of the *María Full of Grace* example. We require, then, that assertions about society that play any significant role in an argument be responsibly argued for – that is, located within the relevant *status quaestionis*.

Many important theories in social sciences and philosophy are reliable and opaque. Thus, the standard theory of comparative advantages in trade (section 2.1) is reliable and opaque. We do not mean to suggest that political deliberation should take this theory for granted. However, any serious public deliberation about trade policy must *confront* the theory of comparative advantages. Similarly, the theory of market failure is reliable and opaque, and, here again, any discussion of government intervention in many areas of human activity must include consideration of that theory. The statistical and other techniques used in empirical research, as well as theories of cognitive psychology and political science discussed in Chapter 2, are also complex and often counterintuitive. And to take a quite different area of politics, serious deliberation about the justice of a particular war must often include a discussion of the doctrine of double effect – a complex discussion, as moral philosophers know. The examples, of course, multiply: tax policy, educational policy, crime control, the conduct of foreign affairs. In all these areas public debate fails to reflect such complexity and often takes for granted positions that most experts reject.

Debate on economic and social policy is particularly vulnerable to discourse failure, because standard economics is opaque. To be sure, the foundation of economics, rational choice theory, is, in its simplest form, quite vivid: Persons do things because they stand to gain by doing them. The central proposition of rational choice theory can thus be seen as a formalization of the vivid folk explanation of motivation for action.[5] However, many claims derived from this apparently trivial postulate are opaque and thus non-evident to the public. The law of comparative advantages (section 2.1.) is an example, as is the proposition that the minimum wage creates unemployment (section 6.10). Analyses based on the Prisoner's Dilemma are likewise opaque: People find it puzzling that self-interested players fail to behave in ways that leave some of them better off without harming any of them.

---

[5] However, as our discussion in section 3.1 shows, it is less obvious how to disentangle the epistemic and instrumental components in the folk explanation.

Because these opaque derivations of rational choice theory can be extended to important areas of social science beyond economics, the public will tend to overlook a vast segment of reliable theoretical analysis of society. We do not claim that rational choice analysis can be extended to all areas of human behavior; we remain agnostic on that issue. It is enough for our purposes to show that people have a systematic incentive to overlook opaque theories that centrally bear on a wide range of public policies, and that many reliable social theories are opaque. If we are right, civic deliberation as an epistemic tool for political decision making cannot get off the ground. Because even deliberators concerned with the truth are sensitive to informational costs, they will often overlook reliable social theories and empirical findings in their political arguments.

There are many examples of opaque social theories that the public rejects despite the fact that they are more reliable than their vivid rivals. We have already indicated that many people reject arguments for free trade and favor various mercantilist alternatives. The public tends to favor the view that rent control will decrease the number of homeless persons over the opposite prediction yielded by standard applications of price theory. Or consider the following two rival policy recommendations: One proposes, as a solution to corruption and bad policies, to educate citizens in civic virtues so that they can elect decent and knowledgeable politicians. The other recommends designing institutions that will discourage politicians from bribery and other forms of corrupt politics and, conversely, encourage them to adopt good policies, whatever those may be. If we are right, citizens will be more persuaded by the educational recipes against corruption than warranted by reliable scholarship.[6] The favored approach is vivid; the approach based on incentives is opaque because it predicts that political actors will benefit society while pursuing individual aims unrelated to the common good.

The deliberative democrat may nonetheless point out that complex social theories can always be recast in simpler versions. For every complex theory, he might say, there is a simplified, popular version that citizens can grasp with little difficulty. On this view, citizens would avoid error because they would have easy access to reliable social theories. Thus, price theory would be available to the general public in a simplified and readable version, in much the same way as the essentials of the theory of relativity were able to reach many readers of Albert Einstein and Leopold

---

[6] For a seminal work in the latter direction, see James M. Buchanan and Gordon Tullock, *The Calculus of Consent* (Ann Arbor: University of Michigan Press, 1962).

Infeld's readable book *The Evolution of Physics*. Unfortunately, this reply overlooks the costs of writing and apprehending those simplified versions, compared with the ease with which people can get in touch with vivid theories or devise them for the consumption of others. We saw that vivid theories come to us naturally as a result of daily experience, possibly reinforced by ingrained cognitive frameworks (themselves perhaps the result of adaptive behavior in tribal societies, where some vivid theories might have accurately reflected much of social life). In contrast, someone *has* to write a simplified version of a complex theory – a task requiring considerable talent and effort. Moreover, those simplified versions are frequently counterintuitive, because, as we have seen, reliable social theories typically postulate opaque mechanisms. Textbooks can certainly simplify, for example, the *formulation* of the law of comparative advantages without much distortion. However, to ensure full understanding of those corollaries of the law that are relevant to policy making, they have to enable the reader to draw, say, the counterintuitive conclusion that unilateral elimination of tariffs increases general welfare, including the welfare of most workers in the country that repeals the tariff. To take another example, if we try to simplify the theory of public goods we cannot possibly avoid the counterintuitive claim that people are unwilling to bear the cost of producing goods from which each of them will obtain net benefits. So, even assuming that the simplified versions will be as available to the average citizen as vivid theories are (a dubious assumption, given the massive everyday evidence in favor of default theories), the creation, propagation, and apprehension of the former are usually costlier. The very preponderance of discourse failure in societies abundant in popular versions of complex theories suggests the extent to which discourse failure enjoys rhetorical advantages.

4.2. Deliberative Institutions

Defenders of deliberative democracy might accept the critiques leveled so far but insist that the correlation between deliberation and truth is a matter of institutional design. The various deliberative defects here explored, they may argue, can be corrected by building institutions that effectively screen out unreliable information and theories. After all, we have reached a better understanding of how the world functions in many areas – the foremost example is natural science. Could not we adopt in politics institutions akin to those that have facilitated scientific progress?

We cannot. Scientific progress has been achieved, not by massive popular deliberation, but by tiny scientific communities' observing stringent rules for the acceptance and rejection of theories and arguments.[7] Deliberativists expect exactly the reverse: For them, the legitimacy of public policies is directly related to political participation. Unfortunately, the rigorous probing of arguments characteristic of scientific procedures is unattainable in even modestly participatory deliberation, let alone massive deliberation. Reliability of the methods of inquiry is partly a function of the size of the deliberative community.[8] As far as we know, reliable methods of inquiry have prevailed only in relatively tiny communities, and there is no reason to think that this will change. A defense of a public policy in an article accepted by a leading journal is likely to be sounder than its counterpart in a televised debate. A typical political argument contains both causal and normative claims. Thus, a defense of affirmative action may rest on the claim that historical harm done to certain groups ought to be redressed. It may also depend on the claim that preferential hiring of members of those groups will not harm them or other group members (typically through indirect, less initially visible effects of the program). We should expect science to settle this causal claim, yet this is not the way in which the claim is decided in political deliberation. This alone means that, in a large class of political issues, namely those whose answers depend, if partly, on causal assumptions, the epistemic credentials of deliberative outcomes are suspect.[9]

The deliberativist, however, may insist that, if institutions were well designed (for example, by giving citizens the opportunity to listen to experts), citizens' ignorance could be overcome. For instance, he may propose to expand the practice of debates among experts with different viewpoints. But actual instances of this proposal are far removed from

---

7 The view that scientific progress was conducted by relatively tiny intellectual traditions or scientific communities that followed stringent argumentation rules is shared by major, and otherwise disparate, philosophies of science such as those of Thomas Kuhn and Karl R. Popper. See Kuhn, *The Structure of Scientific Revolutions*, op. cit., and Popper, *Conjectures and Refutations: The Growth of Scientific Knowledge*, fourth ed. (London: Routledge and Kegan Paul, 1972), esp. pp. 27 and 127. Of course, the credibility of epistemic arguments for political deliberation will a fortiori diminish if not even paradigmatic instances of scientific deliberation approach us to the truth. For an influential version of radical skepticism on scientific method, see Paul Feyerabend, *Against Method: Outline of an Anarchistic Theory of Knowledge* (London: NLD, 1975).

8 Restricted forms of deliberation, such as legislative debates, are ineradicably plagued by discourse failure, because, as we have seen, of electoral incentives to posture and distort.

9 See also sections 6.5 and 6.7. We also leave for later consideration (section 6.6) the possibility of moral error.

ideal deliberation, as formulated by deliberativists themselves. Consider the following real-life story:

Some years ago, the distinguished international-trade economist Jagdish Bhag-wati was visiting Cornell University, giving a lecture to graduate students during the day and debating Ralph Nader on free trade that evening. During his lecture, Prof. Bhagwati asked how many of the graduate students would be attending that evening's debate. Not one hand went up. Amazed, he asked why. The answer was that the economics students considered it to be a waste of time. The kind of silly stuff that Ralph Nader was saying had been refuted by economists ages ago. The net result was that the audience for the debate consisted of people largely illiterate in economics and they cheered for Mr. Nader.[10]

This episode is instructive. It suggests that even under deliberative conditions well above the average (Cornell is a leading university), the audience may show no willingness to dispassionately listen to conflicting viewpoints. Rather, it just takes advantage of the occasion for expressing its antecedent ideological preferences. As is well known, this is not an isolated episode. Moreover, both the absence of students of economics and the dominating presence of politically committed individuals suggest that the ordinary citizen will not take advantage of these deliberative fora. People trained in economics have little reason to attend the debate; for them, it means only rehearsing elementary refutations of widespread economic fallacies. We conjecture, then, that the audience was composed of some combination of economically illiterate students (as suggested in the story) and political careerists, in a broad sense that includes people who help their own careers by sending appropriate ideological signals. The rational ignorance effect explains quite straightforwardly the economic illiterates' cheering for Nader: They just fell prey to the vividness of his views.[11] The political careerist is typically posturing. Both cases are manifestations of discourse failure. The expansion of *these* fora surely cannot approach us to the deliberative ideal.

The deliberativist may join us in criticizing the kind of forum just described. His point may simply be that the state should make everyone deliberate in an appropriate manner. For example, he may propose mandatory periodic attendance by high school or college students to debates or seminars conducted by knowledgeable social scientists. These debates would be subsidized by the government, who might offer high

---

[10] Thomas Sowell, "Low Taxes Do What?" *The Wall Street Journal*, February 24, 2004.

[11] For Nader's views on trade, see www.votenader.org/issues. For an evaluation, see Alex Rothenberg, "Nader's Anti-Free Trade Rhetoric Draws Crowds, but Disregards Basic Economic Principles," September 26, 2000, available at www.theshortrun.com/articles.

fees to attract leading scholars. The organizers will make sure that students have ample opportunities to see common types of discourse failure refuted. But why would the government be in a good position to organize these debates? Government is a major engine of discourse failure. Politicians trade on the public's ignorance and error for electoral purposes. Moreover, we have seen (section 2.6) that discourse failure sometimes affects academics too – that is, the very people whose job description is searching for the truth. We can hardly expect politicians – who, whatever they are for, do not have truth as their overriding concern – to support truth-sensitive deliberative fora.

Some writers have proposed to overcome this problem by creating new and improved deliberative structures. The main idea (although there are many variations) is to assemble random groups of citizens to deliberate on an issue and provide them with expert information, appropriate deliberate settings, and so forth. To counter some of the rational ignorance effect, participants would be paid. Proponents of this view claim, based on controlled experiments, that the public has the capacity to deal with complex public issues, but it lacks the incentives to do so.[12]

The idea is that, if these deliberative polls were widely established, rational ignorance would be reduced, among other reasons because they will rely on expert information. And presumably, the citizenry at large, informed of the recommendations by the polls, would use their improved understanding to reshape their political positions and, ultimately, vote wisely. However, successful implementation of these proposals faces enormous difficulties, even ignoring some obvious preliminary obstacles.[13] Citizens will have to interpret the conclusions reached by the representative audience, and all the forces that contribute to discourse failure will mediate such interpretation. Take, for example, Fishkin's reports on the variations in public opinion after conducting deliberative polls on the causes of crime.[14] After participating in the deliberative polls recommended by Fishkin, respondents show an increased acceptance of the

---

[12] See Bruce Ackerman and James Fishkin, *Deliberation Day* (New Haven, Conn.: Yale University Press, 2004), p. 4. This work builds on Fishkin's research. See James S. Fishkin, *The Voice of the People: Public Opinion and Democracy* (New Haven, Conn.: Yale University Press, 1995); id., *Democracy and Deliberation: New Directions for Democratic Reform* (New Haven, Conn.: Yale University Press, 1991).

[13] Those are: their expense and the uncertainty about whether the results of the polls after deliberation have indeed been influenced by it. See Martin Gillens, "Political Ignorance and Collective Policy Preferences," *American Political Science Review*, Vol. 95, no. 2 (June 2001), p. 379.

[14] See Fishkin, *The Voice of the People*, op. cit., pp. 178–81.

view that reducing unemployment can effectively lower crime rates. This may well be a good idea, but it is hard to see how the citizenry, even if fully in agreement with these results, will pick up the best policies to reduce unemployment – a choice that is far from obvious. At *that* stage, politicians and special-interest groups will predictably use the mass media to play into the public's default theories.

A supporter of Fishkin's schema might retort that deliberative polls can settle all policy questions – in the foregoing example, not only the question of crime control but also the question of unemployment. That is, further deliberative polls might enlighten participants about various alternatives to reduce unemployment, and then those results could be applied to the crime control issue. We can imagine a rather long chain of deliberative polls, each addressing implementation problems left unresolved by the previous link.

Unfortunately, even if Fishkin's proposal could successfully overcome these difficulties, it could not survive further objections. To begin with, the public would have to weigh the merits of the results of the deliberative polls vis-à-vis alternative proposals affected by discourse failure. Those who benefit from discourse failure will either resist the implementation of Fishkin's mechanisms or prevent them from working successfully. In particular, they will discredit the expert information to which Fishkin's deliberators were exposed, and this maneuver is likely to succeed because, if we are right, expert information will be more opaque and harder to fit into the public's default vivid beliefs. Consider, for example, decriminalization of drugs. Assume that a deliberative poll has, on the basis of expert information, reached the conclusion that, while drug use is often harmful, the current criminalization of drug use increases certain forms of crime.[15] Once the issue reaches the citizenry, those who benefit from prohibition will try to discredit the expert information on which the reports were based. If we are right, the theories by default to which special interests will appeal in that effort have rhetorical advantages over the expert information. For example, they will insist that drug use is immoral, harmful to addicts, and a major cause of crime, and as such it ought to be banned. The vivid theory here is that legal prohibition effectively reduces undesirable behavior, without ulterior unpalatable effects. To be sure, the fact that Fishkin's deliberators are randomly chosen citizens will raise the costs of challenging the polls. It is an empirical question, in any

---

[15] See, for example, Mark Thornton, *The Economics of Prohibition* (Salt Lake City: University of Utah Press, 1991).

such setting, who will prevail. Still, it is not farfetched to hypothesize that those wielding vivid theories will have the upper hand (after all, libraries are full of well-publicized reports by expert panels that the public has systematically ignored).

Moreover, deliberative polls face a number of daunting practical difficulties. For example, who will select the expert information and formulate the questions? Let us concede, for the sake of argument, that Fishkin's deliberators can feasibly study and debate propositions of reliable social science, as defined in section 4.1. Consider the following candidates for issues to be submitted to the polls. (i) How to promote general welfare, (ii) what to do about unemployment, (iii) whether a certain inflation rate is worth a certain unemployment rate, (iv) whether unemployed single mothers should be subsidized, (v) how to fight crime, and (vi) whether guns should be controlled. It is unclear how Fiskin's system deals with the situation where the conclusions reached by a poll contradict those of another. For example, do we need an additional deliberative poll to settle a possible disagreement between the recommendations of poll (i) and poll (iii)? Are additional polls necessary to decide *whether* any of (i)–(vi) have produced conflicting results, and, if so, determine which prevails? An example of another type of problem is whether poll (i) is inappropriate because of excessive abstraction. These problems suggest that deliberative polls have to proliferate indefinitely in order for citizens to be able to overcome, finally, their rational ignorance. Because of this web of questions and meta-questions, the system of deliberative polls will have to be very complex. And because reasonable persons may prefer different ways of organizing the system, those who design it (the government?) will need interpretive leeway to solve the foregoing problems. If such interpretation is to be left to democratic procedures, all the forces of discourse failure will be at work. To see this, consider again a possible conflict between the recommendations of polls (i) and (iii). Assume that deliberators in poll (i), after seriously studying the *status quaestionis* in reliable social science, conclude that free markets will promote the general welfare. Assume further that deliberators in poll (iii) go through an analogous process and conclude that full employment demands high inflation through massive government intervention in the economy, and that full employment is worth that intervention. If this inconsistency is decided by submitting it to democratic procedures, the mutually reinforcing interaction between ignorance and posturing (section 2.2) will favor vivid ways of resolving the contradiction. In our example, people will predictably favor government intervention because they can easily empathize with the tangible hardships of the unemployed in a market economy, rather than with the unpredictable ways in which hardship will befall large segments of the population once welfare maximization is no longer a goal of public policy.

4.3. Good Policies, Bad Reasons

Sometimes a policy grounded on the best available social theories is supported by the public for bad, vivid reasons that are nevertheless better than the bad rival reasons that the public may have endorsed before deliberation. One possible example is the health care debate in the 1990s in the United States. The parties to the debate appealed to vivid stories: Democrats conjured up the image of the jobless person's finally gaining access to health care thanks to governmental compassion, while Republicans instilled the fear of the faceless bureaucrat's denying us the doctor of our choice. Of course, both positions were far less rigorous than, and sometimes inconsistent with, the complex economic, political, and philosophical scholarship about health care.[16] But, arguably, competition between the rival positions in the political arena modestly increased the public's understanding of the issue, in part because politicians had the incentive to expose the weaknesses of the rival position. This is so, even if that competition need not have substantially increased epistemic value, because having better reasons for a certain policy does not entail having the most reliable reasons, and even if politicians have an incentive to expose *what the public will perceive as weaknesses* of the rival position, not *actual* weaknesses. For citizens may become aware, thanks to deliberation, of relevant issues theretofore ignored. Another example may be Franklin D. Roosevelt's "fireside chats," in which he justified the New Deal by appealing to vivid oversimplifications of Keynesian economics (e.g., the idea that public works will create one-quarter of a million jobs, without loss of jobs elsewhere), which many experts then deemed to be the most reliable theoretical framework. Similarly, Ronald Reagan's vivid justifications for deregulation measures (e.g., the idea that private citizens use money better than bureaucrats do) were certainly more appealing to the

---

[16] See, for example, Charles R. Shipan, "Individual Incentives and Institutional Imperatives: Committee Jurisdiction and Long-Term Health Care," *American Journal of Political Science*, Vol. 36, no. 4 (November 1992), pp. 877–95; Norman Daniels and James Sabin, "Limits to Health Care: Fair Procedures, Democratic Deliberation, and the Legitimacy Problem for Insurers," *Philosophy and Public Affairs*, Vol. 26, no. 4. (Autumn 1997), pp. 303–50.

public than the opaque tenets of supply-side economics[17] that inspired Reagan's economic advisors.[18]

This concession, however, does not undermine our argument. It shows at best that social knowledge improves modestly in some cases. The point that sometimes political competition leads citizens to endorse unreliable, vivid views on issues theretofore ignored presupposes one of our central claims, namely that deliberation selects vivid theories or reaffirms those that the public holds by default. The views the public adopted in the foregoing cases are certainly defective in the light of even simplified versions of scholarly treatments of the issues involved. The fact that occasionally the clash of arguments makes people see salient issues that had gone unnoticed before is incidental to a truth-insensitive deliberative process. As we have repeatedly observed, that same process normally leads people, through the discourse failure mechanisms we have diagnosed, to regard as salient features that play no role in the relevant reliable social theories. Political competition will reinforce the citizen's unreliable default views by presenting as salient those facts or processes that easily fit into those views. Under those conditions, there is little hope that political competition among vivid views will increase veritistic value. If a vivid theory held by default competes with an opaque, counterintuitive theory, the former will predictably win in the political arena. This dooms epistemic defenses of political deliberation, because, as we have seen, many crucial social theories are opaque. Moreover, of two rival vivid theories, the one more strongly held by default, and not the one that approximates the truth, will prevail. Consequently, the epistemic gain here discussed is limited to the situation in which the victorious vivid theory has mimicked a true or plausible theory. In the health care example, a political argument that appeals to the image of long waiting lists for transplants may have made apparent to the public a cost that, according to reliable social theory, might ensue from universal health care. Unfortunately, this harmony between vividness and truth does not hold across the board in politics. Critics of farmer subsidies, for example, lack an argument vivid enough both to make transparent

---

[17] Consider the thesis, central to Reagan's economic policy, that reductions in tax rate will, up to a point, increase tax revenue. This thesis is entailed by the *Laffer curve*, which represents the functional relationship between tax rate and tax revenue. Economists disagree about the validity of the Laffer curve; however, our point is simply that it must be considered in any serious discussion of tax policy.

[18] We are grateful to Robert Keohane for the point and the examples in this paragraph.

to the general public the total cost of farmer subsidies and to offset the rhetorical force of rival vivid views, such as those that appeal to "the need to protect our countrymen's jobs" or "the preservation of that repository of American values, the farmer's way of life."

It might be claimed that the deliberative forum facilitates the adoption of reasonable *policies*, whatever *reasons* citizens offer to support them. Consider, for example, two arguments for privatizing a state-owned telephone company. The first says that privatization will increase general welfare because it will force the company to provide better and cheaper telephone services. The second argument says that privatization will threaten wasteful companies with bankruptcy; as a result, a more efficient, welfare-enhancing allocation of resources will take place.

We predict that most people will endorse the first rather than the second argument, even though the latter receives stronger support from reliable theories.[19] For one thing, the second argument is opaque: It is not immediately evident to the average citizen why the public will benefit from a regime in which firms might undergo bankruptcy. For another, the first argument suggests net gains for everyone. It recommends privatization because privatization will presumably result in better and cheaper telephone services. Citizens will naturally believe that this will enhance general welfare. Yet this is a non sequitur, because the optimal level of telephone service might well be *below* the one currently offered by the state-owned company. Possible links between the reduction in telephone service and the gains in other sectors of society are, for most people, hard to see. Citizens are here led, for bad reasons, to favor policies that are appropriate in terms of their own goals (here, enhancing general welfare).

But, someone may protest, to the extent that people adopt good policies for the bad reasons that they came to believe through deliberation, what is wrong with deliberation? Good results are what matter, after all. But this is unconditional surrender. It concedes that deliberation does not yield sound arguments; instead, it is contingently conducive to good policies. The deliberative democrat must overcome the obvious presumption that arguments premised on unreliable theories normally lead to bad policies. More important, even if he can discharge this burden, he is not recommending here any practice that is recognizably deliberative. For here deliberation is no longer a reason-giving process: Unreliable

---

[19] The authors of this book saw this prediction massively borne out by the public rhetoric that supported the privatization of the Argentine telephone company in the early 1990s.

theories cannot possibly provide *reasons for* anything, including good policies. No political theorist who prizes deliberation as a reason-giving process can offer this defense of deliberative democracy. Public opinion may well support good policies for bad reasons,[20] but a process that makes people form true beliefs on inappropriate grounds cannot be recognized as *deliberative*.

The deliberative democrat might object that this reply is purely verbal. He might accuse us of defining deliberation as a process that tends to exclude bad reasons. A weaker understanding of deliberation would have people reach good policies whatever their reasons. The good reasons supporting such policies are not necessarily the reasons why deliberators endorsed them. In this way, the deliberative democrat attempts to preserve an epistemic element in his defense of deliberation. The only thing that matters is that deliberation makes truth prevail: Conclusions, not premises, matter.

How can bad reasons possibly yield good policies? Here is an example: Let us assume that the good crime control policy is some combination of liberal and conservative measures. On drunk driving, for example, assume that the good policy is to impose a high fine in the absence of harm and a mild prison sentence if death or injury results. (We need not be concerned in this context about what makes these two policies good ones.) Let us also assume that the median voter favors these policies. Finally, assume that citizens routinely offer bad reasons for the various options in the given range. This reason-giving process results in a certain distribution of citizens along the range of positions. Recall now the median voter theorem, to which we referred in section 2.3. By virtue of this theorem, under these circumstances the good policy will be selected by majority rule, because, for reasons unrelated to the merits of the policy, the winning strategy is for candidates to be attentive to the preferences of

---

[20] Here are some examples of (arguably good) policies defended with bad (or relatively weak) reasons. Take the argument that raising tariffs is bad because our trade partners will retaliate. While of course this claim might be true, it distracts listeners from the main reasons for promoting free trade, which are of course opaque (see section 4.1). Alternatively, consider the defense of environmental legislation on the grounds that it will enhance the quality of our *environment* (thus implying that no negative side effects will ensue). Politicians give this dubious argument because of the opacity of two considerations whose combined force warrants *a certain amount of pollution control*: the theory of externalities (i.e., a type of market failure) and the fact that environmental regulation is costly (typically, in terms of economic growth). For further thoughts on discourse failure in environmentalist rhetoric, see section 2.3.

the median voter. So we have here a case in which deliberation conducted on the basis of bad reasons leads to a good policy.[21]

Leaving aside the fact that this defense of deliberation bears a pale resemblance to the original theory, it is still unpersuasive. It remains wholly mysterious why bad reasons will in general lead to good policies. Moreover, deliberation plays no heuristic role in this argument. If the deliberative democrat already knows what a good policy is and argues that citizens will endorse it for bad reasons, then deliberation is epistemically superfluous. The deliberative democrat must show, then, that political processes that select good policies somehow necessitate deliberation. He has to make sense of his institutional proposals (such as increasing the frequency of neighborhood and town-hall meetings, or establishing appropriate rules for congressional debates), given his admission that when deliberation succeeds in selecting good policies it does so for bad reasons. He is then caught in a dilemma. If he promotes deliberative democracy with an eye to encouraging people to give *good reasons*, his enterprise is utopian for the reasons we have seen: Bad reasons are more likely to prevail anyway. If, on the other hand, he wants deliberative democracy to generate good policies, his institutional proposals, by hypothesis, will have to promote certain patterns of unsound reasoning – namely, those that are most conducive to good policies.[22] It is hard to see, then, on what bases institutional design would proceed. In any event, institutions designed to allow bad reasons with the hope that they will lead to good policies will not foster deliberation as commonly understood by theorists of deliberative democracy – that is, as a reason-giving process whose non-incidental outcome is the selection of better rulers and policies.

When people reject a good policy because of a vivid theory (*VT*), a supporter of the policy cannot successfully counter with a good opaque theory (*OT*), because, as we saw, *VT* will have rhetorical advantages given widespread ignorance. So he will have to find *bad* persuasive reasons. He may have a hard time convincing citizens that his reasons are better than those provided by *VT*. Moreover, the rhetorical disadvantage that *OT* has in relation to *VT* is a source of further competitive disadvantage for *OT*. This occurs when the very *fact* that some people publicly *oppose VT* (or the

---

[21] The example should be qualified in view of the possibility (section 2.3) of disharmonies between winning rhetorical strategies to gain office and winning policy strategies to remain in office.

[22] We are taking for granted here, as deliberativists do, majority rule over a wide scope of distributive issues. We will argue in Chapter 9 that discourse failure could drastically be reduced by replacing redistributive majoritarianism with consensual arrangements.

policies based on them) *lends support*, in the public's eyes, to *VT*. People may naturally believe, for example, that critics of *VT* argue in bad faith – a belief that supporters of *VT* may in turn reinforce with further vivid theories aimed at uncovering the critics' spurious motivations. It is no surprise, then, that vivid theories breed conspiracy explanations. In these cases, political deliberators rarely take at face value challenges to their deeply rooted and vivid beliefs. Rather, they often *reinterpret* those challenges as evidence for the existence of the very conspiracy that, according to the theory they hold, blocks the realization of the values they cherish. Thus, some protectionists see free-trade proposals as a plot of big business to drive out domestic small industries and thus, in its quest for profit, hurt the poor. On that view, they might very well tag a defender of free trade as an agent of big business. Protectionists of this sort will regard the very fact that someone defends free trade as confirming the conspiracy. They believe that big business gets richer at the expense of the poor.[23] They cannot conceive that anyone would honestly defend free trade, so they will naturally see free traders as the mouthpiece for the rich. For them, the *fact* that someone dares to defend free trade is evidence for their view that the rich have managed to spread an ideology that justifies harming the poor. In that scenario, then, attempts to deliberate compound discourse failure. It is not just that someone's emotional attachment to a theory blocks his serious examination of the merits of the contending arguments: The very fact that his (deeply held) beliefs are challenged will reinforce his original mistake rather than prompt him to critically examine opposing views. So, to win the public's favor, bad reasons for good policies must not only be easier to understand than their competitors. They must overcome what we may call *the bootstrap argument* offered by their adversaries: Public defense of the good policy is part of the evidence that the adversaries invoke. The history of religions and state-imposed ideologies abounds in bootstrap arguments: The very opposition to such religions or ideologies, no matter how well argued it is, is seen as evidence of "possession" by the devil, "superstructural" expressions of class warfare, and so forth. Opposition to the vivid theory reinforces belief in it. Conspiracy explanations are not only a natural complement to vivid theories: They immunize them against refutation.[24]

---

[23] See our more extended discussion in section 2.1.

[24] For the relationships between the idea that "truth is manifest" and conspiracy theories of ignorance and error, see Popper, *Conjectures and Refutations: The Growth of Scientific Knowledge*, op. cit., pp. 3–30. For a general theory of "immunization" strategies, see

Bootstrap arguments are common in current liberal democracies, although they are less common and much less effective there than in undemocratic societies. Unlike theocratic or totalitarian regimes, liberal democracies cannot resort to massive uses of coercion and one-sided propaganda. At the very least, in a democracy both sides in a dispute can use bootstrap arguments. More generally, societies differ in how much they honor a deliberative attitude in politics – in particular, a disposition by the public to take seriously reasons that might militate against their own. We conjecture that deliberative attitudes are mostly the result of historical accident. A public forum may reach a discursive equilibrium where the attempt to argue seriously is rewarded. Perhaps many public fora in the United States instantiate such good equilibrium. Other societies, however, have generally reached quite opposite equilibria, where critical thinking is penalized in many settings, including "academic" ones. Perhaps most public fora in Argentina (our native country) instantiate such bad equilibrium.[25] We cannot pursue this further, however.

A politician who wants to enlist support for free trade must not only concoct a bad reason for free trade (he cannot rely on the counterintuitive, opaque law of comparative advantages, discussed in section 2.1). In addition, he has to make citizens listen to his *arguments*. This will be hard to do when many citizens, as we have seen, may have been led to believe that the public *utterance* of such arguments is evidence for their belief that supporters of free trade are lobbyists for foreign industries. (How can anyone defend free trade despite its "obviously" disastrous consequences for workers in the protected industries, with no offsetting effects?) The free trader has no symmetrical persuasive counter-argument available. Even if he convinced citizens that protectionists were lobbyists for domestic producers at the expense of domestic consumers, the "fact" would remain, in the public's eyes, that free trade would increase unemployment, here and now. The ordinary citizen believes (correctly, we think) that, *other things being equal*, unemployment is worse than moderate price increases in the protected goods. But, crucially, the supporter of free trade has no

Hans Albert, *Treatise on Critical Reason*, tr. Mary Varney Rorty (Princeton, N.J.: Princeton University Press, 1985).

[25] For an analysis of good and bad equilibria, see Robert Cooter, "The Rule of State Law Versus The Rule-of-Law State: Economic Analysis of the Legal Foundations of Development," in E. Buscaglia, W. Ratliff, and R. Cooter, eds., *The Law and Economics of Development* (Greenwich, Conn.: Jai Press, 1997), pp. 101–48. For a discussion of how the notion of multiple equilibria helps explain the emergence of social norms, see Sugden, *The Economics of Rights, Co-operation and Welfare*, op. cit., pp. 19–33.

rhetorically effective way of showing, in actual deliberation, that other things are *not* equal in ways that would change citizens' minds on the issue. He has no vivid way of showing that free trade may well decrease both overall *and domestic* unemployment (while certainly increasing both overall and domestic welfare). Our point here is not merely that mainstream economics is correct in this matter, although, as we said in section 2.1, we think it is. It is also that, even if the matter were controversial, feasible deliberation in current liberal democracies is systematically biased toward vivid theories irrespective of their plausibility.

4.4. Shortcuts

Some writers have claimed that citizens can acquire relevant political information at low cost to themselves by taking shortcuts. For example, citizens may gather information just by participating in everyday life: by exchanging views at a party, by talking about politics at lunchtime, and even by conducting personal financial transactions that may educate them about the economy.[26] Another suggestion advises the public to follow the cues from opinion leaders and other experts, including the views communicated to the public for free by political parties, special-interests' spokespersons, and the like.[27]

The problem of shortcut theories is that there is no inexpensive way for the citizen to identify reliable opinion leaders. In virtually all important political issues, the citizen faces self-appointed experts who disagree. Let us assume that only one of them expresses views that are supported by reliable social science. Identifying that one opinion leader requires an investigation that the average citizen will not undertake, for the same reasons that he will not become properly informed about politics generally. Nevertheless, suppose, for the sake of argument, that somehow the citizen managed to identify the reliable experts. Even then, if the experts differ, he will have no inexpensive way to establish whose opinion is worth following. For, unlike the scholar, he will have insurmountable difficulty understanding the reasons offered by those experts and striking a balance among them in order to take a stance. The kind of information

---

[26] For a summary and critique, see Ilya Somin, "Voter Ignorance and the Democratic Ideal," *Critical Review*, Vol. 12, no. 4, Fall 1998, pp. 413–58, at 420–1.

[27] See, for example, Page and Shapiro, *The Rational Public*, pp. 365, 387–8; Richard D. McKelvey and Peter C. Ordeshook, "Information, Electoral Equilibria, and the Democratic Ideal," *The Journal of Politics*, Vol. 48, no. 4 (November 1986), pp. 909–37, esp. pp. 911 and 934.

that citizens need effectively to take these shortcuts is precisely the kind of information they lack.[28] We are told that citizens can overcome their unwillingness to invest in political information by selecting opinion leaders, yet they would have to make such an investment to select the right opinion leaders. This position is hardly consistent.

Other kinds of shortcuts fall prey to similar objections. Thus, citizens might be thought to learn from an administration's failure; presumably, this is all they need in order to vote bad governments out of office.[29] Yet, voters cannot normally tell whether present bad conditions are the result of policies pursued by incumbent politicians, let alone whether the opposition would perform any better. Bad conditions may have been caused by earlier administrations or by factors outside governmental control. Similarly, it might be claimed that many citizens become knowledgeable about *specific* political issues.[30] The hope is that votes cast on the bases of such pieces of knowledge will somehow select the best policies. But here, again, the opacity of the relevant causal connections misleads single-issue citizens. There is no such thing as exhaustive knowledge of "an issue" that exempts the citizen from investigating (sometimes distant) causal connections with "other issues." Take the case, nicely discussed by Ilya Somin, of someone interested in civil rights.[31] It is not immediately obvious what the civil rights *issue* has to do with the *issue* of Social Security reform. Yet, it can be argued that Social Security involves a major hidden redistribution from poor blacks to longer-lived white retirees. Rationally ignorant citizens are not likely to see this connection.[32]

---

[28] See Michael Delli Carpini and Scott Keater, *What Americans Know About Politics and Why It Matters*, op. cit., p. 45.

[29] The classic locus for this argument is Morris Fiorina, *Retrospective Voting in National American Elections* (New Haven, Conn.: Yale University Press, 1981). Others have argued that voters are likely to vote prospectively – that is, based on predictions about what the candidates would do if elected. See Michael B. Mackuen, Robert S. Erikson, and James A. Stimson, "Peasants or Bankers? The American Electorate and the U.S. Economy," *American Political Science Review*, Vol. 86, no. 3, 1992, pp. 597–611.

[30] Phillip Converse made this suggestion in his seminal "Belief Systems in Mass Politics," in David E. Apter, ed., *Ideology and Discontent* (New York: Free Press, 1964), pp. 245–9.

[31] Somin, op. cit., pp. 428–9.

[32] Larry Bartels has challenged the hypothesis that uninformed voters using these kinds of shortcuts act as if they were fully informed. See Larry M. Bartels, "Uninformed Votes: Information Effects in Presidential Elections," *American Journal of Political Science*, Vol. 40, no. 1, February 1996, pp. 194–230. Lau and Redlawsk, "Advantages and Disadvantages of Cognitive Heuristics in Political Decision-Making," op. cit., pp. 952–3, cast doubt on too quick a reliance on one version of shortcut theory, "low information rationality," suggested by the cognitive psychology literature. See section 2.3.

It is instructive to compare political shortcuts with nonpolitical instances where shortcuts work well. Consider medical doctors. People routinely consult them and trust their advice, notwithstanding the fact that the scientific theories underlying that advice are usually very opaque, and for that reason difficult to grasp. Is not this fact a refutation of the contention that opacity plays a major role in political error? Not so. Opacity alone does not trigger discourse failure. People err in politics because the modest stake they have in the outcome discourages them from learning the complex theories and facts needed to understand the ways in which society works. They have no incentive to overcome opacity. In contrast, patients want to consult the best doctors. Patients will not make the effort to study medicine: They inductively know that doctors generally give accurate health advice. Furthermore, most of us were exposed early on to examples of the physical, chemical, and biological theories on which medicine rests. The availability of popular information (e.g., television documentaries) may reinforce that learning. In contrast, there are few, if any, materials in the media, let alone in early formal education, about economics, political science, sociology, philosophy, and other social disciplines characterized by opaque explanations. In particular, media audiences are hardly ever exposed to even the most elementary social *theory* (e.g., price theory) that they would need to understand the facts in the news. To the contrary: The media are often a major outlet for the interaction between politicians and citizens that fuels discourse failure. Again, early formal education is largely silent on opaque social theories. It should be no surprise, then, that in general the medical patient, unlike the citizen, not only has a strong interest to find the truth: He also finds it.

When these facts are properly taken into account, we can see why most citizens do *not* consult economists or other experts in social theory to improve their electoral choices. The same logic explains why big firms usually *do* consult economists to learn about the general economic situation. They do this not out of civic duty to become informed but because they internalize the benefits of that knowledge.

A final point. Citizens lack incentives to become informed *qua* voters, but, interestingly, they sometimes have incentives to acquire political information relevant to their success in displaying *discourse failure*. Thus, successful lobbyists usually bear significant costs to obtain information about, say, which politician is likely to be persuaded by their arguments, or what piece of legislation will maximize their gains.

4.5. Deliberation, Free Speech, and Truth

Can the deliberative democrat take advantage of the Millian defense of free speech? The deliberative democrat might claim, with Mill, that uncensored political speech makes truth prevail. Just as freedom of speech allows the truth to emerge, so political deliberation is conducive to the adoption of better social policies. In *On Liberty*, Mill wished to argue for the *freedom* to express ideas, including the freedom to deliberate. The deliberativist may share Mill's epistemic optimism[33] (although, as we will see, he may defend deliberation on non-epistemic grounds). Yet, he does not merely want to sustain a right against censorship but rather advocate that citizens use speech in a deliberative manner.

We want to examine here the Millian claim, endorsed by deliberativists, that "truth has the best chance to emerge . . . if ideas are allowed to compete freely in the marketplace."[34] Deliberativists might attempt to trade on this idea in order to counter the diagnosis of discourse failure that we have offered so far: If Mill is right, discourse failure will be progressively eradicated in a free society. Following Goldman, we distinguish two interpretations of the "marketplace of ideas" thesis. Sometimes it refers literally to economic markets, in which case the argument is that free markets are the best institutional means for the promotion of truth. Just as free competition among producers of shoes leads to more, better, and cheaper shoes, so free competition among ideas should lead to more, better, and readily available ideas. Other times, however, "marketplace of ideas" is a metaphor that "construes the marketplace of ideas as a market-like arena, in which debate is wide, open, and robust, in which diverse views are vigorously defended." Goldman correctly points out that this kind of arena may or may not result from market mechanisms: Sometimes government action might be required to secure it.[35]

---

[33] Mill takes a sympathetic (although still guarded) approach to deliberation in *Considerations on Representative Government*. See section 1.1.

[34] The formulation, without endorsement, belongs to Goldman, *Knowledge in a Social World*, op. cit., p. 192. Justice Holmes endorsed the "free market of ideas" argument in his famous dissent in *Abrams v. United States*, No. 316, 250 U.S. 616; 40 S. Ct. 17; 63 L. Ed. 1173; 1919 U.S. LEXIS 1784, Argued October 21, 22, 1919, Decided November 10, 1919. Gutmann and Thompson cite Mill and Aristotle for the epistemic value of deliberation, *Democracy and Disagreement*, op. cit., p. 44; so does Thomas Christiano, *The Rule of the Many*, op. cit., p. 84. According to John Dryzeck, Mill is the grandfather of "contemporary liberal constitutionalist deliberative democracy." John S. Dryzeck, *Deliberative Democracy and Beyond: Liberals, Critics, Contestations* (Oxford: Oxford University Press, 2000), p. 9.

[35] Goldman, *Knowledge in a Social World*, p. 192.

Goldman rejects the proposition that free-market rules for speech promote the truth. His main point is that whether truth is advanced or not will depend on whether citizens have a preference for true messages. Free markets respond to consumer preferences, not to some predetermined qualities of the product. He also suggests that truthful public speech is a public good, and thus a private market will predictably underproduce it.[36] We add that citizens may acquire false beliefs through the mechanisms of discourse failure already outlined. So Goldman's point, that more speech is unlikely to increase veritistic value in society, is reinforced by the argument we offer here.[37]

An additional reason why Goldman rejects this literal version of the "marketplace of ideas" thesis is that ideas are not goods in the economic sense. He claims that ideas are not literally produced and consumed, as other goods are. For example, viewers pay nothing for the right to view billboard messages – and this is not because they are free riding on others. He adds that there is no difference between the "consumption" of the viewer who believes the message and the one who does not. This makes it hard to regard such consumption as resulting from a demand for truth. Finally, "the producer/seller of the message does not get paid for it, even by those who 'consume' it."[38] If true, this point of Goldman's may strike at the heart of the argument of this book. The theory of discourse failure relies on how costly it is for someone to come to believe certain things about society. This suggests that we are treating citizens' political ideas as commodities, governed as such by the laws of economic theory. It might be thought that if Goldman is right, we are wrongheaded.

But this charge is unwarranted. Whether or not ideas expressed in public are goods in the economic sense, it is perfectly legitimate to say that the costs of acquiring different sorts of information (and, as a result, of forming the corresponding beliefs) vary. In this sense, economic analysis helps detect patterns of political beliefs. While, as Goldman rightly observes, the notion of buying and selling ideas is problematic when taken literally, human choices have costs, even if those choices are not part of any exchanges.[39] In politics, various agents make theories available to the

---

[36] Goldman, p. 197.

[37] Someone may think that this endorsement of Goldman's theses is inconsistent with our support of market arrangements as devices against discourse failure in Chapter 9. We will see in section 9.2 that the inconsistency is merely apparent.

[38] Goldman, p. 203.

[39] See James Buchanan, *Cost and Choice: An Inquiry in Economic Theory* (Chicago: University of Chicago Press, 1969), esp. pp. 38–50.

public, and then individuals accept those they deem the best ones, given their relative difficulty. This process does not involve an exchange in a usual sense. Imagine that Friday, unnoticed by Robinson Crusoe, puts at Robinson's disposal every day a basket of fruit. The availability of fruit allows Robinson to spend more time fishing and hunting. The opportunity cost (i.e., the forsaken fruit) of these activities has decreased thanks to fruit's now being plentiful. Predictably, Robinson will now spend more time fishing and hunting, and little or no time gathering fruit. Similarly, ordinary citizens (even those who want to know "what's going on" in politics) will spend little or no time studying social problems. We have already seen the reasons leading them to behave in this way. First, politicians and rent seekers will make readily available to ordinary citizens certain views about society. Second, it is rational for ordinary citizens to believe those views, given the theories they hold by default. Finally, the net personal benefits for citizens of testing their default views and obtaining reliable political information is low, given the high opportunity costs of doing so and the low probability of affecting political outcomes. Using the notion of the opportunity costs of various activities with an eye to predicting behavior does not presuppose market dealings or trade in the ordinary sense.

As Goldman correctly points out, however, the "marketplace of ideas" is better understood metaphorically. After all, it is important for deliberativists to have a robust debate in society, and such robust debate need not emerge spontaneously in the market. Using various examples from U.S. law, Goldman argues that if we are concerned with truth, then perhaps a cautious state regulation of speech will have higher veritistic value.[40] One reason for this is that in order for debate to spread truth in society, two conditions must be fulfilled. First, the premises of the arguments have to be true, and second, "all hearers of the debate [must] have a correct appreciation of the support relations between premises and conclusions."[41] Goldman argues that, because these are very stringent conditions, quantity of debate does not assure quality of debate. He uses courtroom procedural rules and peer reviews for professional journals as examples of controlled speech that is preferable, on epistemic grounds, to total inclusiveness.

Goldman is right that certain forms of speech regulation increase the epistemic value of the outcomes. In fact, the examples provided by

[40] Goldman, pp. 205–17.
[41] Goldman, p. 210.

Goldman are perfectly in line with our thesis that deliberation may well have epistemic virtues in controlled, specialized settings. In contrast, discourse failure is unavoidable in politics. In that setting, those who benefit most from discourse failure are those who hold the political power that is supposed to implement truth-sensitive controls on deliberation: Herein lies, in our view, the major flaw in the otherwise perceptive analysis by Goldman. Government regulation of deliberation for epistemic purposes will fail because government is a primary source of discourse failure. Government failure (i.e., inefficiencies traceable to political decision making[42]) is, here as elsewhere, largely an epiphenomenon of discourse failure. For suppose Goldman is right that there is a speech regulation R that will increase veritistic value. This does not entail that *transferring to government the powers* necessary to enact R will guarantee that the government will enact precisely R. Perhaps social knowledge would be advanced by banning government from any regulation whatsoever of speech markets. From the fact that there is a potential legal solution to a social problem it does not follow that it is a good idea, in order to address that problem, to empower legislators to enact the requisite law. Indeed, public-choice analysis has eroded the hopes that governments will use their powers to achieve public-spirited aims.[43] Rather, more often than not politicians will enact special-interest legislation at the expense of dispersed groups, such as consumers and taxpayers.[44] Rational choice assumptions account also for the rhetoric engrafted onto this political dynamic. Because government officials often have aims unrelated to the truth, their rhetoric will likewise be truth-deficient. This behavior is often facilitated by the fact that appropriate specifications and applications of R involve conceptually and causally contestable matters,

---

[42] See note 120, Chapter 2, and accompanying text.

[43] The literature on capture of regulatory agencies by special interests is vast. See, for example, Robert B. Ekelund and Robert D. Tollison, *Mercantilism as a Rent-Seeking Society: Economic Regulation in Historical Perspective* (College Station: Texas A&M University Press, 1981), and the essays in Tollison, ed., *The Political Economy of Rent Seeking* (Boston: Kluwer, 1988). For a thorough theoretical analysis of the kinds of rules that can hold hope of overcoming government failure, see Geoffrey Brennan and James M. Buchanan, *The Reason of Rules: Constitutional Political Economy* (1985), reprinted in Geoffrey Brennan, Hartmut Kliemt, and Robert D. Tollison, eds., *The Collected Works of James M. Buchanan*, Vol. 10 (Indianapolis: Liberty Fund, 2000).

[44] See Mancur Olson, *The Logic of Collective Action: Public Goods and the Theory of Groups* (Cambridge, Mass.: Harvard University Press, 1965), and *The Rise and Decline of Nations: Economic Growth, Stagflation, and Social Rigidities* (New Haven, Conn.: Yale University Press, 1982).

and correspondingly wide discretionary interpretive powers.[45] The analysis of discourse failure draws attention to the rhetorical processes that contribute to government failure.

To summarize: If Mill's "marketplace of ideas" argument is understood not merely as a defense of freedom of speech but as supporting a strong positive correlation between deliberative robustness and the spread of true beliefs among citizens, then it is mistaken for the reasons we, as well as Goldman, have given. (This does not exclude that sometimes, on some specific issues, deliberation may contribute marginally to the public's enlightenment, as we noted earlier in this chapter.) If citizens already hold mistaken theoretical beliefs about society, deliberation will often reinforce error because political agents will benefit from spreading among the citizenry further theories and information, however unreliable these may be, that fit those beliefs.

However, we can rescue two epistemic reasons in support of free speech. First, saying that error is unavoidably widespread among the citizenry is consistent with saying that free speech is a fundamental prerequisite of *scientific* progress, including progress in the social sciences and the humanities. Censorship prevents scientists from discovering facts that are relevant to their research. For example, government may prevent social scientists studying poverty from having access to relevant data.[46] Second, and more important, free speech is instrumental to making the public aware of the danger of collective tragedies, and so thwarting their occurrence. Nothing we have said so far denies that beyond a certain threshold of disaster the consequences of mistaken policies become visible even to rationally ignorant citizens. No genocide or commensurate avoidable humanitarian disaster has ever occurred in a free-speech environment.[47] (Free speech is further supported by non-epistemic arguments, such as

---

[45] See Guido Pincione, "Market Rights and the Rule of Law: A Case for Procedural Constitutionalism," *Harvard Journal of Law and Public Policy*, Vol. 26, no. 2, Spring 2003, pp. 397–454.

[46] Censorship of positions resulting from what we call "discourse failure" would certainly thwart the empirical testing of hypotheses that we advance in this book.

[47] See Amartya Sen, *Development as Freedom* (New York: Knopf, 1999), p. 152. As Hardin points out, "major actions – significant policies or abuses – can commonly cross the threshold of a citizen's perception without need of any effort on the part of the citizen to find out what is at stake." See "Democratic Epistemology and Accountability," *Social Philosophy and Policy*, Vol. 17, no. 1, Winter 2000, pp. 110–26, at p. 125. Sometimes the public learns from catastrophes: Think about Germany after World War II or Hungarians after communism. It is implausible to think that public deliberation was the engine of such beneficial changes, vis-à-vis individual reflection on the ills of such regimes – especially given the fact that they banned free public deliberation.

appeals to individual autonomy and respect for persons. Attempts by government to muzzle citizens evince grave disrespect for their autonomy and the public's ability to decide what they want to see and hear. We will discuss in section 7.1 autonomy-based defenses of political deliberation.)

The epistemic advantages that free speech confers on scientific research do not accrue to public discussion of political issues. Thus, in the foregoing example, rationally ignorant citizens concerned about poverty will neither gather accurate information about nor acquire reliable explanations of poverty. In contrast, usual procedures for the acceptance or rejection of scientific views (e.g., the rules for manuscript acceptance in scientific journals) will largely shield the scientist from factors that make people err in politics. Furthermore, scientists are mostly self-selected on the bases of their interest in the truth – a trait that appears much less frequently in political deliberators, let alone in most politicians and other posturers. So, while there are epistemic grounds to support open and widespread deliberation, these grounds do not help the typical epistemic defenses of political deliberation. Political deliberation, as we have suggested, is likely to be distorted, yet it is the appropriate environment for scientific circles to enhance the reliability of their beliefs. For the reasons we discussed, however, those circles are bound to be politically ineffective. The epistemic argument for free speech does not help, then, the deliberative democrat.

4.6. Deliberation as a Regulative Ideal

The deliberativist may claim that his proposal is normative. He might agree with much of our criticism of current deliberative practices and yet insist that he precisely envisions a society free of discourse failure. On this view, the fact that present democratic societies do not instantiate proper deliberative practices is not fatal to his thesis. He may regard deliberation as a regulative ideal toward which society, aided by his theory, should incrementally tend. Ideal, not actual, deliberation enhances the quality of political debate and decision making. This appeal to the notion of a regulative ideal acknowledges the reality of discourse failure and asks citizens to deliberate better and more. The injunction may be coupled with praise of deliberation as a civic virtue. The hope is that many citizens will be morally motivated to deliberate.

Unfortunately, this contention is vulnerable to a charge of utopianism, because the proposed remedy increases the already high costs of informed political participation. Moreover, multiplying political debates under widespread rational ignorance compounds political error. The deliberativist may concede that under current conditions citizens will err but insist that people have a civic duty to inform themselves, even at considerable effort. The fact that acquiring information is difficult does not excuse citizens from civic ignorance, especially given the importance of political issues. As in any other area of morality, people must act even at high personal cost. In particular, virtuous citizens are expected to bear informational costs. Because civic virtue requires citizens to become properly informed, political error might reveal moral shortcoming on their part and be therefore inexcusable.[48]

When is error inexcusable? Cases that immediately come to mind are those like the following. A physician who wants to cure diabetes treats patients with an as yet untried drug. He tries this drug in a trusting patient and kills him. This physician cannot excuse himself by saying that he really wanted to heal the patient but was mistaken about the actual effects of the drug. We would not excuse this physician even if he made some effort to work out the effects of the drug on patients – say, by an isolated experiment in which a treated rat got better. We would strengthen our critique if we learned that he infringed legal standards for the testing of new drugs. The deliberativist has to assimilate citizens' ignorance to the physician's failure to obtain relevant information. Just as the doctor cannot be excused for not becoming properly informed before using the drug, so the citizen cannot be excused for not becoming properly informed before participating in politics. If the citizen errs, it is his fault. On this view, the theory of deliberative democracy is normative in the sense that it enjoins citizens to overcome this error. If people complied with their civic duty, there would be no discourse failure. Deliberativists may supplement this idea with institutional proposals to help, or even force, citizens to obtain relevant information – this is the analogue to the legal standard of care for physicians. Just as responsible legislatures should regulate drug testing, so should they promote civic education, including citizens' willingness to become properly informed. An appropriate mix of public-spiritedness and state coercion would overcome the discourse failure that pervades modern societies.

There are important differences, however, between the irresponsible physician and the ignorant citizen that make the latter's, but not the former's, error excusable. The main reason why the physician cannot be

---

[48] For further discussion of deliberation as civic virtue, see sections 3.1, 4.1, 6.1, and 7.5.

excused is that he is familiar with reliable scientific theories about the effects of drugs and with reliable procedures for the testing of new drugs. His failure to use that knowledge is inexcusable; he acted negligently. In contrast, the citizen who, rightly or wrongly, feels motivated by a strong duty to deliberate will predictably display the forms of discourse failure we have identified. To see this, let us concede to the deliberativist his optimism about the motivating force of his ideal of civic duty. Citizens are so inspired by this ideal that they are willing to spend much time and effort to learn about politics and deliberate. If we are right, however, they will not read reliable social science. Instead, they will watch political debates on television, attend political meetings, and read newspapers editorials – precisely the sources most affected by discourse failure. This is because they hold by default vivid theories about society, and the sort of information furnished in *those* sources (and not in reliable social theory) *would* be the relevant one should those theories hold. Compare again with the physician: He holds theories selected through truth-sensitive processes.[49] He learned those theories in medical school because he knew he would benefit from practicing medicine. His medical knowledge and the harm caused by medical mistakes justify society's holding him responsible for those mistakes. In contrast, the citizen is unable to reap the benefits of his heightened political literacy. As we saw, he will typically remain ignorant about politics. Moreover, his vote will be inconsequential. It seems unreasonable, then, to blame him for his political ignorance.

Another version of the regulative-ideal argument merits discussion as well. The deliberativist may propose to reduce the cost of political deliberation for citizens. For example, he may propose legislation allotting more television prime time to political debates. This, he thinks, will reduce the cost of deliberation because many people routinely watch prime time television. Similarly, the deliberativist may propose legislation establishing mandatory school time for moot parliaments and similar programs. If the mass media or the schools could become vehicles for the exchange of political ideas, citizens would no longer have to study hard to understand how society works, and discourse failure would be less pervasive.[50]

Yet, the facts do not bear out such optimism. The past couple of decades have witnessed an explosion of information and public fora in

---

[49] For a philosophical discussion of biasing factors and their bearing on objectivity, see Nozick, *Invariances*, op. cit., pp. 94–9. Of course, the costs involved in overcoming innate propensities to err (section 2.3) reinforce our charge of utopianism.

[50] In another context, we offer some remarks on campus deliberation in section 4.2.

the media and the Internet. However, it is by no means clear that the quality of political debate is better today than it was more than a century ago.[51] Indeed, the types of discourse failure that we have identified reflect the major trends in political debates in a typical contemporary democracy – that is, precisely after the media and Internet explosion. We have seen that suppliers of political information trade on citizens' ignorance and error. Politicians and special interests generally stand to lose by challenging the vivid beliefs that the public holds by default. Why think that an increase in the supply of political information will reduce people's tendency to err, rather than reinforce belief in defective explanations? Anti–free-trade activists face now much lower organizational costs. They can summon a political rally by Internet. And the rally will be quickly and massively broadcast, so that the public at large will be exposed to the vivid rhetoric used by those activists. Because, as we have seen (section 2.1), protectionism relies on vivid premises (e.g., "We ought to protect our jobs"), and standard trade theory is noticeably opaque, default errors about the effects and dynamics of international trade are reinforced and magnified as the costs of spreading vivid theories decrease. Unless the deliberativist proposes that the state silence many of the groups that stand to gain from improvements in communication technology, we do not see how he expects the "information revolution" to curb the expansion of political error.

The perverse interaction between donors and receivers of political information teaches us a lesson about regulative ideals. One can think of a regulative ideal as a model of society to which we should tend, even if it is likely that we will never reach it. On this interpretation, it makes sense to take steps toward the ideal. Positing a regulative ideal is thus one way to avoid the charge of utopianism. However, epistemically valuable deliberation is not a regulative ideal in this sense. For, if we are correct, the deliberativist's ideal cannot be *approached*. Multiplying feasible deliberative fora will multiply error. Rather than approach the epistemic ideal, the typical recommendations by deliberativists (expanding deliberative fora) will get us further from it. Our charge of utopianism, then, is not predicated on the *difficulty* of implementing the deliberativists' institutional proposals, although that difficulty may be serious enough. Proposing more deliberation to cure discourse failure is simply counterproductive.

---

[51] For indications that the quality of nineteenth-century debates may well have been better than it is today, see Somin, "Voter Ignorance and the Democratic Ideal," op. cit., pp. 434–5.

Contrast this with regulative ideals that do have practical import, such as free trade. It may well be the case that free trade is an unattainable goal. However, partial trade liberalizations, at least when they are stable, demonstrably get us closer to the realization of the values that underlie the regulative ideal of free trade.[52] Or consider the ideal of eliminating violent crime in society. In most cases, that ideal can be approached.

A general difficulty with presenting deliberation as an ideal that society should constantly try to approach is this: Sometimes efforts to approach an ideal take us further away from it. Paradoxically, increased efforts to acquire political information may lead people away from the truth. Imagine two political candidates, Smith and Jones. Smith, let us assume, proposes policies based on opaque, reliable social science, while Jones proposes policies based on vivid, unreliable social science. Imagine, further, two voters, Kyle and Betty. Kyle is illiterate and does not watch any television or listen to radio. Let us assume that he would flip a coin to choose between Smith and Jones. He has a 0.5 probability of picking the right candidate, Smith. Betty is instead much concerned about politics. She is literate, watches television, reads the newspapers, and so on. She wants to become as politically knowledgeable as possible. Unfortunately, because both these sources of information and her selection and interpretation of it are affected by discourse failure, Betty will predictably vote for the wrong candidate, Jones. Her effort to become politically educated has driven her away from the truth. This should suffice to cast doubt on the view of deliberation as a regulative ideal.

4.7. Deliberative Democracy, Condorcet, and Bayes

Our analysis so far shows that discourse failure is a serious obstacle to epistemic defenses of deliberative democracy. We close this chapter by considering how discourse failure prevents deliberativists from using some formal results in social choice theory and the theory of inductive inference. Some authors invoke the Jury Theorem, stated by Condorcet, to vindicate the epistemic value of majoritarian decisions.[53] This theorem states that if we assume that, in a given voting group, the probability of each voter's independently holding a true belief on a binary choice

---

[52] See Fernando R. Tesón, "Global Justice, Human Rights, and Trade" (forthcoming, 2006).

[53] As Goldman points out, this line of argument can be traced back to Rousseau's conception of the "general will" expressed by the vote cast by a public-spirited citizenry. See Goldman, op. cit., pp. 315–16.

is greater than 0.5, then the probability that the view selected through majority rule will be true will be greater than 0.5, and it will tend to 1 as the number of voters increases to infinity.[54]

As a preliminary matter, the Condorcet theorem supports democracy, but *not deliberation*. This is because, in order for the theorem to work, voters need to satisfy the condition of mutual independence. They should not base their views on the views of others. Only when each voter has deliberated "within" can we say that the law of large numbers supports majority vote as a truth-tracking device, because only in that case can we compute the (alleged) greater-than-even chance that *each* citizen has of being right. If votes are correlated, the Condorcet logic cannot apply. Independence requires that citizens do not confer with one another, remain immune to opinion leaders, lack similar experiences or training, and share no common information.[55] This is, of course, the exact opposite of deliberation. The mutually reinforcing dynamics of error and posturing characteristic of discourse failure involves massive violation of the independence requirement. Moreover, if voters do not reach their conclusions independently of one another, the chances of collective mistake will be equal to the chances of individual mistake. Because discourse failure affects voters' choice of the opinion leader, the chances of the majority's getting it right will be low.

But deliberativists hope that the condition of independence can somehow be relaxed to render the logic of Condorcet compatible with deliberation. The argument is that the condition of independence is met as long as citizens vote their conscience after having deliberated.[56] Let us

---

[54] For a numerical example, see Larry M. Bartels, "Uninformed Votes: Information Effects in Presidential Elections," *American Journal of Political Science*, Vol. 40, no. 1, February 1996, p. 199, n. 3. See also Luc Bovens and Wlodek Rabinowicz, "Complex Collective Decisions: An Epistemic Perspective," *Associations*, Vol. 7, no. 1, 2003, p. 39; and Robert E. Goodin, *Reflective Democracy*, op. cit., pp. 91–108. Goodin shows that the theorem holds even if we relax some presuppositions that appear in usual formulations; for example, it also holds for plurality vote.

[55] See Krishna K. Ladha, "Information Pooling Through Majority-rule Voting: Condorcet's Jury Theorem with Correlated Votes," *Journal of Economic Behavior & Organization*, Vol. 26, issue 3, May 1995, p. 354. The mutual independence condition is required in all versions of the Condorcet Theorem. See Goodin, op. cit., p. 98.

[56] Jeremy Waldron, for example, points out that the condition of independence is not violated by citizens' reading the same newspapers, listening to the same debates, and so forth. What matters is what occurs *after* the exchange of information – after deliberation. See Jeremy Waldron, "Democratic Theory and the Public Interest," *American Political Science Review*, Vol. 83, no. 4 (December 1989), pp. 1327–8. In the same sense, see Goodin, *Reflective Democracy*, pp. 125–7.

concede this, for the sake of argument. Nevertheless, a corollary of the theorem is that, if each voter has a probability *lower* than 0.5 of holding a true belief about the question submitted for a vote, the probability of a majoritarian decision's being true will be *even* lower – in indefinitely large electorates, it will tend to zero (call this corollary the *Reverse Condorcet Theorem*). This is precisely the scenario we should expect, given discourse failure. If political debate is plagued by discourse failure, the optimistic premise of the theorem (that each voter is more likely than not of being right) does not hold, and therefore error will be magnified in a pool of large numbers of voters.

Nor can epistemic democrats appeal to the Condorcet theorem as a truth-tracking device where there are more than two options before the electorate. Robert Goodin and Christian List have shown that the theorem still holds in case each voter has a probability higher than $1/k$ of holding a true belief about the question submitted for a vote, where k is the number of options. In large numbers, the probability of a *plurality* vote favoring the true position will be even higher.[57] Thus, if option A is the correct choice among three options before each voter, and each voter is 0.4 likely to choose option A, and 0.3 likely to choose each one of the incorrect options B and C, plurality vote will ensure that option A will win in indefinitely large electorates.[58] However, here, too, the corresponding version of the Reverse Condorcet Theorem frustrates the epistemic aspirations of democracy for the range of issues contaminated by discourse failure – a wide range, if we are right. The theory of discourse failure suggests that each voter's chances of picking the right option (or even the one closest to the truth) are lower than her chances of picking some other option. A distribution of probabilities more in line with the discourse failure hypothesis might be: option A (correct), 0.3; option B (incorrect), 0.3; option C (incorrect), 0.4. Clearly, by the Reverse Condorcet Theorem, plurality vote will converge, as the number of voters increases, toward incorrect or false political views.

Moreover, discourse failure affects not only the probabilities of voting for the right or true option but, crucially, the *nature* of the options and their relative salience in the eyes of the voter. The American voter's salient electoral options are conservative and liberal policies. Let us

---

[57] See Robert E. Goodin and Christian List, "Epistemic Democracy: Generalizing the Condorcet Jury Theorem," *Journal of Political Philosophy*, Vol. 9, 2001, pp. 277–306, offered in simplified version as chapter V of Goodin, *Reflective Democracy*, op. cit., pp. 91–108.

[58] See Goodin, *Reflective Democracy*, op. cit., p. 99.

suppose that Karl Marx's economic theory, as presented in *Das Kapital*, is true. Suppose, also, that the policy recommendations most naturally derivable from *Das Kapital* are substantially at variance with conservative and liberal recommendations. If we are right, discourse failure will have led American voters to frame their options as conservative and liberal: Even sketchy expositions of *Das Kapital* will have to refer to opaque, invisible-hand, complex processes, whereas the typical electoral contest between Republicans (the more conservative) and Democrats (the more liberal) is of course abundant in the various mechanisms of discourse failure that we have identified. So discourse failure crucially determines the framing of the issues in a way that puts the true option (in our hypothetical, Marxist economics) at a disadvantage. Therefore, we cannot here simply apply Condorcet as a truth-tracking device, because the very options were selected through a truth-insensitive process. This conclusion is reinforced by the phenomenon of strategic voting: Given the salience of the conservative–liberal framing, believers in the Marxist alternative who do not want to waste their votes will favor either of the salient alternatives (for example, voting conservative in order to accelerate the collapse of capitalism theorized in *Das Kapital*). To put it differently: In order to get off the ground, the logic of Condorcet requires that one of the options submitted to the voters be true. This is the case in the jury setting used by Condorcet to illustrate his theorem, where the defendant *is* either guilty or innocent. In an important class of cases submitted to majoritarian decisions in modern democracies, however, the alternatives are not jointly exhaustive and mutually exclusive. Because of discourse failure, only options resting on mistaken views will be salient. When the alternatives are not jointly exhaustive and mutually exclusive (as in the conservative–liberal example previously given, where by construction a third alternative is true), epistemic democrats cannot invoke the Jury Theorem to assert that the majoritarian coalition is right, or even that it is significantly close to the truth.

Another attempt to establish the epistemic value of democracy on formal grounds relies on Bayesian logic, which lays down mathematical procedures to update one's beliefs in the light of new evidence. Goodin uses Bayesian logic to argue that the very fact that a majority is voting for a certain candidate, proposal, or party is evidence that counts for revising people's previous views on the matter.[59] Rational, Bayesian voters are

---

[59] See Goodin, op. cit., pp. 109–21.

prepared to revise their opinion in the light of such evidence. There are two fatal objections to the use of Bayesian logic here. First, if (i) we were all Bayesian, (ii) the fact that other disagree with us were evidence that we are wrong, and (iii) all looked for the truth, there would never be any disagreements. If you disagree with us, we should take that as evidence that we are wrong and we should update our position (and vice versa, assuming we each think that we are equally intelligent or well informed.) For example, Bayesian deliberators would have no reason to have more than *one* conversation on trade (see section 2.1). The fact that there are persistent disagreements in society suggests that we are not Bayesians of this sort, in which case the Bayesian argument for democratic deliberation is inapplicable. But suppose nonetheless that we were all Bayesians *simpliciter.* In that case, we would simply defer to the best-informed or most intelligent persons and discontinue deliberation and voting, in which case democracy is epistemically inferior to technocracy or some other kind of rule by elites.[60]

But second, even if Bayesian logic can be unproblematically applied to political deliberation, there is no reason to treat *votes* as "reports" (to use Goodin's term) that are more likely to be right than wrong.[61] In fact, if we are right, the opposite is likely to be true. Goodin's application of Bayesian logic cannot get off the ground: Votes are irrelevant as evidence for or against the prior probabilities we assign to our political beliefs. Truth is correspondence with facts (or coherence with other beliefs), and we cannot see how, say, majority support of protectionism would count as evidence for the truth of protectionist views.[62]

---

[60] We are indebted to Jon Klick for calling our attention to this point. The point was made first by Robert J. Aumann, "Agreeing to Disagree," *The Annals of Statistics*, Vol. 4, no. 6, (1976), pp. 1236–9. See the discussion in Tyler Cowen and Robin Hanson, "Are Disagreements Honest?" available at hanson.gmu.edu/deceive.pdf.

[61] Most of the time, Goodin takes the fact that majorities vote in a certain way as evidence for Bayesian updates on beliefs. This leads him to devote the entire Chapter 7 of *Reflective Democracy*, op. cit., to "rationalize persisting opposition" – that is, to make sense of voting with the minority in apparent neglect of Bayesian procedures. Oddly, however, in a few passages he suggests that votes are not as important as "the factual underpinnings of the reasons that people give for their votes" and adds that "this provides yet another argument for extended discussion" (p. 145). If we are right, however, the mutually reinforcing interaction of rational ignorance and posturing will make Bayesian updates of political beliefs work perversely in such discussion.

[62] Indeed, Goodin acknowledges that "the Bayesian power of majorities" does not hold for someone who attaches negative credibility to the reports of others. Op. cit., p. 137.

We remain neutral about the validity of Bayesian procedures generally.[63] Given our polemical purposes, it is nevertheless tempting to apply Bayesian logic to the theory of discourse failure itself. This means that we should update our initial assignment of probabilities to the theory as we observe, say, that most politicians prefer to use visible-hand, zero-sum rhetoric, rather than their invisible-hand, positive-sum counterparts in reliable social theory. Because we (the authors of this book, at least) did observe such facts, we feel entitled, on Bayesian grounds, to increase our a priori assignment of probabilities to the discourse-failure hypothesis. Observation of deliberation and voting reinforces, via Bayes, the belief that the public is mistaken in systematic ways.

---

[63] For a survey of the ongoing controversy, see David Papineau, "Methodology: The Elements of the Philosophy of Science," in A. C. Grayling, ed., *Philosophy: A Guide through the Subject* (Oxford: Oxford University Press, 1995), pp. 166–71. See also James Joyce, "Bayes' Theorem," *The Stanford Encyclopedia of Philosophy* (Winter 2003 Edition), Edward N. Zalta, ed., URL http://plato.stanford.edu/archives/win2003/entries/bayes-theorem/.

5

Symbolism in Political Argument

5.1. Self-Defeatingness as Symbolism

Deliberativists have several strategies available to counter our critique. One is to reinterpret political deliberation as a non-epistemic enterprise. Citizens, they might claim, do things other than seek the truth when they talk to one another. Those speech acts perform very important functions in society. Through deliberation, citizens not only try (clumsily, perhaps) to reach the truth, but, as importantly, they express their commitment to values or principles. Seen in that light, their factual errors are of secondary significance, and hence the charge of discourse failure is less damaging than we have claimed so far. In this and the next chapter we examine two versions of this strategy: the view that deliberation involves symbolic behavior, and the view that apparent factual error can be explained away as a respectable moral position, respectively.

We begin our analysis of symbolism in politics by examining an odd and frequent case. Many people seem insensitive to the fact that the public policies they support in their political deliberation might frustrate the values in the name of which they support those policies. For example, many people support minimum wage laws by invoking the plight of the poor while simultaneously believing that those laws may well hurt the poor.[1] Some writers have argued that only a nonstandard, symbolic model of rationality can vindicate this puzzling behavior as rational. On their

---

[1] Witness the number of politicians, journalists, and other public figures who express unqualified support for the minimum wage in the name of helping the poor even though they *passed* economics courses where they were exposed to the standard reasons why such laws may well harm the poor. See section 6.10.

view, many people support minimum wage laws to symbolize or express concern for the poor. For these authors, political theory has overlooked the fact that many people act not to achieve some identifiable political end but to express a commitment to values or principles.[2] They do not act instrumentally but expressively or symbolically. Such discursive behavior is quite common in political deliberation. In our example, the deliberator who supports minimum wage laws in the name of helping the poor yet believes that those laws hurt (or, at least, may well hurt) the poor does not aim primarily at helping the poor but at expressing symbolically her concern for the poor. On this view, she is rational despite the fact that she seems to act counterproductively. Our aim in this chapter is to show that ordinary models of rationality provide the best account of self-defeating political deliberation. Such models confirm the diagnosis of discourse failure that we offered so far. Many people whose political behavior would seem incomprehensible given their stated aims and values are actually displaying an ordinary, instrumental sort of rationality.

5.2. Symbolic Behavior in Politics

We define *symbolic behavior* as behavior intended by the agent to express adherence to a principle without such behavior's falling under the principle.[3] We are interested here in the relationship between symbolic behavior and some kind of principle, especially of a moral sort. An agent may instantiate the principle or may express his support for it or do both. For example, suppose that I consider myself bound by the principle "Be faithful to your spouse." I instantiate this principle when I refuse to yield to temptation of betrayal (it is unclear whether I instantiate the principle every time I fail to betray). In contrast, I express support for the principle when I say how important fidelity is, or when I give my spouse a wedding anniversary gift. Perhaps one can say, with Nozick, that whenever I instantiate a principle I also express support for that principle.[4] Be that as it may, the relationship does not seem to work the other way around: The

---

[2] See Robert Nozick, *The Nature of Rationality* (Cambridge, Mass.: Harvard University Press, 1993), pp. 25–30; Elizabeth S. Anderson and Richard H. Pildes, "Expressive Theories of Law: A General Restatement," *University of Pennsylvania Law Review*, CXLVIII (2000), pp. 1503–75; Cass Sunstein, "On the Expressive Function of Law," *University of Pennsylvania Law Review*, CXLIV (1996), pp. 2021–53.

[3] We are grateful to David Copp for this definition. Similar definitions result from referring to values or goals rather than to principles.

[4] Robert Nozick sees things in that way in *The Nature of Rationality*, op. cit., p. 33.

fact that I have expressed support for a principle does not mean that I have instantiated the principle. My symbolic or expressive[5] behavior is not yet compliance with duty. The symbolic act does not cause the state of affairs recommended by the principle. Rather, it expresses approval of, or appreciation for, the principle itself.

Symbolic meaning may be *social* or *subjective*. In the first case, the agent is doing something that is conventionally regarded as showing adherence to a principle. In the second case, the agent is doing something that shows to himself that he is adhering to a principle. The agent who subjectively expresses adherence to a principle is endorsing the principle. The agent whose behavior is socially seen as symbolizing a principle may or may not endorse the principle.

We confine our discussion to symbolic behavior in political deliberation – more specifically, to (seemingly) self-defeating attitudes toward laws, policies, and other public measures. Public measures have social consequences. Yet symbolic agents who deliberate publicly do not recommend laws because of their valuable social consequences but because in doing so they express support for or adherence to a principle. So an agent who supports a law for symbolic reasons is expressing adherence to the (moral) principle that presumably informs that law. She may or may not will the causal consequences that ensue from that law. A typical political agent A who acts symbolically

(1) publicly expresses adherence to principle P by supporting law L.

We shall say that A supports L in the name of P. A *self-defeating* symbolic political agent is one who recommends a public measure (such as a law) in the name of a principle that, so he believes, would be frustrated (either directly or in virtue of behavior performed in response to the threat of sanctions) by the enactment of that law. A self-defeating political agent, therefore, in addition to (1),

(2) believes that L, if enacted, would frustrate the realization of P (that is, would frustrate the state of affairs enjoined by P).

Call this agent a *self-defeating reformer* (SDR). Note that the sense in which this agent's behavior is self-defeating is that she believes the law

---

[5] We use "symbolic" and "expressive" interchangeably, although the distinction between the two might be useful in a different context. Thus, we may say that someone may want to express herself without communicating anything – this may be called expressive behavior. Symbolic behavior, on the other hand, can be defined as communicative. The difference matters for a distinction we make later between self-defeating reformers and self-defeating *performers* – that is, persons who seem to act counterproductively but want only to express themselves.

she supports would frustrate the realization of the principle in the name of which she acts.[6] She does not necessarily believe that *her act of support* is detrimental to the principle. Nor do we assume in this definition that she endorses *P*. All we assume is that her behavior may conventionally express adherence to *P*; as we noted earlier, symbolic meaning may be social, subjective, or both. Someone may object that agents who satisfy (1) and (2) need not be really self-defeating. For example, an insincere agent (that is, one who does not care about *P*) would not be really self-defeating. This objection, however, leaves untouched the puzzle that we want to examine – namely, why rational persons would support counter-productive political measures, whether or not we call them self-defeating agents.[7]

5.3. Symbolic and Causal Utility: Nozick's Challenge

Nozick claims that people who perform an act to express adherence to a value while simultaneously believing that the act frustrates the realization of the value can nonetheless be acting rationally.[8] They can be rational because they derive symbolic utility from that behavior. Nozick thinks that standard decision theory is incapable of uncovering the rationality of such people because it works exclusively with causally derived utilities, thus ignoring symbolic utilities.

Nozick uses two examples from politics. We've already mentioned the first: Someone publicly supports minimum wage laws in the name of the principle that we ought to help the poor, even when he believes that those laws actually hurt the poor.[9] He still does so because the act of supporting minimum wage laws symbolizes concern for the poor. He derives utility

---

[6] For stylistic reasons, we will refer to agents who believe such propositions, meaning to include those who believe that such propositions are plausible. Our argument holds for both cases.

[7] Indeed, as we will argue, most SDRs are instrumentally rational, so they are not self-defeating in any sense that denies instrumental rationality. The self-defeating quality of their behavior is that the political measures they support would, if enacted, frustrate the values they invoke to justify such support.

[8] *The Nature of Rationality*, op. cit., pp. 26–8.

[9] Sunstein also uses that example, though in a normative context. He concludes that people who believe that minimum wage laws hurt the poor should not, as a matter of political morality, support them just for symbolic reasons ("On the Expressive Function of Law," op. cit., pp. 2046–7). In their defense of expressive theories of law, Anderson and Pildes nonetheless say that the view that expressive evaluation somehow requires people to ignore the consequences of action is absurd ("Expressive Theories of Law: A General Restatement," op. cit., p. 1513).

from expressing support for that principle ("We ought to help the poor"), quite apart from whether or not those laws help the poor.[10] In the second example, someone publicly supports anti-drug measures without paying attention to evidence that those measures increase drug consumption and crime. Here again, the act symbolizes the moral condemnation of drug use and the crime associated with such use (what could be more symbolic of the revulsion for drug use than prohibiting it?). In both cases, the agent (the deliberating citizen) derives symbolic utility from supporting those measures, notwithstanding his belief that they may prevent the (subjectively) valuable outcome that his support is symbolizing.

Nozick claims that symbolic rationality cannot be reduced to instrumental rationality. He endorses the standard view that rational agents maximize utility or value but distinguishes between *causal* and *symbolic* utility.[11] Symbolic utility is a further strand, a distinct, noncausal concept. The agent performs an act because it has symbolic value for him. That the act is symbolic means that it stands for something else – a

---

[10] We use the example of self-defeating support of minimum wage laws, where the agent whose rationality we assess happens to adopt a view against free labor markets. The argument here does not depend on the proposition that minimum wage laws hurt the poor or, for that matter, on any pro-market or libertarian political view. What is important here is that the self-defeating agent *believes, or at least regards as plausible*, that minimum wage laws hurt the poor. On the plausibility of this view, see section 6.10. One can easily think of examples of pro-market or libertarian self-defeating agents. Imagine someone who opposes deregulation of utilities in the name of efficiency. Suppose further that economists convince him that, because of market failure, the deregulation he proposes will produce inefficient outcomes. Yet this agent may persist in his support of deregulation if he believes that such behavior socially symbolizes commitment to efficiency. In our terminology, this person is a self-defeating political agent.

[11] Nozick discusses a third kind of utility as well – evidential utility (*The Nature of Rationality*, op. cit., pp. 45–59). Decision theorists propose evidential principles to accommodate some intuitions about what it is rational for an agent to do in situations where his payoffs depend on what others do or have done on the basis of a correct prediction of his decision. The Prisoner's Dilemma and Newcomb's Problem, respectively, illustrate those situations. The strand of decision theory that plays a role in the account of seemingly self-defeating political utterances that we shall offer in section 5.6 is causal in nature. Causal decision principles inform also the rational ignorance hypothesis and, more generally, the *explanations* of patterns of discursive behavior advanced in this book. We take no sides on the extent to which evidential, causal, or other decision-theoretic principles can accommodate *an observer's intuitions* about what it is rational for an agent to do in various settings. For this latter, normative question, see the discussion by Susan L. Hurley in "A New Take from Nozick on Newcomb's Problem and Prisoner's Dilemma," *Analysis*, Vol. 54, no. 2, pp. 55–72 (arguing that a weighted combination of causal and "cooperative" principles best accommodates our intuitions about what it is rational to do in Prisoner's Dilemmas and Newcomb's Problems, with no need to appeal to evidential concepts).

principle, or value, or something desirable. Crucially, however, the act does not cause the state of affairs recommended by the principle, the value, or the desirable thing. What the act symbolizes (that "something else") has value for the agent, and that value is imputed back to the act, thus "giving *it* greater utility than it appeared to have."[12] Nozick recognizes, of course, that utility can be imputed back along causal lines: Action A may have value for the agent because she believes that A causally contributes to an outcome O that she (instrumentally or ultimately) values.[13] The metaphor of "imputing back" attempts to show that the value of A is parasitic on the value of O. For Nozick, then, A is valuable either because it causes O or because it symbolizes O. In the latter case, A borrows value from O because A stands for O. This will be true even when A does not contribute causally to O – in fact, it will be true, according to Nozick, even when A frustrates the realization of O. Thus, a citizen who in public deliberation defends, say, drug prohibition in the name of fighting crime need not care about the fact that those laws, if enacted, would increase crime. All that matters is that those laws socially *symbolize* opposition to crime.

Nozick observes that standard decision theory cannot easily explain symbolic utility and thus cannot explain what he views as the anomalous case: the SDR case. An SDR believes that the policy he advocates frustrates the realization of the symbolized principle. Nozick claims that an SDR acts irrationally under standard decision theory, yet he argues that we can salvage his rationality by appealing to irreducibly symbolic utility. For Nozick, traditional decision theory has overlooked the fact that symbolic utility is independent of causal utility: An act's utility may be noncausal – purely symbolic, as it were. Its value for the agent does not depend, even partly, on the probabilities of its causing future situations that actualize the symbolized value. Nozick thinks his view is supported by the fact that many people persist in doing something "in the face of strong evidence that it does not actually have the presumed causal consequences."[14] The symbolic, rather than the (putative) causal connection to an outcome plays a central role in the decision to do it. In our example, an SDR derives symbolic utility from supporting minimum wage laws in the name of the principle that one ought to help the poor, even though he believes that those laws will hurt the poor. Nozick observes that perhaps

---

[12] *The Nature of Rationality*, op. cit., p. 26.

[13] The variable O here may range over states of affairs or attitudes: Agents may want to symbolize subjective attitudes as well as desirable outcomes.

[14] Op. cit., p. 27.

a rational agent should choose a different act to express his adherence to the principle, one that does not have these bad consequences. But simply refraining from performing that act (that is, without replacing it with another symbolically appropriate act) would deprive people of its symbolic utility – something, Nozick thinks, they are unwilling to let happen.[15]

Why does Nozick believe that his account improves on traditional decision theory? He may be assuming a plausible adequacy condition for a theory of rationality: the theory must treat most behavior as rational.[16] The fact that many people defend self-defeating positions in politics may suggest that, given the standard account of rationality, they are crazy or irrational. However, a theory of rationality under which most people were crazy would not be attractive. So Nozick feels compelled to introduce a symbolic, nonstandard form of rationality in order to account for the inordinate number of citizens who seem to behave in a self-defeating way in the political arena. Because it has been a major burden of this book to show that such behavior can be explained by resorting to a standard, instrumental account of rationality, we must show why our account is preferable to Nozick's.

5.4. Symbolizing as the Intended Outcome

We interpret judgments about rationality as relying on testable hypotheses about an agent's means and goals. We also assume that people who defend symbolic behavior use testable hypotheses as well. We thus avoid the use of ad hoc or circular notions of utility. That is, we shall not say that someone who prefers to do *x* rather than *y* is rational because he *eo ipso* derives more utility from *x* than from *y*. In order to assess people's rationality we do not simply work with their revealed preferences: We have to know more about their goals and beliefs. We avoid ad hoc judgments of rationality.[17]

We do not believe that in order to explain self-defeating political behavior we should amend standard decision theory, which evaluates and explains behavior within the framework of actions causing outcomes. A rational agent believes that her action will (be likely to) cause an outcome that she values. This view of rationality is, therefore, instrumental:

---

[15] Ibid.
[16] We use the terms "decision theory" and "theory of rationality" interchangeably in this chapter.
[17] See also our discussion of circularity in section 3.2.

A rational agent chooses what she regards as efficient means to her goals. But surely there is a sense of "action" in which *the action itself* can be the desired outcome. An agent may derive utility or value from doing *A*, where *his doing it* is the outcome he intends. He may take an interest in his own action, as something different from further causal consequences of the action. It is natural for him to believe that doing that action is an efficient means to satisfy such interest. For example, many people value playing tennis quite independently of further causal consequences that they expect to achieve (for example, improved health, better bodily appearance). So the fact that an action is the very outcome sought by the agent does not prevent standard rational choice theory from explaining the agent's behavior: The action itself has utility or value for the agent. The agent who acts symbolically, then, draws value or utility from expressing his adherence to a principle. His expressive act is what he values.

As we have seen, Nozick observes that often an action is valuable (has utility for) the agent because it symbolizes something valuable, and so the action borrows utility from the symbolized thing. The value of the symbolized thing is imputed back to the action. We believe, however, that this does not undermine the basic rational choice analysis: The agent draws utility from the state of affairs he causes. Sometimes the causal chain is very short: The agent who derives symbolic utility from a ritual dance causes the relevant outcome (i.e., his dancing) in a very straightforward way. But this should not be more mysterious than deriving utility from more distant outcomes, as in dancing for money. The two examples differ only in the lengths of the respective causal chains, and this difference is irrelevant to decision theory. What complicates the issue in Nozick's analysis is that there are two kinds of valuable outcomes in his examples. One is the action itself (from which the agent derives value directly, as it were), and the other is the principle symbolized by the action. Presumably, the agent would say that the reason he values the action is that it symbolizes that principle (for example, the duty to help the poor), but the fact remains that the agent derives utility from his doing the symbolic action. Nozick's challenge to traditional decision theory trades on the fact that there is no causal relation between the action and the instantiation of the principle or value in the name of which the action is undertaken. The suggestion is that we need to postulate a new relationship between action and outcome to explain what is otherwise mysterious. We think this view overlooks the fact that there is a causal relation, a relation of means to ends, and thus no mystery, once we acknowledge that the symbolizing is itself the end. The symbolic political deliberator, in particular, values his symbolizing, not necessarily the symbolized thing.

Another way to put this is as follows: We value things and events because of some of their properties. Sometimes such properties are causal in character, as when we value a political revolution because it has brought about justice. But this need not be so. I may value a car because it *is* fast. Moreover, we often value something because of its noncausal relational properties; for example, I may value John because he is a member of the Red Cross. Shall we say that I *impute back* to John the value I ascribe to the Red Cross *along membership lines*? Yes, provided that this does not mean anything different from saying that I impute back to the car the value that I find in the car's speed (along a nonrelational property). In both cases, a property grounds a value judgment and renders rational any cost-effective undertaking aimed at instantiating that property (e.g., my producing such a car, my advising John to become a member of the Red Cross). Similarly, the fact that I value *S* because it symbolizes *T* renders it rational, in the standard sense, for me to (cost-effectively) bring about *S*. What matters here is that sometimes my own actions instantiate *S*. As David Christensen[18] says, "the utility comes from the *symbolizing* of the situation," from the act of communicating something to others.[19] Nozick is correct that this utility is independent of the expectation of the symbolized situation coming to pass, but his assertion that the utility flows from the situation back to the act wrongly suggests an anomaly for standard decision theory. It is not that the symbolized situation generates utility for the agent but rather that the symbolic act does. When a citizen acts symbolically, we do not know yet if he is really prepared to honor the principle on behalf of which he acts. All we know is that he values his (social or subjective) expression of support for the principle.

As we anticipated, we assume that judgments about rationality are not ad hoc. So the foregoing account of symbolic behavior requires us to have independent evidence about the agent's utility functions. In the dancing example, attributing to the agent the ultimate end of dancing would be ad hoc if we did not have independent evidence that he has such end. But, as we said, we are not defending the rational choice model in this way.

---

[18] Book Review, *Noûs*, XXIX (1995), pp. 259–74. See also Gerald F. Gaus, "Goals, Symbols and Principles: An Evaluation of Nozick's Theory of Practical Rationality," presented at the Colloquium on Political Philosophy held at Universidad Torcuato Di Tella Law School, Buenos Aires (June 7, 2000), now published in David Schmidtz, ed., *Robert Nozick* (New York: Cambridge University Press, 2000).

[19] Op. cit., p. 265.

In order to say in an interesting way that the dancing itself is the agent's ultimate end, we need to have independent evidence: He might have paid for dancing lessons in the past, he might have told his friends that he loved dancing, and so on. Because conceivably the available evidence may tell against such a hypothesis, our analysis makes room for irrational behavior. However, as we extensively argued (and summarily repeat in section 5.6), most counterproductive political behavior conforms to testable rational choice assumptions.

5.5. Are Self-Defeating Reformers Rational?

The ordinary rationality of SDRs can be best seen by distinguishing several cases of apparently self-defeating political behavior. Imagine a citizen who sincerely endorses the principle that one must help the poor. When deliberating with his fellow citizens, he supports minimum wage laws yet believes that these laws, considered in isolation, would hurt the poor. He does not believe, however, that *his act* will hurt the poor, all things considered. He chooses publicly to support minimum wage laws because he thinks he thereby instantiates a symbol that, in turn, starts a causal chain resulting in the betterment of the poor. He may or may not derive utility from symbolizing the principle he endorses. But he does believe that his act (that is, his public support of those laws) will have other consequences that are beneficial to the poor: People will be encouraged to give more to charity or will support public causes or politicians who are committed to helping the poor. This citizen believes that the measures he supports are counterproductive in terms of the value he cherishes, but that *his support* for those measures is not. The agent we are imagining adds the expected symbolic utility (if any) of his supporting the laws to the expected causal utility of those other consequences and subtracts the expected utility of the possible enactment of the laws he supports. (The latter expected utility is negligibly negative, given that public support of laws is normally causally irrelevant to their being enacted.) If the balance is positive, he performs the symbolic action.[20] One major reason why a rational agent will be tempted to perform the symbolic act is that it is within his power, something he can do for sure, here and now (as

---

[20] We employ the terms "addition," "subtraction," and (later) "algebraic sum" loosely, for terminological convenience. We do not mean to endorse a cardinal view of utility. But our account does assume, however, intrapersonal ordinal rankings of utility. "Addition" and "subtraction" allude to the agent's subjective balancing of alternatives.

opposed to bringing about the improvement of the poor, which is outside his power).

So this agent, in addition to satisfying the dyad (1)–(2) above, meets the following two conditions:

(3) He endorses *P* as his overriding principle.
(4) He thinks that his supporting *L* (as something different from *L* itself) will conform to *P* or advance the values that underlie *P*, all things considered.

Call this person the *consistent agent*. It seems safe to conclude that this agent is rational because he does not think that his behavior, as something different from the laws themselves, harms the poor, all things considered. He maximizes his utility by doing what he believes is causally conducive to that end – he is instrumentally rational.

But suppose a citizen is not primarily interested in the causal consequences of his act of symbolism. Conceivably, his overriding goal may be the symbolizing itself. Normally, this agent (the *expressive agent*) will maximize his utility quite straightforwardly – he just does the symbolic act (for example, he wears a ribbon, he publicly supports a principle, and so on). We can say that the utility derived by the expressive agent is symbolic in the sense that he performs an action because of its being a symbol of something (socially or subjectively) valuable. Under our definition of symbolic behavior, the agent who acts symbolically does something in the name of, or for the sake of, a value or principle without instantiating that principle. The agent who acts symbolically brings about something that is valuable to him – namely, an act that has symbolic meaning (i.e., that stands for something else, however we construe such relation). Accordingly, symbolic behavior possesses the same instrumental structure that we find in nonsymbolic contexts. The agent causes the symbol (the act) to occur (brings it about, performs it), just as an agent who derives utility from dancing causes (brings about, performs) acts falling under the description "his dancing."

It might be useful to compare the consistent agent with the expressive agent. Both the consistent agent and the expressive agent are SDRs: They satisfy the foregoing propositions (1) and (2). The consistent agent is attentive to consequences, because he values the fact that his symbolic behavior, apart from having utility or value in itself to him (and maybe others), does (in his view) help the poor, all things considered. By contrast, the expressive agent is less attentive to those consequences: He does not want, primarily at least, to help the poor. Unlike the consistent agent, the expressive agent does not believe that his behavior helps the poor, all things considered. He satisfies neither (3) nor (4) above. He derives utility from supporting minimum wage laws because his support symbolizes helping the poor. He derives utility from an instance of this symbolic connection (from being on the right side, as it were). We may say that the utility he derives from the act of supporting minimum wage laws exceeds whatever (negative) utility he derives from the enactment of minimum wage laws, discounted by the probability of such enactment given his support. Of course, under normal circumstances such expected (negative) utility is very low because his support is causally irrelevant. So in ordinary cases the cost to the expressive agent of being on the right side (measured by the expected disutility, if any, he might derive from the fact that the poor will be hurt as a result of his present behavior) is very low. The consistent agent, on the other hand, sincerely cares about the poor. Given his belief that the laws are unlikely[21] to be enacted, he may safely support minimum wage laws.

The upshot of all this is that an SDR remains rational in the sense of traditional decision theory. Neither in the consistent-agent case nor in the expressive-agent case need we assume that utility is noncausally imputed back to current behavior. In particular, there is no "imputing back" along symbolic connections. The consistent agent and the expressive agent are, therefore, rational under standard decision theory. They differ only in the value they assign to the symbolic action vis-à-vis its consequences.

To be sure, these citizens' behavior is puzzling because the policies they support are counterproductive in terms of the values they ostensibly invoke. Here, again, we should distinguish between the consistent agent and the expressive agent. The consistent agent's behavior coheres: He believes he ought to help the poor, and he knowingly behaves to achieve just that. By contrast, the expressive agent's behavior may be incoherent. If he actually endorses[22] the principle in the name of which he acts, his behavior is incoherent: He believes he ought to help the poor, but he knows that his behavior will not achieve that end. To the extent that he values helping the poor more than he values the symbolizing itself, in some scenarios he may be instrumentally irrational.[23] But if the expressive

---

[21] Politicians, and especially legislators, may significantly influence the outcome. But for very rare cases of irrationality, standard decision theory can explain their behavior along the lines we suggested in our analysis of discourse failure, summarized in section 5.6.

[22] Recall that we did not stipulate that an SDR necessarily endorses the principle in the name of which she acts. See proposition (1), section 5.2.

[23] He need not be, however. Assume he would get 100 units of utility from helping the poor as a class and 10 units of utility from symbolizing his concern. Now suppose that

agent does not endorse as paramount the principle in the name of which he acts, his behavior coheres: He does not believe that what he does will help the poor, but helping the poor is not his primary goal. His primary goal is the symbolizing itself.

What about people who (a) advocate policies that they foresee will be detrimental to their values, (b) have as their reason for such advocacy the fact that those policies (or advocacy of them) express a commitment to those values, but (c) do not behave in that way *in the name of realizing* such values? Consider this case: A woman stands by her sick son's bed. She knows that his chances of recovery are small. Terribly moved by her son's plight, she embraces him, knowing that this will kill him immediately (the *poignant case*[24]). What are we to make of the mother's rationality? She is not an SDR. She does not fit our earlier definition of self-defeating behavior, because she is not supporting a course of action in the name of things she deems valuable. Perhaps we can attribute to this mother the intention to express adherence to a value, such as the value of having healthy children, and in this sense hers is a symbolic action. But, unlike the consistent agent and the expressive agent, what she does is something other than supporting specific measures in the name of the value. Call this behavior *symbolic**, to distinguish it from the sort of symbolism discussed so far and defined at the outset of section 5.2. Unlike the act of supporting something, the mother's embracing her son is symbolic* in that it lacks propositional implications, so it makes no sense to assess it in terms of how favorable or detrimental to (non-expressive) goals her act is. We can call this mother a *self-defeating performer* (SDP). Because an SDP is, as such, not supporting or advocating anything, she is not an SDR.

The mother in the poignant case satisfies the conditions laid down for X in the following dyad:

(I) X believes that her doing A symbolizes* valuable thing T.
(II) X believes that A causes outcomes incompatible with T.

none of the actions open to him has much probability of actually helping the poor. The correct policy (the one that, if enacted, would help the poor) has a 0.01 chance of being enacted, while a mistaken policy (one that, if enacted, would not help the poor) has a 0 chance of being enacted. However, the mistaken policy's probability of successful expression is high – say, .9 – while it is low for the correct policy – say, .3. He then performs the expected utility calculations: (a) advocating the good policy: $.3(10) + 0.01(100) = 4$; (b) advocating the mistaken policy: $.9(10) + .0(100) = 9$. So even if he values helping the poor more than symbolizing his concern, it is rational for him to support the mistaken policy.

[24] We are grateful to Geoffrey Brennan for suggesting this example.

Note that, unlike the formulation offered in section 5.2, this one makes no reference to X's supporting measures that frustrate her ends. So her behavior should not be confused with that of the expressive agent. While the expressive agent primarily values his symbolizing, his behavior has a causal component in that he supports political measures, and this support is conventionally understood as entailing that those measures are instrumental to the realization of the principle in the name of which he acts. Thus, when confronted with someone who supports minimum wage laws in the name of helping the poor, most people will reasonably infer that this agent believes that minimum wage laws help the poor. On the other hand, an SDP, like the mother, displays purely expressive behavior, as it were, so there is no potential for incoherence. In short, her expressive behavior is symbolic*, not symbolic. Unlike an SDP, an SDR supports a policy in a political context. As such, he takes a moral stance in the sense that he is committed to justifying his views if need be. This makes room for incoherence – the SDR acts in the name of principles whose realization may be frustrated by the policy he advocates. To be sure, the SDP is still acting in a kind of self-defeating way because she knowingly engages in behavior that frustrates her values. But she does not instantiate the symbol in the name of a principle; she just expresses her values, as it were.

Is the SDP instrumentally rational? There is no definite answer: All depends on how we fill out the description of the case. If, in the poignant case, the mother's overriding end is to help heal her son, then she is arguably irrational in the standard sense: She fails to maximize her utility given her beliefs.[25] If the expected utility she derives from embracing her son is greater, then she is rational in the same sense.

Can ostensibly self-defeating political discourse be modeled in terms of the SDP? If the answer is yes, then prima facie counterproductive political deliberators would not be displaying self-defeating behavior, and a fortiori they would be instrumentally rational. As we have just seen, unlike the SDR, the SDP is not supporting anything. She expresses adherence to a principle or value, but, to the extent that she does not advocate measures in the name of a principle or value, there is nothing in her behavior to be inconsistent with. If this were the correct model for political agents (for example, the supporter of minimum wage laws and drug prohibition), then they would not be self-defeating, and their symbolic* behavior would not by itself allow us to decide whether they are rational or not. Contrary to what seems a natural interpretation of their conduct, those people

[25] Remember that we are using a noncircular notion of utility (see section 5.4).

would not be properly supporting anything: It would be more accurate to view them as *embracing* a valuable cause.[26]

We doubt, however, that many agents whose political discourse sounds counterproductive are really SDPs. Embracing a cause is not like embracing a person. Support of political measures is not simply expressive of commitment to values or principles; it is also performed in the name of values or principles. As we said, an agent who supports laws in the name of values or principles is committed to endorsing causal beliefs. Thus, support of minimum wage laws in the name of the principle that we ought to help the poor conventionally implies a commitment to the causal belief that such laws help the poor (or, at the very least, that those laws do not harm the poor). Contrast this political attitude with that of the mother in the poignant case. She may be expressing her love for her son, but she is not behaving in the name of a principle that mandates helping her son survive. So we conclude that the only irrational political agents are those SDRs who sincerely endorse as of paramount value the principle in the name of which they act. We suspect that these agents are very rare.[27] Let us substantiate this suspicion in the next section.

5.6. Why Political Deliberators Appear to Neglect Consequences

As we pointed out in section 5.3, we expect a theory of rationality to explain the way most people behave. But we also required of such explanations that they not be ad hoc (section 5.4). Therefore, we need to offer independent evidence of why in politics a surprisingly large number of people seem to act symbolically, even at the cost of self-defeatingness. We showed that symbolic political agents typically value their act of symbolizing, but not necessarily the symbolized thing. They need not care much about the consequences of the laws they support for symbolic reasons. This will be true whether or not their behavior is self-defeating – that is, whether or not they believe that the laws they support would, if enacted, frustrate the principle in the name of which they act. What could then possibly motivate people to act symbolically in politics in disregard of the social consequences of the policies they advocate?

---

[26] Symbolism* may play a role in moral assessment. Depending on the circumstances, symbolic* reasons might exonerate otherwise objectionable behavior: Like the mother, political agents would be moved by terrible facts (for example, unsatisfied dire needs, extreme violence).

[27] So is the poignant case, and for this reason it should not threaten standard decision theory, even assuming that the mother is typically irrational.

Our theory of discourse failure supports two conjectures in response. The first is that in many cases people whose behavior may appear self-defeating are ignorant of or mistaken about the relevant causal connections. Suppose someone supports minimum wage laws in the belief that they will help the poor. This agent is not self-defeating: He does not satisfy (2) above; that is, he does not believe that the measures he supports will frustrate the goals in the name of which he acts. This person, however, might seem to act in a self-defeating way because, on a plausible reading of economic theory (see section 6.8), minimum wage laws might well hurt the poor. His apparent self-defeatingness is even more noticeable when he is unwilling to consider relevant evidence and arguments. Obviously, if many people neglect relevant evidence, chances are that false beliefs about society will be pervasive, and this in turn may lead those people to advance seemingly counterproductive political proposals.

Why would so many people hold mistaken social theories? We offered the answer in the preceding chapters of this book. Political interaction creates incentives for people to err. Citizens tend to remain ignorant about politics, and rationally so.[28] In the minimum wage example, even a citizen who is morally motivated to help the poor will, if rational, remain ignorant of relevant facts and theories about effective political ways of helping the poor. It certainly makes more sense for him to help the poor through charity, for example, than trying to help the poor through his informed participation in the political process. We saw that citizens will predictably rely on quickly and easily understandable theories and "facts," because the personal cost of grasping them is low. If our argument in the preceding chapters is correct, we can see why many people seem to act in a self-defeating way in politics. They do not behave in this way because they want to symbolize values. Rather, they are simply mistaken about the relevant causal connections.

Now consider politicians. They have an electoral incentive to know these facts about people's beliefs. Hence, they will predictably employ rhetoric based on short or simple causal chains and on the other sources of vividness we discussed[29] – otherwise, they will find themselves competitively disadvantaged in the struggle for rationally ignorant votes. As we have seen, rational error stems from the same logic as rational ignorance. The rational behavior of both politicians and voters explains why certain general views about the workings of society tend to prevail. Differential

[28] See note 16, section 2.2., and accompanying text.
[29] See sections 2.2 through 2.6.

incentives to acquire and spread political information lead citizens to accept or reject social theories through a truth-insensitive process. Under these conditions, and assuming that sometimes the right explanation of a social phenomenon is hard to understand, we should expect widespread acceptance of false theories. The upshot is that we do not have to appeal to symbolic reasons to explain the spread of apparently self-defeating public positions among citizens. Neither do symbolic reasons account for the politicians' truth-insensitive[30] rhetoric: They are utility maximizers in a causal sense, whatever their utility functions (for example, maximization of political power, or votes[31]), and they often choose to lie in the pursuit of their goals.[32] So, prima facie SDRs are likely to be rationally ignorant or mistaken if they are ordinary citizens, whereas they are likely to be rationally insincere if they are (successful) politicians. We reach this conclusion without assuming that utility can be imputed back along symbolic lines. We rely instead on standard rational choice assumptions.

The second conjecture is that many people have incentives to appear on the side of what is socially perceived as right. Being so perceived is usually associated with various kinds of benefits: success at work, acceptance in certain circles (political or otherwise), and in general the psychological and material rewards accruing from social prestige. As our analysis of academic discourse failure (section 2.6) showed, dissenting from widespread views is often costly. An SDR who wants to appear on the right side in public deliberation might or might not be concerned about his self-defeatingness. That is, he might or might not care about the fact that his support, say, for minimum wage laws in the name of helping the poor is coupled with his belief that those laws hurt the poor. We can imagine an SDR's thinking as follows: "I believe that minimum wage laws

[30] Politicians do have an incentive to care about truth when falsehood is transparent to voters. Our point is that political competition provides politicians with an incentive to care about truth in this incidental sense only.

[31] Such utility functions are compatible with ascribing public-spirited ultimate ends to politicians. We do not take sides here with any particular view about the contents of those ends.

[32] We saw in section 1.2 that rational choice models of voting behavior have difficulty explaining voter turnout. For an unsympathetic survey of the literature on rational choice explanations of voter turnout, see Donald P. Green and Ian Shapiro, op. cit., pp. 47–71. Notice, however, that expressive models of voter turnout are compatible with our analysis of discourse failure. Perhaps symbolic utility draws the voter to the polling booth, but her vote will still be rationally ignorant or mistaken. Whatever the best explanation of voter turnout may be, we believe that the rational ignorance/error effect accounts for the behavior of sincere and rational individuals who look like SDRs. We need not appeal to symbolic reasons.

will be likely to hurt the poor, but I support them because my overriding goal is to be seen by others as promoting those laws out of concern for the poor. So I pretend that I do not have that belief (otherwise, my support would not have such symbolic meaning). I would prefer that the poor not be hurt (and probably they will not be hurt because the likelihood of enactment is low), but at any rate I draw value from the social approval I get thanks to the symbolic significance that I convey by my action." Let us call this citizen the *posturer*. He seeks social esteem as his primary goal and uses his expressive behavior in political deliberation to earn it. He values his expressive behavior instrumentally, and in this he differs from the purely expressive agent (see previous section). To the extent that the posturer does not believe that he has benefits-for-the-poor grounds for supporting laws, the coherence of his behavior is saved. Insincerity sustains coherence. He asserts but does not believe the following proposition, entailed by his advocacy of minimum wage laws in the name of the poor: "Minimum wage laws help the poor." He also asserts (or implies) that his goal is to help the poor, but he does not really have that goal, at least as his overriding goal. This citizen is thus doubly insincere.

Does the posturer's insincerity affect his rationality? We do not think so. Citizens who are insincere in this way are instrumentally rational. The instrumental rationality of an act does not turn on the means employed by the agent to bring about his preferred outcome. Insincerity, in particular, may be the citizen's means of conveying the symbolic message associated with his support of minimum wage laws. Only if sincerity is a definitional feature of the symbolic act can insincerity frustrate symbolic meaning. But there is no substantive constraint (including mental constraints, like sincerity) in successful symbolizing.[33] As we have seen, an agent may instantiate a symbol without endorsing the symbolized value or principle. So nothing in rational behavior rules out insincerity. We conclude, then, that ostensibly counterproductive behavior whereby the citizen gets social esteem by being insincere is instrumentally rational.[34] Again, a citizen's desire to posture seems to us a much more plausible explanation of apparently self-defeating political positions than the citizen's desire to instantiate valuable symbols. While posturing is something that we would

---

[33] Nor is there any such constraint in Nozick's account.

[34] Is not the consistent agent (see section 5.5) also insincere? Recall that this agent believes that his support for minimum wage laws will help the poor, all things considered, yet he also believes that the laws themselves will harm the poor. It depends on how one defines insincerity. Unlike the posturer, the consistent agent is faithful to the goal or value to which he declares adherence.

expect given rational ignorance and the incentives of various political actors, a desire to instantiate valuable symbols in a self-defeating manner seems both ad hoc and mysterious.

To summarize, most people who engage in self-defeating political symbolism display an instrumental sort of rationality. Symbolic political deliberators typically value instrumentally the act of symbolizing. When seen in this light, their behavior is no longer puzzling. To be sure, many people seem simultaneously to attach overriding force to the principle they invoke while behaving counterproductively with respect to that principle. If this appearance turned out to be reality, our argument in this chapter would have expelled too many people from the realm of rationality. But things are not as they seem. Rational ignorance or error, along with political insincerity (in short, discourse failure), accounts for most counterproductive political behavior. The remaining counterproductive agents are so few that they should not subvert standard accounts of rationality.

6

Discourse Failure and Political Morality

6.1. The Moral Turn

We have argued that theories of deliberative democracy are utopian because the mechanisms that generate discourse failure prevent citizens from deliberating in the manner recommended by deliberativists. This chapter explores and rejects a reply that deliberativists may offer to the charge of utopianism: that citizens who seem to ignore complex empirical matters involved in the choice of policies are really advancing moral positions to which such empirical matters are irrelevant. The argument (which we call "the moral turn") runs as follows: Discourse failure affects only matters of fact. The public may ignore who the public officials are and how they behave, the mechanics of complex economic transactions, the functions of many institutions, and so forth. Political disagreement is, in contrast, primarily moral in character.[1] Public debate on most political issues (regulatory policy, abortion, education, affirmative action, drug

---

[1] See Gutmann and Thompson, *Democracy and Disagreement*, op. cit., esp. pp. 11–51, and John Rawls, *Political Liberalism* (New York: Columbia University Press, 1991). Rawls's insistence that the stability of a just society depends on citizens' using public reasons alone in political deliberation suggests that the most divisive and serious disagreements are moral in nature (what he calls conflicts among "comprehensive views"). This tendency to focus on moral disagreement is evident in Rawls's discussion of the ideal of democratic citizenship (pp. 216–20). In the same vein, Carlos Nino locates the value of democracy in the "moralization of people's preferences." *The Constitution of Deliberative Democracy*, op. cit., p. 107. Amy Gutmann and Dennis Thompson's opening sentence in their "Why Deliberative Democracy Is Different," *Social Philosophy and Policy*, Vol. 17, 2000, p. 161, reads: "In modern pluralist societies political disagreement often reflects moral disagreement, as citizens with conflicting perspectives on fundamental values debate the laws that govern their public life." A dissonant voice among those who favor deliberative practices is

policy, euthanasia, and so forth) reflects a clash of values among different sectors of the citizenry. In deliberation, citizens try to clarify, refine, and correct *moral* views. Moral views are not affected by citizens' ignorance of complex factual issues because those views are normative. The idea is that moral principles tell citizens in a relatively straightforward way what policies they ought to support in the public forum. Because the most frequent and important political disagreements are moral in character, citizens may fruitfully deliberate even if they lack incentives to investigate complex matters of fact. On this view, positions that apparently evince empirical ignorance are just respectable moral positions.[2]

We reject this view. This chapter will show that relatively few political positions are genuine moral stances, that principles of political morality have by themselves no obvious implications for policy making, and that even the few political proposals that are genuinely moral are affected by rational ignorance – this time, of a moral kind. Discourse failure in politics affects empirical and moral beliefs. Many political positions brought to the deliberative forum are affected by the various forms of discourse failure already discussed. The moral turn imports plausible traits of morality into areas of politics where they lose their appeal, and when they remain appealing, their use in public deliberation suffers from cognitive flaws of its own. More generally, we will argue that many important political controversies involve complex empirical matters, independently of whether they also involve matters of principle. In one natural sense, then, we will challenge all overmoralized views of politics. And even where controversies are primarily moral in character, citizens will err. As a result, the moral turn cannot save deliberativism from the charge of utopianism.

We extensively illustrated our argument in the previous chapter with the case of people who support minimum wage laws in the name of helping the poor, despite the fact that reliable economic theory tells those people that in many scenarios the minimum wage hurts the poor.[3] We characterized in section 5.2 such positions as self-defeating.

Pettit, who warns against the electoral incentives underlying moralistic politics. See Pettit, "Depoliticizing Democracy," op. cit.

[2] Political agents who seem insensitive to the bad consequences of their proposals need not be ignorant: As we have repeatedly observed (e.g., section 2.1), they may (also) be posturers. We say that the discourse failure hypothesis is the best explanation of this kind of behavior, which includes those who are ignorant and those who posture.

[3] Actually, such laws tend to hurt the worst-off – typically the unemployed, who would otherwise earn the lowest salaries. For stylistic reasons, we throughout talk of "the poor," meaning "the worst-off." We briefly discuss the economics of the minimum wage in section 6.9.

Self-defeatingness is a particularly blatant case of inconsistency with goals embraced by the speaker. Indeed, even if it were *controversial* that minimum wage laws hurt the poor, there would be a self-defeating flavor in these utterances, for in this case these persons would have to *qualify* their support for minimum wage laws.

A speaker may make a proposal that is inconsistent with valuable goals in a weaker sense. Such proposals may frustrate valuable goals (for himself or for his audience) other than those in the name of which the speaker advances them. Imagine someone who proposes protectionist measures for automakers in Detroit invoking the need to preserve jobs in that industry, and assume that such measures will effectively do that. To that extent, the proposal is not self-defeating in the narrow sense. However, given the theory of comparative advantages, the proposal predictably will harm other sectors of the economy.[4] We will use the term "counterproductive" to refer to positions suffering from either kind of inconsistency.

One might think that these are just instances of rational ignorance – that is, that these agents simply overlook relevant causal connections. Deliberativists, however, might reply that the citizen need not be sensitive to the bad consequences of a public policy. They may offer two alternative accounts. They might say, first, that many supporters of minimum wage laws are not primarily interested in helping the poor. Rather, they intend to *symbolize* or *express* their concern for the poor. "Symbolic" or "expressive" behavior here means behavior intended by the agent to express her support for a principle without falling under the principle.[5] The previous chapter showed that counterproductive political agents are better understood as either ignoring relevant causal connections or posturing, rather than as symbolic agents.

The deliberativist's second strategy, which we examine in this chapter, is to recast apparently counterproductive positions as moral. On this

---

[4] See section 2.1.

[5] We use the minimum wage laws example again in this chapter because it helps the deliberativist's reply. As we will see in section 6.4, he can rely on intuitions about exploitation to characterize the support for the minimum wage as a moral position. We could profitably use many other examples of political stances that are arguably counterproductive (especially if they contain no qualifications): protectionism in the name of reducing general unemployment, rent control in the name of reducing homelessness, deregulation of an industry pervaded by externalities in the name of efficiency, and so on. We think those examples would make the deliberativist's reply even harder because they do not involve a clear analogue to exploitation. Admittedly, our use of the minimum wage example will not convince those readers who find the standard economics of the minimum wage utterly implausible. See section 6.9.

view, taking a stance on public policy primarily depends on moral considerations. Thus, if citizens, after deliberating, come to believe that the duty to help the poor overrides general welfare (a moral matter), such agreement would settle, for example, the debate between supporters of minimum wage laws and free marketeers in favor of the former.[6] People's views on political morality, the deliberativist may argue, are unaffected by their ignorance. Challenging public positions because they are self-defeating or otherwise factually mistaken overlooks, he might say, that such positions often are moral in nature.

We have seen that rational ignorance and posturing are mutually reinforcing and give rise to many counterproductive positions, such as widespread support for the minimum wage. Accordingly, the public will generally support proposals that are consequence-insensitive. Throughout this chapter, we shall refer for convenience to this view as the *discourse failure (DF) hypothesis*. The alternative explanation of consequence-insensitive political discourse – the moral turn – is particularly noticeable in theories of deliberative democracy,[7] but it is by no means confined to them. Non-utilitarian political philosophers sometimes seem to derive concrete political proposals from general moral theses *alone*. For example, Will Kymlicka describes liberal egalitarianism (as defended by John Rawls and Ronald Dworkin) as the doctrine seeking distributions that are sensitive to people's choices but not to factors outside their control.[8] But when he discusses the policy recommendations that follow from liberal egalitarianism, he presents as the only alternatives worth exploring the welfare state and "property-owning democracy" (i.e., a scheme that "seeks greater equality in the redistribution of property and skill endowments"[9]). More specifically, Kymlicka suggests that liberal egalitarians should be committed to "quite radical policies, such as affirmative

---

[6] In their effort to show how moral principles have policy implications, Gutmann and Thompson extensively discuss whether the state ought to fund liver transplants for terminally ill indigents. They give an affirmative answer based on a *moral* reflection about basic opportunity. See *Democracy and Disagreement*, op. cit., pp. 201–29, esp. 220.

[7] It is certainly a major theme in Gutmann and Thompson's *Democracy and Disagreement*, op. cit. A related theme in the literature on deliberative democracy is the connection between deliberation and moral truth or validity. See note 15, Chapter 2.

[8] Will Kymlicka, *Contemporary Political Philosophy: An Introduction*, second ed. (Oxford: Oxford University Press, 2001), Ch. 3.

[9] R. Krouse and M. McPherson, "Capitalism, 'Property-Owning Democracy,' and the Welfare State," in Amy Gutmann, ed., *Democracy and the Welfare State* (Princeton, N.J.: Princeton University Press, 1988), p. 84, cit. by Kymlicka, *Contemporary Political Philosophy: An Introduction*, op. cit., p. 89.

action, basic income, employee self-ownership, 'stakeholding,' payment to homemakers, compensatory education investment, and so on."[10] The assumption here is that if you value distributions that are sensitive to people's choices but not to factors outside their control, you'd better limit the market in important ways. Kymlicka never contemplates the possibility that free markets may realize liberal egalitarian values better than the alternatives he discusses.[11] And Kymlicka is not alone here. Another example is Simon Blackburn's discussion of John Rawls's theory of justice in *Ruling Passions*. Blackburn writes that Rawlsian ideal contractors would "choose a legal and economic system closely resembling those of modern western welfare-state democracies, with a substantial budget of freedoms under the law, and a substantial welfare floor." Interestingly, Blackburn criticizes Rawls for begging the question against, among others, the "free-marketeer." Blackburn apparently excludes, then, the possibility of a Rawlsian defense of free markets – that is, a defense of free markets on the grounds that they best help the poor, and that helping the poor is paramount in a just society.[12]

---

[10] Will Kymlicka, *Contemporary Political Philosophy: An Introduction*, p. 89.

[11] To be sure, Kymlicka refers to the "New Right" as the view that wishes to cut back on the welfare state on the grounds that it rewards the lazy and incompetent, and suggests that liberal egalitarians should respond more adequately to this line of argument than they have done so far. But he does not address defenses of free markets on the grounds that they may help the otherwise undeserving poor. Id., pp. 92–6. See next note.

[12] See Simon Blackburn, *Ruling Passions: A Theory of Practical Reasoning* (Oxford: Clarendon Press, 1998), pp. 273–4. Rawls himself has a more complex approach to this issue. On pages 239–42 of *A Theory of Justice* (Cambridge, Mass.: Harvard University Press, rev. edition, 1999), he observes that his difference principle, according to which social and economic inequalities should work for the greatest benefit to the least advantaged, is agnostic about economic systems, thus allowing for the possibility that free markets may sometimes be required by justice. But in the very next section he repeatedly refers to transfer payments and other redistributive devices as the institutional means to implement the difference principle (pp. 242–51). It is unclear whether Rawls intends these remarks to be just examples of the requisite policies, but in any event they are remarks that have contributed to the dissemination of the reading indicated in the text. To be sure, Rawls rejects the "system of natural liberty" (roughly, a free-market economy constrained by equal liberty and formal equality of opportunity) on the grounds that it "permits distributive shares to be improperly influenced by" natural talents and abilities – that is, factors that are "arbitrary from a moral point of view" (pp. 62–3). Interpreters disagree, however, about the exact relationships between this argument against the free market and Rawls's appeal to the difference principle as a criterion of justice for society's basic institutions. This criterion prevents us from rejecting the system of natural liberty without an investigation into its distributive consequences. For opposing views on the relationships between these two themes in *A Theory of Justice*, see Kymlicka, op. cit., pp. 67–75, and Samuel Scheffler, "What Is Egalitarianism?" *Philosophy and Public Affairs*, Vol. 31, no. 1, Winter 2003, pp. 5–39.

Kymlicka and Blackburn must be assuming that the controversy between the supporter of state intervention and the supporter of free markets is essentially normative or evaluative in a sense that immunizes both positions against causal challenge. For example, we can see the parties to this controversy as imbued with different degrees of concern for the poor. If Kymlicka and Blackburn did not assume something like this, their policy proposals would not merely be obvious non sequiturs: Their proposals might well frustrate the achievement of the stated goals.[13] Here the moral turn is coupled with the idea that, at least sometimes, policy proposals are moral stances that *directly* derive from abstract values or principles of political morality. The deliberativist may offer this idea as a rival to the DF hypothesis to vindicate many consequence-insensitive political proposals that we find in ordinary political discourse. Thus, if citizens came to believe that the duty to help the poor overrides general welfare (a moral matter), they would be committed to, say, supporting minimum wage laws (rather than, say, free labor markets). The suggested upshot is that challenging public positions because they are counterproductive or otherwise empirically mistaken overlooks the fact that such positions are often moral in nature.[14]

Before proceeding, we need to dispel two possible worries. First, as far as we know, the argument we criticize (that political positions which seem counterproductive are really plausible moral positions) has not been specifically advanced by deliberativists. They have identified moral disagreement as the centerpiece of deliberation, but they have not used

[13] Some influential economists claim that free markets best serve the poor. See, for example, Milton and Rose Friedman, *Free to Choose* (New York: Harcourt, second edition, 1990). For a well-documented argument that the welfare state in the United States has in fact spawned poverty, and that the previous welfare provision through organized private charity better attended to the needs of the poor, see David Schmidtz, "Taking Responsibility," in David Schmidtz and Robert E. Goodin, *Social Welfare and Individual Responsibility* (Cambridge: Cambridge University Press, 1998). For a discussion that emphasizes the shortsightedness and nationalism of usual defenses of the welfare state that invoke the plight of the poor, see Tyler Cowen, "Does the Welfare State Help the Poor?" op. cit., pp. 36–54. Our point is not that the Friedmans, Schmidtz, or Cowen is correct. Rather, as we will argue, it is that we should not jump from abstract principles of justice to policy conclusions without addressing opposing reasonable views about the empirical matters involved.

[14] We saw in the previous chapter that some writers try to vindicate counterproductive political proposals through a symbolic account. We treat the moral turn separately from the symbolic account, without pausing to discuss to what extent moral behavior may also be symbolic. Robert Nozick claims that behavior that conforms to a principle "stands for" continuous compliance with that principle and is, to that extent, symbolic. See his *The Nature of Rationality*, op. cit., pp. 14–21.

this claim to resist the charge of utopianism. This being so, we might be accused of fighting a straw man. Not so. On the one hand, deliberativists have not responded to the charge of utopianism. This chapter discusses a reply that they could offer should they recognize the relevance of citizens' ignorance in the first place. That is, a natural move for them is to claim that apparently counterproductive views are really moral stances that are immune to causal objection. So, the fact that deliberativists do not specifically make those replies is to their detriment, not to ours. On the other hand, the argument in this chapter reaches even genuine moral arguments in politics, as they, too, fall prey to discourse failure. So we challenge both the attempts to overmoralize political deliberation (i.e., to treat causal disputes as if they were moral disputes) and the belief that political disputes that are moral in character are relatively simple and thus immune to discourse failure.

The second worry is this: Someone may object that our argument presupposes narrow self-interest on the part of citizens. It seems more realistic to assume that people act politically for all kinds of reasons, including moral reasons. This objection, however, does not affect our thesis in this chapter. The charge of utopianism is not premised on citizens' being self-interested or selfish – or, for that matter, on any specific view about what citizens value. Suppose an altruistic person wants to help the poor and asks us how best to achieve that goal. Our first reaction may be to tell her to do concrete things to help the poor, such as giving away money to them. But suppose she replies that that is not what she had in mind: She would like to become properly informed in order to deliberate with other citizens about the best ways in which society can help the poor. She adds that, in her view, civic virtue requires that she act this way (as opposed, or in addition, to helping the poor directly).

This attitude is somewhat puzzling,[15] but let us assume, for the sake of argument, that this person genuinely believes that civic duty requires her to deliberate with others and not just to act individually. Indeed, many

---

[15] It seems more plausible for this person to discharge her duty of beneficence by doing concrete things, such as acts of charity, rather than taking the time and effort to become informed in order to engage in political deliberation. An ungenerous interpretation of her position is that she wants *others* to incur the cost of helping the poor. A generous interpretation, which we adopt for purposes of argument, is that she genuinely believes that as a citizen of a democracy she has the civic duty to deliberate in order both to do her share in discharging a *collective* duty to help the poor and to *express* in deliberation her *public* adherence to the relevant moral principle – something that would be lost in individual charitable behavior.

deliberativists think that citizens committed to civic virtue, as something different from other forms of altruism, have reasons for deliberating in an informed manner.[16] It is true that citizens sometimes embrace civic virtue. However, deliberativists overlook the fact that virtue sometimes demands costly behavior, and that most persons are sensitive to such costs. For example, whether someone has a duty to rescue a drowning person depends in part on whether the rescuer's life or health is at risk. High personal cost may override the duty to rescue. Of course, becoming informed in politics does not entail such dramatic costs. Yet, deliberating in an informed way is arguably so costly that the average citizen will simply not do it.[17] Civic virtue thus understood has a high price. Most of us have better or more urgent things to do, including discharging other moral duties, than to invest our time and energies to become properly informed in politics – something that presupposes learning many complex theories and facts. It is even dubious that using our time and energies in this way is virtuous, given the valuable activities we would be forced to forgo. Because the exercise of virtue is costly, rational ignorance is a barrier to achieving political truth through deliberation. This is so independently of how many people are morally motivated or of the mix of moral and nonmoral motives in those who come to deliberate.[18]

In this chapter, we argue that the DF hypothesis is superior to the moral turn as an account of ordinary political discourse that seems inattentive to relevant facts. We will proceed in the following sequence. In section 6.2, we lay out a test (The Display Test) to determine whether a political proposal is genuinely moral or rather is attributable to rational ignorance or posturing; we use this test to show what is wrong with two versions of the moral turn, one resting on the idea of moral balancing and the

---

[16] See, for example, Stephen Macedo, *Liberal Virtues: Citizenship, Virtue, and Community in Liberal Constitutionalism* (Oxford: Clarendon Press, 1990), esp. 272–7. Jon Elster identifies John Stuart Mill as the forerunner of this view. See Jon Elster, "The Market and the Forum: Three Varieties of Political Theory," in Bohman and Rehg, eds., *Deliberative Democracy*, op. cit., pp. 23–4.

[17] As we have seen (section 2.2 and Chapter 4), rational ignorance is deep and pervasive. The problem cannot be fixed easily – for example, by recommending that people spend twenty minutes a day reading newspapers. As our example of minimum wage legislation indicates, citizens' political positions crucially depend on theoretical frameworks the understanding of which requires study that goes well beyond reading newspapers. See also section 4.4 for a critique of proposed shortcuts to political knowledge.

[18] Thus, the effort by Christiano to reject the self-interest postulate as a prelude to his defense of deliberative politics, even if successful, would not undermine the DF hypothesis. See *The Rule of the Many*, op. cit., chapter 4.

other on the idea of deontological constraints. In section 6.3, we argue that an appeal to deontological constraints does account for *both* positive *and* negative results of The Display Test. Section 6.4 criticizes a version of the moral turn based on the notion of autonomous responsibility in evildoing. In section 6.5, we present some examples that suggest how easy it is to underestimate the role of causal complexity in political argument, and, as a result, to make an unwarranted leap from principles or values to policies. Section 6.6 shows that even the most plausible candidates for the category of purely moral political proposals are best explained by the DF hypothesis, if only because enforcing morality gives rise to complex causal issues. The last section summarizes our argument and presents a caveat on the scope of the DF hypothesis.

6.2. Balancing, Deontology, and the Display Test

The following example may be thought to support the moral turn. Suppose someone believes he ought to decrease the number of intentional killings in society. He also believes that the death penalty, through deterrence, would decrease intentional killings overall. However, he opposes capital punishment. He may believe that his behavior, and, by extension, the behavior of a just government, ought not to be informed by certain intentions, such as the intention to kill a human being. That the government not act on such an intention is for him an overriding imperative – no amount of good consequences (not even reduction in the total number of intentional killings) may override that constraint. There is a sense of self-defeatingness that applies to this agent, because (a) he believes he has a duty to decrease the number of intentional killings in the world, and (b) he believes his proposal does not decrease the number of intentional killings in the world. Yet, this position is quite reasonable. Many people would say that this agent legitimately ignores facts he may regard as decisive in other contexts, because such facts lack enough purchase here. Why not think that this position illustrates the structure of many ostensibly counterproductive political positions? If so, a genuine moral concern, rather than rational ignorance or posturing, motivates such positions. The intended upshot is that the discursive behavior of this abolitionist lends support to the moral turn.

This argument sounds plausible because an agent who endorses more than one principle may find himself under conflicting recommendations. If he chooses to follow one of those recommendations, he takes the principle that grounds it as overriding the competing principle. This agent has struck a balance between principles. Thus, the abolitionist believes that preventing the state from intentionally killing human beings is more important than decreasing the number of intentional killings overall. He might say that he wants to decrease the number of intentional killings but not at the cost of endorsing immoral behavior by the state. This position does not look unduly counterproductive. Similarly, people who support the rights of the criminal defendant typically do not invoke the need to reduce crime, even if they believe that crime ought to be reduced and know that stringent procedural rights will increase crime. The discursive behavior of these agents cannot, then, be part of the evidence for the DF hypothesis. Rather, it supports the moral turn: The abolitionist's overriding moral commitments authorize him to ignore consequences he himself deplores.

But the capital punishment example is not a good model for most counterproductive political positions. A sincere person should acknowledge, if need be, the bad consequences of the positions she endorses. Well-informed and sincere political speakers should publicly disclose those bad consequences. If the capital punishment model is correct, they should not be embarrassed for doing so.

Let us say that a speaker who is willing to disclose the bad consequences of a proposal meets The Display Test. More precisely: Someone passes The Display Test if and only if he publicly acknowledges the downsides of his political proposal or, if he did not publicly acknowledge them, he would insist on the proposal if exposed to those downsides. For present purposes, we stipulate that a downside of a political proposal is any feature of it that, if disclosed, would likely reduce the audience's support for it. Such downsides are not only those outcomes that are *predictable* on the grounds of the most reliable theories available. They include, in addition, the *uncertainties* about the proposal's bad effects (given the most reliable theories available). Those who pass The Display Test, then, do not publicly conceal or overlook the proposal's downsides; typically, they feel no embarrassment by the recognition that it may frustrate some worthy goals. On the other hand, those who fail The Display Test are either ignorant or dishonest. They may be simply people who would withdraw their proposals if exposed to their downsides, in which case they are ignorant. Alternatively, they may fail to recognize the problems with their proposal because they seek rhetorical advantages, as something different from winning the audience's informed approval. In the latter case, they are probably posturers who take advantage of the audience's rational ignorance. The Display Test is then clearly relevant to our investigation. We are trying to assess, remember, the merits of the DF hypothesis vis-à-vis the moral turn as accounts of apparently counterproductive political utterances. The Display Test helps us identify political stances that are genuinely animated by moral commitments, because the agent is willing to disclose those bad consequences that his moral commitments authorize him to accept (reluctantly, perhaps) as the price of doing the right thing.

We submit that the abolitionist meets The Display Test, while the protectionist and the supporter of minimum wage laws fail it. Imagine the abolitionist making the following statement: "I am committed to decreasing the number of intentional killings in society. I also believe that the state never ought to intentionally kill a human being. Under the circumstances, I can't achieve both goals. Because I believe that the first principle ought to cede when it conflicts with the second, I support the abolition of capital punishment. I regret to do this, because I know that I am supporting a measure that will increase the number of intentional killings in society." Although some people may reject this position, it is certainly reasonable, as we have indicated. The agent is prepared to pay the price of increased crime in society for the sake of avoiding immoral behavior by the state, and to openly recognize that. The abolitionist, then, meets The Display Test.

This is not true of the supporter of minimum wage laws. Consider how she would defend her position in a manner analogous to the way the abolitionist did. She would say: "I am committed to helping the poor. I am also committed to using legal coercion to prevent employers from underpaying workers. Under the circumstances, I can't achieve both goals. Because I believe that the first principle ought to cede when it conflicts with the second, I support minimum wage laws. I regret to do this, because I know that I am supporting measures that will hurt the poor." Most of us would find this position bizarre. We would expect that a supporter of minimum wage laws would want to benefit, not hurt, the poor. We believe, that is, that supporting the minimum wage has an ineradicable causal component. This is why the typical[19] supporter of minimum wage laws fails The Display Test. Failing The Display Test in turn shows why the position cannot, without distortion, plausibly be portrayed as purely or mainly moral: Someone advancing a moral view that he actually holds is

---

[19] Bear in mind that we are testing the relative merits of the discourse failure hypothesis and the moral turn as analyses of public, non-academic, political discourse. We henceforth assume this qualification.

prepared to pay the cost of being moral, as it were. A *sincere* moral stance is transparent.

Five points about The Display Test: First, the capital punishment and minimum wage examples may mislead us into thinking that satisfying The Display Test is an easy task. It is precisely because the facts to be displayed are transparent only to those who are familiar with opaque social theories that people can so easily overlook or conceal them. Consider David Schmidtz's critique of Peter Unger's defense of a world in which "whenever well-off folks learn of people in great need, they promptly move to meet the need, almost no matter what the financial cost. So, at this later date, the basic needs of almost all the world's people will be met almost all the time."[20] Schmidtz writes (we quote *in extenso* because we find no way to improve on the grace and concision of Schmidtz's prose):

> Imagine what our community would be like if a lot of us voluntarily did as Unger asks. There were about five thousand people in the nearest town when I was growing up on a farm in Saskatchewan. Suppose farmers gave up that part of our crop we would have cashed in to buy movie tickets. The Towne Theater goes out of business. No big deal, perhaps. The half dozen employees seek work elsewhere, although suffice it to say that in a town of five thousand, opportunities are limited. Maybe they find work at the Princess or Lucky Cafés. Fine, but we are not done. We also stop cashing in grain for hamburgers at the café, instead sending that part of our crop abroad. The cafés close, over a dozen people are out of work, and we exceed our town's ability to find work for them.
>
> Unger says we would not have nice cars and nice homes. . . . We send away that part of our crop that would have bought new cars. Fine. The car dealers and their employees are out of work. They no longer send money to foreign countries; nor do they support local merchants, critical services aside. The furniture shop and the clothing store shut down. They stop repaying business loans. Their employees stop making mortgage payments. Banks begin to foreclose on houses. There is no one to buy the houses, though, so the banks close too, and I don't know what happens to their employees. Perhaps they become refugees.[21]

Schmidtz's story is about people wholeheartedly trying to do their duty. Political proposals are about creating *legal* duties – duties enforced by the state. Legal enforcement of the moral duties defended by Unger would arguably bring about even *worse* results, because legal enforcement has costs of its own, in addition to whatever moral costs are involved in the

---

[20] Peter Unger, *Living High and Letting Die: Our Illusion of Innocence* (New York: Oxford University Press, 1996), p. 20.

[21] David Schmidtz, "Islands in a Sea of Obligation: Limits of the Duty to Rescue," *Law and Philosophy*, Vol. 19, no. 6, 2000, pp. 701–2.

use of coercion (even to enforce morality).[22] Those who propose such legal measures would meet The Display Test if, at the very least, they took the trouble to *address* the (types of) facts mentioned by Schmidtz – to say, that is, where he might have gone wrong. Assuming that the story told by Schmidtz is relevant to assess Unger's proposal (as it seems obvious to us that it is), those who advance this proposal while ignoring that type of story fail The Display Test. Or, more precisely: Those who advance a political version of Unger's proposal while remaining silent about the kinds of facts mentioned in Schmidtz's story, or at least showing no willingness to indicate what is wrong with stories such as Schmidtz's, fail The Display Test.

Second, a comparative assessment of the DF hypothesis and the moral turn should look at *actual* political deliberation.[23] This is so because we are trying to ascertain which of the two hypotheses better accommodates widespread cases of apparently counterproductive political discourse. Thus, in the minimum wage debate, one question relevant to the availability of the moral turn would be this: Are union leaders and politicians who support minimum wage laws willing to publicly acknowledge that those laws hurt the poor, or at least that it is unclear whether they do so? It would be no counter-example to our critique of the moral turn the case of a philosopher or a social scientist who, in a scholarly seminar, puts forth a plausible case for minimum wage laws that includes a recognition that they may have bad consequences.[24] In realistic deliberative politics, nobody is willing to make such concessions. Willingness to display those consequences of a proposal that others may take as reasons to reject it is surely relevant to determining whether that proposal is attributable to ignorance, posturing, or moral concerns.

Third, the fact that, in a natural sense, The Display Test heeds to the consequences of a political proposal does not commit us to utilitarianism. Someone may flunk The Display Test by failing to acknowledge consequences of his position that are inconsistent with the non-utilitarian political theory (Dworkinian, Nozickian, Rawlsian, among others) that he endorses. Thus, if I support a social program in the name of Rawls's difference principle, I should be sensitive to the fact (if it is a fact) that the program would worsen the situation of the worst-off groups. The point

---

[22] We shall briefly discuss the moral relevance of legal enforcement in section 6.7.

[23] Deliberativists insist that actual political deliberation adds to the legitimacy of laws and policies. See, for example, Gutmann and Thompson, *Democracy and Disagreement*, op. cit., p. 229; "Why Deliberative Democracy Is Different," op. cit., p. 168; and Habermas, *Between Facts and Norms*, pp. 29–30.

[24] See our caveat in note 55, this chapter.

of The Display Test is to bring to the surface those consequences of a political proposal that the audience may take as morally relevant; it is not to suggest that the only relevant such consequences are those sanctioned by utilitarianism.

Fourth, the supporter of the minimum wage cannot escape the oddity in her position by hiding its consequences. No plausible moral-political theory allows people to hide the bad consequences of a political proposal. The Display Test is precisely sensitive to the demands of transparency. Indeed, if there is a place where transparency matters, it must be in any deliberation capable of conferring legitimacy to political decision making.[25] Deliberative transparency requires a citizen to disclose all those consequences of his proposals that others may find relevant to assessing those proposals. For example, someone who declares that he does not wish to condone injustice (say, the underpayment of workers) should concede that the measure he proposes will hurt the poor. Unfortunately, counterproductive political agents rarely make such admissions,[26] and many of them seem reluctant to do so even if asked to take a stance toward the consequences of their proposals.[27]

Fifth and finally, an agent may fail The Display Test even if, according to reliable social science, it is *unclear* whether his proposal will have bad consequences.[28] This will be typically the case when public

---

[25] This is especially so on accounts of deliberation that see it as constitutive of moral truth. See Habermas, "Discourse Ethics: Notes on a Program of Philosophical Justification," in *Moral Consciousness and Communicative Action*, trans. Christian Lenhardt and Shierry Weber Nicholsen (Cambridge, Mass.: MIT Press, 1990), pp. 43–115; and Nino, *The Constitution of Deliberative Democracy*, esp. pp. 117–28. Similarly, Christiano says that rational deliberation involves participants "guided by a concern for truth and reasoned consensus" and thinking of others "as potential contributors to that pursuit." *The Rule of the Many*, p. 117.

[26] We find it hard to imagine genuine exceptions to the tendency to silence relevant information (problems, doubts, etc.) in political debate. Highly professional discussions in academic contexts may well be one of them. At any rate, we do not confine our skepticism to politicians and other public figures. There is a lot of discourse failure in, for example, cocktail parties and the academic settings we discussed in section 2.7.

[27] Of course, authenticity is no carte blanche to side with any law or policy whatsoever.

[28] Some writers have argued that, because societies are too complex, social science cannot yield accurate predictions. See, for example, Gerald Gaus, "Why All Welfare States (Including Laissez-Faire Ones) Are Unreasonable," *Social Philosophy and Policy*, Vol. 15 (June 1998), pp. 1–33, and "Social Complexity and Moral Radicalism," unpublished. The connection between complexity and predictive unreliability was first theorized by Friedrich A. Hayek in "The Theory of Complex Phenomena," in Hayek, *Studies in Philosophy, Politics, and Economics* (Chicago: University of Chicago Press, 1967), pp. 22–42, reprinted, with added references, from Mario Bunge, ed., *The Critical Approach to Science and Philosophy: Essays in Honor of K. R. Popper* (New York: Free Press, 1964). Recall that

acknowledgment of the uncertainty would have rhetorical disadvantages. In order to meet The Display Test, those who propose minimum wage laws would have to be willing to acknowledge that *many* specialists argue that the laws will increase unemployment – academic consensus on this proposition was somewhat undermined only recently.[29] Because the typical supporter of minimum wage laws in actual deliberation does not say that it is at least uncertain whether the laws help the poor, he fails The Display Test. Of course, typical public support for minimum wage laws during the many decades when the pessimistic prediction went undisputed by economists flunked The Display Test and was, therefore, symptomatic of discourse failure.

At this juncture someone may object to our insistence that, to avoid committing discourse failure, a speaker should acknowledge evidence against a proposition he utters in public. This requirement may be too demanding, because someone may have honestly formed a belief on the basis of available evidence yet be prepared to revise it in the light of *strong* evidence to the contrary. For example, a professional philosopher may have gathered enough evidence to subscribe to evolutionary biology but is not perfectly acquainted with all the problems attendant to the theory in the specialized literature. Nevertheless, she takes for granted evolutionary biology in her arguments on the philosophy of religion or ethics. To insist that this person express her opinion in a manner and with a conviction commensurate with the evidence, the objector concludes, is to carry The Display Test too far.

We have two replies. First, we do not think that this person behaves like most people who keep silent about evidence against a political view they state in public. On the contrary, the distribution in the general population between opinions on each side of an issue is not commensurate with how strongly reliable social science supports any of them. As we saw, the public

our formulation of The Display Test takes the uncertainty about the bad effects of a proposal as a downside of it (section 6.2). Predictive skepticism about social science would accordingly be evidence for the discourse failure hypothesis, and against the moral turn. We should note, however, that the prevailing view holds that, while there is of course considerable predictive uncertainty in many areas of the social sciences, we can *sometimes* tell what the *likely* effects of *some* policies will be on *suitably abstract* variables. For a classical statement of the view that radical skepticism about prediction in social science rests on confusions about the logical structure of prediction, see Ernest Nagel, *The Structure of Science: Problems in the Logic of Scientific Explanation* (New York: Harcourt, 1961), esp. pp. 459–73 and 503–20.

[29] See section 6.9.

systematically adopts the view that is supported by vivid theories. The DF hypothesis better explains the discursive political behavior we observe. Second, the philosopher in the evolutionary theory example presumably would concede that the theory has problems, once she is shown those problems, so she would pass The Display Test. Someone passes the test, then, when she *would* be prepared to admit, or at least to address, the weaknesses of her view were she to become so informed.

Is our discussion of The Display Test consistent with our analysis of discourse failure? Consider: How would a rationally ignorant public even understand that a policy has the sort of bad consequences that lead speakers to conceal them? It may be thought that the very opacity of consequences predicted by social science will make them unrecognizable by the public (should the speaker display them). In the minimum wage case, the public will have a hard time connecting the enactment of the laws with an increase in unemployment. This seems to cast doubt on our contention that disclosing the fact that minimum wage laws will increase unemployment is likely to erode support for the proposal.

We answer by drawing a distinction between *what* a politician says and *his saying it.* Even if the objector is right and the public is not likely to understand the mechanisms through which a proposal brings about bad consequences, it will nonetheless register the fact that a politician is making concessions against interest and so will predictably hold the admission against the politician. This is because the public has massive evidence that politicians primarily seek power. Citizens have experienced countless occasions on which politicians have lied or breached promises. The view that politicians are primarily power seekers is a default belief that citizens hold with little effort. It is therefore all too natural to conclude that politicians will not make public concessions against interest unless they are *really* true – unless, for example, the politician believes that "the game's up." Given all this, any disclosure of bad consequences, however opaque, is likely to hurt a politician.

When is it morally justifiable to ignore unpalatable consequences? On an influential view, a moral agent is committed to constraints on the pursuit of aggregate goals. Philosophers often use the language of rights to convey such constraints, and the terms *deontological ethics* or *Kantianism* describe such positions. Rights-based moralities, unlike utilitarianism, hold that individuals ought to respect rights even when doing so is suboptimal from the point of view of welfare. Now, welfare is not the only conceivable aggregate goal. An individual may have the goal of minimizing *rights violations,* no matter who commits them. Sometimes the achievement of this goal requires that an agent violate rights. For example, terrorists may credibly threaten someone with killing two innocents unless he kills one innocent. If this agent must not kill even in cases of this sort, he is under a *deontological constraint* on killing innocents. It might be thought that the idea of deontological constraints offers a better defense of the moral turn than that offered by the balancing model at work in the capital punishment example. The overriding moral goal of the deontological agent is to refrain from bringing about states of affairs in which *he* is killing innocents (even when bringing about such states of affairs minimizes the number of killings of innocents, whoever perpetrates them). In the terminology used by some philosophers, the agent in the terrorists example is governed by an *agent-relative* reason not to kill innocents.[30] This reason contrasts with the *agent-neutral* reason to minimize the number of killings of innocents.[31] It may seem that this conceptual framework allows us to say that our agent-relative duty not to hurt specific poor people in specific ways (e.g., underpaying workers) prevails over everyone's (ourselves' included) duty to refrain from hurting the poor. It might be thought that these positions lie beyond the reach of the DF hypothesis, because, typically, deontological agents need not know complex facts and theories in order to discharge their duties. The victim of the terrorists' threat must know only how to avoid killing a particular agent – something that in most situations is very easy for him to know. He is prepared to tolerate the bad consequences of his choice (the terrorists'

---

[30] We are *characterizing* here deontological constraints, without taking sides on whether or how they can be *justified.* The fact that deontological constraints are agent-relative need not imply that the justification of such constraints is agent-centered instead of victim-centered. On the justification issue, see the classic treatment by Bernard Williams, "A Critique of Utilitarianism," in J. J. C. Smart and Bernard Williams, *Utilitarianism: For & Against* (Cambridge: Cambridge University Press, 1973), esp. pp. 94–5. See also F. M. Kamm, *Morality, Mortality,* Vol. II (New York: Oxford University Press, 1996), pp. 207–353; Thomas Nagel, *The View from Nowhere* (Oxford: Oxford University Press, 1986), ch. 9; Robert Nozick, *Anarchy, State, and Utopia,* op. cit., pp. 30–3; Samuel Scheffler, *The Rejection of Consequentialism,* rev. ed. (Oxford: Clarendon Press, 1994); Horacio Spector, *Autonomy and Rights* (Oxford: Oxford University Press, 1992), ch. 5; and Eric Mack, "Deontic Restrictions Are Not Agent-Relative Restrictions," *Social Philosophy and Policy,* 15 (1998), pp. 61–83.

[31] Some philosophers use the term *consequentialism* to refer to agent-neutral moralities. See, for example, Derek Parfit, *Reasons and Persons* (Oxford: Clarendon Press, 1985), pp. 26–7. We prefer not to use this term because it is sometimes meant to refer to utilitarianism, especially in contexts where utilitarianism is contrasted with rights-based theories. In any event, no substantive point turns on this terminological decision.

murder of the innocents).[32] Deliberativists should welcome this agent's manifest rationality. They may rely on this conception of moral agency to resist the charge of utopianism. If counterproductive deliberative proposals evince this type of rationality (i.e., the usual rationality involved in deontological constraints), then rational political deliberation may be a feasible goal, notwithstanding the deliberators' apparent neglect of relevant causal consequences.

Moreover, if the deontological duty is negative (that is, a duty to refrain from doing something), the agent is trivially knowledgeable of the relevant facts. At least in ordinary settings, he knows, say, how to avoid killing a human being. By contrast, if his deontological duty is positive (typically, a duty to help others), he ordinarily needs to have more complex causal knowledge. Even so, he will be excused from understanding even more complex or remote consequences of his behavior. For example, I might recommend that the state help, here and now, poor schoolchildren by sending books to a public school. Arguably, this proposal will not be affected by rational ignorance, because the information that state officials need to supply the books is manageable. But the distinctive feature of this duty is that the donor may safely overlook how these acts of charity affect the poor overall (including how others will behave toward the poor). Typically, then, these agents will be neither irrational nor particularly ignorant. Deliberativists may draw on this fact to complete their defense of the moral turn. They may say, that is, that these positions are not counterproductive because deontological agents need not know complex facts and theories in order to discharge their duties.

However, the idea of deontological constraints is of no avail to the deliberativist who wants to downplay citizens' ignorance and resist the charge of utopianism based on discourse failure. Contexts in which deontological constraints are intuitively appealing are quite different from contexts in which counterproductive political behavior occurs. The victim of the terrorists' threat may justify his refusal to kill as follows: "I perfectly know that I could prevent two killings of innocents by killing this innocent. Faced with this tragic choice, I decide to follow the maxim

---

[32] This formulation is not fully satisfactory, however. Saying that I do not kill somebody if I do not yield to a credible threat of killing others depends on the claim that the intervention of a third party displaces my responsibility for an evil outcome. In other words, someone may claim that I do kill those innocents when I refuse to yield to the threat. Our example in the text assumes the typical case in which the person who refuses to yield to a terrorists' threat answers to agent-relative reasons not to kill innocents in ways that do not require the intentional intervention of others.

never to kill an innocent person." Many of us would say that the soundness of this justification is *not* weakened by the agent's acknowledgment of the bad consequences of his decision. It is therefore reasonable for us to expect this agent to meet The Display Test.

Contrast this with an analogous defense that a supporter of minimum wage laws may offer: "I perfectly know that I could propose measures that help the poor by recommending that employers be allowed to pay lower salaries. Faced with this tragic choice, I decide to follow the maxim never to take public positions that tolerate *exploitation* of workers." On a natural reading of this position,[33] the employer who underpays workers *wrongs* those very workers, in the sense that he hurts them in impermissible ways – he violates their rights, he exploits them. So construed, the objection is compatible with the belief that minimum wage laws hurt the poor in *less* objectionable ways. Avoiding exploitation is, on this view, more important than helping the poor.[34]

This agent believes that exploitation ought to be prevented even at the cost of creating unemployment or otherwise worsening the situation of the poor. His aim is to provide a moral defense of minimum wage laws that does not involve neglecting relevant facts. Indeed, he has eradicated the problematic causal component from that position. To the extent that citizens could make similar maneuvers to rescue other political positions that look counterproductive, the moral turn would gain credibility vis-à-vis the DF hypothesis. The deliberativist should welcome this conclusion.

The problem here is that few citizens in *actual* deliberative fora will accept a defense of the minimum wage formulated in this way. This position loses most of its appeal in any realistic deliberative setting once its proponents disclose its bad consequences, and for this reason in most cases it fails The Display Test. Most people regard as misguided at best someone who supports minimum wage laws while openly conceding that those laws may well hurt the poor. The public concession that minimum wage laws may well hurt the poor yet is needed to prevent exploitation is

---

33 Alternatively, the agent may condemn exploitation because it promotes poverty. If so, because he believes that the measures he supports will hurt the poor, his position is incoherent. Or he may believe that the laws will have no definite impact on the poor. Our point stands too in this variant. We henceforth omit it for stylistic reasons.

34 Remember that, in order to preempt explanations based on the DF hypothesis, the defender of the moral turn must claim that apparently counterproductive agents are *not* ignorant. In our example, the agent believes that minimum wage laws may well hurt the poor.

odd, and that is why no electoral platform of any ideological persuasion defends the minimum wage in *this* way.[35] By contrast, the DF model does no violence to these facts about political discourse.

We remain neutral on whether wages below some minimum are exploitative. Rather, our point is that very few citizens advance that position in deliberative politics in ways that meet The Display Test. Most citizens regard proposals for minimum wage laws as sensitive to the plight of the poor. The balancing and deontological models we have discussed are, then, overmoralized pictures of many self-defeating political positions. As such, they are of no avail to defend deliberative democracy from the charge of utopianism based on the rational ignorance effect and the other sources of discourse failure we have identified.

6.3. Direct Involvement in Evildoing

We saw in the previous section that the supporter of the minimum wage fails The Display Test while the abolitionist passes it. What explains this difference? Unless we offer a principled distinction between the two cases, those who take the moral turn may claim that the capital punishment case models most ostensibly counterproductive political positions. If this move succeeds, most of the time people could safely advance counterproductive political positions. The fact that political positions are primarily moral would accordingly allow deliberators to downplay unpalatable consequences of their proposals.

Let us compare the minimum wage example with the terrorists example. In the latter, the agent is concerned with his own involvement in evildoing – namely, intentionally killing an innocent. In contrast, in the minimum wage example the agent is not herself involved in evildoing – namely, underpaying workers. Her behavior is discursive. Because her personal involvement in evildoing is not at stake, she is not in this context under deontological constraints on hurting the poor. Therefore, we would expect her to care about an aggregate outcome – namely, the overall effect of her proposals on the poor, including reducing the number of

---

[35] Most people who defend the minimum wage in the popular press on moral grounds deny that it causes unemployment. See, for example, Peter Dreier and Kelly Candaele, "A Moral Minimum Wage," *The Nation*, December 6, 2004, available at www.thenation.com/doc.mhtml?i=20041220&s=dreier. The AFL-CIO's support of minimum wage makes no reference to unemployment, nor does it hint at the argument in the text (that the minimum wage, while it hurts many people, should nonetheless be enacted to prevent exploitation). See /www.aflcio.org/yourjobeconomy/minimumwage/talkingpoints.cfm.

instances of what she calls "exploitation." Her position is best understood as grounded on an agent-neutral requirement (i.e., that the poor not *be* hurt) rather than on deontological constraints (i.e., that *she* not hurt the poor in specific ways), because, unlike the victim of the terrorist threat, hurting others (here: the poor, by underpaying them) is not among her options. Deontological constraints seem at home in the terrorists context, but quite unnatural here.

In contrast, the deontological model can accommodate the abolitionist case. The abolitionist who believes that intentionally killing human beings is wrong even for the sake of preventing further intentional killings will apply this judgment to the state. In his view, the state may never intentionally kill a human being, even for the sake of deterring murder, in much the same way as the person threatened by terrorists is governed by a deontological constraint on killing innocents. Both positions are coherent and plausible. By contrast, if the overriding concern of the critic of capital punishment were the minimization of intentional killings, *whoever* commits them, his position would sharply differ from that of the agent threatened by terrorists. For in this case his position would be this: "I oppose capital punishment in the name of the principle that mandates reducing the number of intentional killings, no matter who commits them. I believe that capital punishment, through deterrence, will reduce the number of intentional killings." This position is obviously incoherent.

While in the capital punishment case the agent objects to killings perpetrated by the state, in the minimum wage case the agent objects to underpayment perpetrated by employers. Because in the latter case the state is not the agent who commits the underpayment, we tend to see its failure to enact minimum wage laws as less objectionable than the exploitation perpetrated by employers. The state might still be doing something objectionable – say, tolerating exploitation. However, we do not think that most people would support minimum wage laws even if they thought it wrong for the state to tolerate exploitation, should they learn about the bad consequences. The claim that we should not tolerate underpayment even when the predictable consequences are that more people will end up earning no salaries (or meager unemployment benefits) is unpersuasive in any ordinary deliberative setting. Few proponents of this position will pass The Display Test, because most people feel that it does not make sense for someone to support minimum wages without thereby being committed to the welfare of the poor. Most of us expect the supporter of minimum wage laws to rely on an impersonal ethical viewpoint. She should be sensitive to evidence that the proposal she advances would, if implemented, hurt the poor. On the other hand, it does make sense for someone who believes that the number of intentional killings ought to be reduced (even that the state ought to reduce it) to oppose capital punishment while publicly acknowledging that its abolition will (regrettably) increase the number of intentional killings. Similarly, this analysis explains why civil libertarians can, without embarrassment, recognize some of the bad consequences that strengthening the protection of civil rights might produce, for example an increase in crime. For them, the protection of civil rights is an agent-relative concern of the state.

Another way of putting this is as follows: The act of tolerating immoral behavior does not itself instantiate that behavior. Suppose someone recommends invading North Korea on the grounds that millions of persons are suffering daily injustices at the hands of the government. If I oppose that recommendation on the grounds that the invasion would make things worse for the very victims it is intended to help, that obviously does not make me an accomplice in the injustices perpetrated by the North Korean government. Many people would regard my position as sensible, even though it entails tolerating injustice. This example shows that the nature of the reasons against tolerating evil is different from the nature of the reasons against evildoing. Perhaps subjecting toleration of evil to an agent-neutral logic is the appropriate response to the fact that toleration *is* an attitude that relates to behavior by *others*. Of course, toleration of evil is sometimes an all-things-considered wrong, but not because the tolerator is violating the same agent-relative requirements that govern the evildoer. Rather, it is because the act of toleration has fallen short of independent, typically agent-neutral moral requirements (imagine a state tolerating widespread spouse beating, or someone who tolerates burglars in her neighbor's house when she could safely prevent the burglary by calling the police).[36]

The same reasoning applies to the minimum wage laws example. The fact that I ought not to *exploit* workers no matter how many acts of exploitation by others I thereby forestall does not entail that I ought not to *tolerate* exploitation by others no matter how many acts of exploitation by others I thereby forestall. (Nor does it entail that I ought not to tolerate exploitation by others no matter how many *instances of tolerating*

---

[36] We do not go as far as to say that all instances of "tolerating *x*" are subject to an agent-neutral logic. A state's obligation not to intervene (and so to tolerate tyranny in another state) may hold even if that would result in a greater number of unlawful interventions by other states.

exploitation by others I thereby forestall.) The Display Test suggests that whether I ought to tolerate exploitation turns on agent-neutral considerations, for example whether I will be thereby minimizing exploitation (or what arguably makes it an evil, such as hurting the poor or increasing poverty). Deontological constraints govern the original immorality (the exploitative employer's), not third parties' response to it, provided that such response does not instantiate the very action-type to which it responds. *Proposing* free labor markets does not *itself* violate a deontological constraint against exploitation. While my violating a deontological constraint places evil under what Thomas Nagel calls "the intensifying beam of my intentions,"[37] my proposing tolerance of evil intentionally done by others does not place my (discursive) behavior under such a beam. When I am not directly involved in a certain type of evildoing, it is natural for me to regard the evils of that type perpetrated by others as equally serious. The Display Test helps us disclose what the relevant consequences are in each context. If, in any realistic deliberative setting, people condemn underpayment because it hurts workers, the fact that most people who advocate the minimum wage fail to point out that it may well increase unemployment should surely count in any comparative assessment of the DF hypothesis and the moral turn.[38] If, as we observed in section 6.2, in any realistic deliberative setting people condemn exploitation because it hurts the exploited, the fact that minimum wage laws will increase unemployment should surely count, on deliberative grounds, against the proposal.

To be sure, sometimes the evil is so serious that the state should actively prevent it, even if by doing so the victims of evildoing will be hurt to a greater extent overall. Consider the claim that private racial discrimination ought to be banned even if it could be shown that the ban would hurt racial minorities overall. Supporting this ban may well be a compelling position even after computing the bad consequences of the ban, if any. Our point here is that The Display Test helps us see whether the moral turn is a plausible account of such positions. Proponents of the ban will pass The Display Test if they are prepared to openly acknowledge whatever bad consequences the ban may have. In this case, they think the

---

[37] Nagel, *The View from Nowhere*, op. cit., p. 180.

[38] Our argument is entirely independent of whether or not paying salaries below a certain threshold really amounts to exploitation or is otherwise unjust. It shows that even if underpayment violates deontological constraints, commonsense political morality does not place the state's tolerance, and a fortiori the agent's discursive behavior, under such constraints.

moral imperative not to tolerate racial discrimination outweighs those bad consequences. Conversely, if those who propose banning private racial discrimination are unwilling to talk about the possible unpalatable consequences of the ban or are merely misinformed about those consequences, they will flunk The Display Test. In these two latter cases, the DF model, rather than the moral turn, would provide the best explanation of their discursive behavior. Their properly displayed position would be vulnerable to causal objection and so would furnish evidence for the charge of utopianism against theories of deliberative democracy.

The abolitionist's position is exceptional in that it forbids the state from intentionally killing persons irrespective of whether capital punishment prevents outcomes that are more serious from an impersonal point of view, including a greater number of intentional killings (perpetrated by other agents or the state itself). By the same token, core personal security rights prohibit government officials from exacting forced confessions, arresting persons without probable cause, and so on,[39] irrespective of whether such prohibitions result in increased crime or other bad consequences, including more state misbehavior. We sometimes convey these ideas by talking about respecting persons, their inviolability, or their special status.[40] Both here and in the capital punishment examples there is a special concern about the state's *violating* rights, as opposed to its *minimizing* rights violations.

But most political positions are *not* like this. Whether the state ought to enact minimum wage legislation, tariffs, or rent-control laws is not a matter of *the state's* complying with deontological principles. In none of these cases is there an identifiable evil (as intentionally killing an innocent was in the terrorists case) that the state ought to avoid perpetrating *itself*. We therefore find it natural for anyone, including state officials, to propose minimum wage legislation *in the name of helping the poor,* tariffs *in the name of reducing unemployment,* rent-control laws *in the name of fighting homelessness.* Unlike the abolitionist's proposal, these proposals do not prohibit the state from doing the same kind of evil it is attempting to minimize. A fortiori, then, purely discursive political behavior is governed in these areas by an agent-neutral morality, because political discourse is even further removed from direct involvement in evildoing. In many areas of

---

[39] This duty of the state is different from the duty to protect individuals from one another. The design and enforcement of criminal legislation is arguably governed by appropriately weighed aggregative considerations (e.g., decreasing crime, optimizing retributive justice, or an appropriate mix of both).

[40] See literature referenced in note 30, this chapter.

politics, the issue is, simply put, one of political craft: *how* to bring about good or just outcomes, as defined by a conception of social justice.[41]

We conclude that many counterproductive political positions do not stem from genuine commitments to deontological principles. Such positions evince discourse failure. They look unattractive once their bad consequences are fully displayed. Their proponents contrast with the victim of the terrorists' threat, the abolitionist, or the civil libertarian, all of whom can, without embarrassment, disclose the bad consequences of their positions.

6.4. Split Responsibility

The moral turn may yet take on another form. Suppose again that someone believes we ought to help the poor. This person also believes that minimum wage laws would help the poor if employers were willing to reduce their profits to keep costs competitive while preserving employment. However, she predicts that employers will lay off workers in response to those laws. She might then say that (a) she has done her share for the cause of the poor, and (b) she cannot take responsibility for the immoral autonomous behavior of others – employers in this case. Is this a legitimate way of ignoring the bad consequences of minimum wage laws?[42]

We do not think so. This objector proposes that the state impose minimum wages *but* permit layoffs. She advocates the use of the coercive power of the state to force employers to pay higher salaries but is *not* prepared to support the use of that same power to prevent the consequence she predicts (layoffs) should markets be left otherwise unhampered. She is prepared to force employers to comply with their moral duty but not to use force to prevent employers from effecting outcomes that are arguably even worse for workers. One may wonder why this agent does not support

---

[41] It may be objected that many important political issues do not involve causal complexities because they are about redressing past injustices. To that extent, those issues would be less affected by discourse failure. Yet political redress of injustice (as distinct perhaps from case-by-case judicial reparation) requires complex causal analysis. Thus, whether affirmative action programs adequately redress disadvantages traceable to injustices perpetrated in the distant past is something that requires complex historical research. It also requires complex normative and empirical inquiry aimed at ascertaining whether affirmative action (rather than, say, monetary reparation to members of victimized groups) is the best way to remedy those injustices.

[42] We are grateful to Seana Schiffrin for drawing our attention to this objection. She developed it in "Paternalism, Unconscionability Doctrine, and Accommodation," *Philosophy and Public Affairs*, Vol. 29, no. 3, July 2000, pp. 205–50.

both a legal prohibition of unjust wages *and* a legal prohibition of layoffs. Of course, few people are prepared to support both prohibitions. A prohibition of layoffs will arguably cause general hardship and thus violate the principle that we ought to help the poor. How many advocates of minimum wage laws would go as far as to prohibit employers from closing down their plants, sending money abroad, emigrating, and so forth? It seems safe to conjecture that, unlike the connection between the minimum wage and unemployment, the downsides attending those other measures will be transparent to most people, however (rationally) ignorant they are about other issues. This explains, we think, why so many people support minimum wage laws but not outright suppression of markets.

One might object that this agent is not committed to endorsing such disastrous policies: She might reject a legal prohibition of layoffs precisely because of its bad effects. But it is odd for this person to appeal to economics at this juncture of the argument, given that she ignored it before. Recall that this agent would have contented herself with doing her share in alleviating the plight of the poor even though she had predicted that employers would not do their share. (She *must* have predicted that employers would not do their share if her behavior were to count as evidence for the moral turn rather than for the DF hypothesis.) She now predicts that outright suppression of markets will hurt the poor – that is, she relies on economics to advise against such a policy. The problem with this is that there is no non-arbitrary juncture at which, to do one's share in helping the poor, one should reject the advice of economics and appeal to legal coercion. Why not use moral persuasion instead of legal coercion to get the employer to pay a just salary in the first place? On the other hand, it seems arbitrary to blame the employer for laying off workers and not the investor for not risking his capital (thereby helping to decrease the rate of unemployment) in a statist economy.

Moreover, what is this agent's "share" in the social responsibility to help the poor? One may sensibly criticize the employer for underpaying workers yet refuse to recommend minimum wage *laws* (because, if enforced, they would hurt the poor). However, it does not seem sensible to go beyond moral judgment and recommend legal coercion when legal coercion (minimum wage laws) will predictably hurt the poor. An agent's "share" surely cannot be to recommend something that will hurt the poor, given how (according to her own beliefs) markets work. (Remember again: If she does not believe that minimum wage laws hurt the poor *and* cannot dispel the economists' doubts on the claim that those laws help the poor, her case cannot be invoked by the deliberativist we are now imagining. That is, she could not attribute to moral commitments, rather than to ignorance or posturing, the insensitivity to consequences that pervades political discourse.[43]) So an agent who wants to do her share in helping the poor and believes that it is immoral to underpay workers should simply urge employers to behave morally and hope that they will do so. It is less defensible to advocate prohibition of underpayment while believing that the consequences of the prohibition will be even worse for the poor.

6.5. Causal Complexity in Political Argument

Other things being equal, the more complex the causal issues involved in the selection of public policies are, the more supported the DF hypothesis will be vis-à-vis the moral turn as an account of counterproductive political discourse. In this section, we briefly illustrate how easy it is to underestimate the role of such causal complexities.

It might be claimed that citizens disagree not only about the morality of capital punishment (where, as we saw, the policy implications are straightforward) but also about abortion, euthanasia, affirmative action, drug policy, the place of religion in society, pornography, gay marriage, military intervention, and many other issues that are distinctly moral in character. The suggested idea is that our analysis is limited to issues of economic policy and perhaps a few others where the respective positions turn on complex facts. The minimum wage issue is one such case. Still, so the objection concludes, many important policy proposals straightforwardly derive from moral principles or values, in much the same way as opposition to capital punishment does.[44]

This view is vastly overstated. Complex causal beliefs permeate most disputes in the political arena, including social issues that are ostensibly moral in character. In most cases, principles of political morality do not *obviously* lead to specific policies.[45] Suppose that two citizens agree that

---

43 In other words, we intend to capture here the case of the deliberativist who believes that *there are nonnegligible chances* that the consequences of her proposal will be even worse for the poor. This person will flunk The Display Test as well. Here, as elsewhere, we do not introduce explicitly this qualification for stylistic reasons.

44 As we have seen, theorists of deliberative democracy tend to attribute disagreement about policies to moral disagreement. See note 1, this chapter.

45 There may well be *moral* complexity, in addition to causal complexity. If so, the scope of the DF hypothesis would be wider than suggested by the Downsian formulation of the rational ignorance effect. See next section.

the state has a duty to mitigate poverty. One of them claims that strong private-property rights will achieve that end. If the other citizen can convince her that private-property rights will increase poverty, the first citizen will have to withdraw her earlier support. This is a causal, not moral, controversy; it can be settled only by measuring the effects of strong property rights on the amount or extent of poverty. Alternatively, the critic of property rights may oppose them on grounds of virtue: For him, say, private property promotes greed. This person would also make the defender of property rights retreat from her position by convincing her that strong property rights would increase poverty. These possibilities illustrate the well-known fact that one can in principle (that is, were people willing to pass The Display Test) dissolve a political dispute by pointing to a causal mistake of an adversary who does not share one's values. What is less obvious is the extent to which the political proposals that citizens make are underdetermined by the moral positions they hold. Our discussion of Kymlicka's and Blackburn's views (section 6.1) illustrates this fact.

There are, of course, purely moral positions. The abortion debate may be an example, because the relevant medical facts are not contested. Likewise, the euthanasia debate, at least in some versions of it, should be classified as a moral controversy. Sometimes it is unclear whether a controversy is moral or causal in nature. The debate over hate speech, for example, can be seen as a purely moral controversy in which supporters of hate-speech laws believe that it is simply wrong to allow certain insults to circulate in a society that respects human dignity and equality. Opponents may claim that free speech is a fundamental right that requires tolerance of unpopular and offensive utterances. Cast in these terms, this is a moral controversy. But if the supporter of hate-speech laws invokes the need to ensure that members of disadvantaged groups enjoy better opportunities, the controversy becomes causal.

Causal disagreement about public policies is large. It affects a significant number of controversies that, as shown by the foregoing debate about property rights, involve a moral disagreement. Even if citizens reached an "overlapping consensus" among divergent comprehensive moral views,[46] many empirical disagreements would remain, as the causal route to the goals laid down by comprehensive doctrines is far from obvious. Thus, Christian ethics (a comprehensive doctrine) tells people to

---

[46] The ideas of overlapping consensus and comprehensive views are discussed by Rawls in *Political Liberalism*, op. cit., Lecture IV, pp. 133–72. See note 8, Chapter 8, for related issues.

help the poor – a goal that, if our analysis is right, many will pursue in counterproductive ways. Once we recognize to what degree political positions depend on complex causal relationships, we realize how pervasive the potential for ignorance and posturing is.[47]

Our point is not that citizens do not disagree about morality. Any defense of a public policy rests on moral as well as causal considerations. Yet deliberativists imply that settling the moral debate provides an easy path to the justification of a public policy. Were they right, they could hope to avoid the charge of utopianism based on rational ignorance. But they are wrong. Complex causal claims are part and parcel of any sound defense of public policies.

6.6. Moral Error

We have shown that most political disputes are causally complex and are for this reason affected by discourse failure. Still, deliberativists might hope to find a place for deliberation in purely moral disputes. They might claim that because these disputes do not involve complex matters of fact, they are unscathed by citizens' ignorance. Furthermore, citizens, however insurmountably ignorant about factual political matters, can elect officials who share their values and trust them to implement the policies best suited to those values.

Deliberators, however, will have difficulty overcoming the specifically *moral* errors that plague purely moral controversies. Deliberation, as understood by its proponents, requires citizens to offer public reasons – that is, that they refrain both from comprehensive premises that not all reasonable persons will accept and from ostensibly self-interested reasons.[48] Yet a rigorous exchange of public reasons very rarely occurs in the public arena. Rather, it might take place in specialized journals and similar elite settings. Anyone can see that the most sophisticated debate on abortion on cable television will be far less rigorous than an average article on abortion published in a good journal. When theorists of deliberative democracy recommend that citizens give public reasons, they should

---

[47] Politicians have an incentive to see moral issues everywhere, because it is easier to posture, to show that they stand for "what is right," than to try complex explanations that they know voters will not make the effort to learn and understand. We might speculate that the insistence in the literature on deliberative democracy on moral disagreement as the main divisive force in modern democracies (see note 1, Chapter 6) stems from taking the politicians' overmoralization of politics too seriously.

[48] See note 17, Chapter 2.

be understood, we think, as recommending that citizens give *good* public reasons. Surely they do not urge citizens to give any reasons whatsoever as long as they are public. Theorists of deliberative democracy thus face a dilemma. If they wish to preserve popular participation, their conditions for ideal deliberation are utopian. Conversely, only elitist, nonparticipatory institutions will approach that ideal, at least most of the time.[49] If our goal is to improve the quality of the reasons given in moral disputes, then relying on the elitist, nondemocratic settings mentioned previously is the best alternative. Our point is not that the body politic should defer to those elitist institutions but rather that the justificatory practices endorsed by deliberativists are unattainable even in purely moral disputes.

Moreover, people have difficulty in making their moral views coherent. The moral debates in the public forum are rarely examples of sound, reflective equilibrium. Again, only discussions among experts may achieve the crispness necessary to understand whether moral views hang together. Often people fail to connect.[50] For example, people often fail to notice that their moral beliefs commit them to other moral beliefs.[51] Judith Jarvis Thomson writes that sometimes this happens when the deduction is complex, but also when "one has strong motives for failing to draw the conclusion."[52] She rightly observes that this is not merely a case of failure to connect but of "positive 'walling off.'" Suppose a managing partner in a law firm believes that excluding Hispanic lawyers from high-profile corporate cases is wrong because it evinces lack of respect for those lawyers. This same person, however, believes that there is nothing wrong with excluding female lawyers from divorce cases. Suppose, further, we ask our lawyer what makes the exclusion of Hispanic lawyers from corporate cases disrespectful. His answer is that such exclusion involves assigning professional responsibilities according to traits that are irrelevant for the successful performance of the task. At this point we will observe that the same principle condemns his exclusion of female lawyers from divorce cases. Perhaps this lawyer was too busy or had never been

---

[49] To be sure, academics and others who participate in these elitist institutions may fall prey to the deliberative pathologies that we described in section 2.7. But we also showed there that those disciplines targeted at uncovering the hidden costs of public policies will be less affected by discourse failure. In any event, for present purposes it is worth noting that the fact that not all citizens participated does not mean that not all interests or relevant reasons have been considered.

[50] We follow here Judith Jarvis Thomson, *The Realm of Rights* (Cambridge, Mass.: Harvard University Press, 1990), pp. 9–33.

[51] *The Realm of Rights*, pp. 25–6.

[52] *The Realm of Rights*, p. 26.

challenged by such questions. If so, the connection was, in Thomson's typology, too complex.

But the lawyer may fail to see the connection even if it would be easy for him to spot. Suppose we find out that some time ago a female lawyer mishandled the lawyer's divorce. Consciously or not, the lawyer had, in Thomson's typology, strong motives (perhaps even a psychological "walling off") to miss the inconsistency between his commitment to a nondiscrimination rule and his mistreatment of female lawyers.[53] People's personal histories or quirks in their psychological makeup are also likely to lead them astray. Surely such mistakes should be added to the sources of discourse failure that we studied previously.

Can the deliberativist reply that deliberation allows citizens to overcome their propensity to err? Mutual criticism can correct mistakes. Indeed, the very fact that people are prone to the sorts of ingrained errors we have just mentioned seems to make deliberation all the more necessary. The problem with this move is that it fails to take seriously the charge of utopianism and the dynamics of discourse failure that sustain it. One consequence of the rational ignorance hypothesis is that citizens will simply ignore many relevant reasons offered in the deliberative forum. As we have seen (section 2.3), they will hold by default vivid political views plagued with error. Surely, the foregoing moral errors will compound discourse failure. But then, the type of deliberation that would be required for the epistemic argument to succeed is too onerous to the ordinary citizen. If anything, a predisposition to err raises the cost of correcting mistakes through deliberation. The very fact that our predisposition to err requires *more* deliberation can hardly be invoked to resist the charge of utopianism.

Someone may have the following reservation against our analysis of moral error. Many people, let us assume, try to act morally in their everyday lives. They will accordingly learn ways to be morally worthy. They will not want to remain ignorant about the best way to achieve their goal of being moral. This moral self-training (seeking moral advice, thinking hard about one's moral duties, conditioning oneself to react properly in various circumstances, and so forth) is *decisive* on the outcome an individual pursues – namely, to become a virtuous person.[54] The

---

[53] Thomson's types of "failure to connect" are the failure to draw a moral conclusion, the failure to connect one moral belief with another, and the failure to connect a moral belief with a nonmoral belief. *The Realm of Rights*, p. 26.

[54] Recall that rational ignorance in politics stems from the fact that, for all practical purposes, nothing the agent can do will help decide the electoral outcome or impinge in

knowledge so acquired may be relevant to political participation. For example, when someone reflects on whether he should authorize a doctor to withdraw artificial life support from a relative, he may become familiar with arguments for and against euthanasia. This expertise, in turn, will serve him well in any public debate about whether or not to legalize certain forms of euthanasia. If a sufficiently large number of people behave in this way, the incidence of moral error in political deliberation may be substantially reduced. The objection, then, is that we may have a nonpolitical reason to become morally literate – namely, our desire to become worthy persons or achieve any similarly public-spirited goal. As a side effect, we can then transfer this knowledge to political life and thus mitigate the rational ignorance effect.

An obvious reply is that few people have had personal experience with all the moral issues that may come up in public deliberation. I might have been involved in a decision on euthanasia, in which case I may have developed an ability to detect morally relevant facts about euthanasia and connect them to the rest of my moral code. But that does not protect me from moral error with respect to other issues. To this, our objector may retort that citizens may develop a *generic* moral sense, valid for reflection on all moral issues. My experience with euthanasia can be transferred to other moral issues because I now have a generic ability to detect and connect relevant moral facts and issues. Now, this conjecture flies in the face of the foregoing failures to connect, and in any event it fails to protect deliberators from the sort of causal mistake that we discuss in the next section.

6.7. Enforcement and Causation

We have assumed, for the sake of argument, that certain political proposals, such as those advanced in the debate about euthanasia, are purely moral. By this we mean that those proposals are about the appropriate response of the law to the fact that euthanasia is morally permissible (or impermissible, as the case may be). Thus, those who propose a ban on euthanasia typically believe that the ban is the appropriate moral response to the fact that euthanasia is morally wrong. This proposal is purely moral because it claims that a legal prohibition is the *morally required response* to

other ways on political outcomes (see section 2.2). By contrast, the kind of moral training we mention in the text obviously helps the agent to achieve his valued outcome – becoming a better person.

the (alleged) fact that euthanasia is morally wrong. It would be a mistake, however, to infer from the fact that X is immoral a moral requirement to ban X. Such inferences are vulnerable to challenges based on causal claims, and to that extent the DF hypothesis can explain their apparent insensitivity to relevant consequences. That extent is large indeed. Let us see why.

Because political deliberation concerns the adoption of binding public policies (i.e. laws), the facts that it should take as relevant differ from those that people should consider in their private capacities. Consider again euthanasia. Someone may face a difficult decision about whether or not to authorize termination of artificial life support of a relative. Whatever conclusions this person reaches, they cannot settle the question about whether or not to *legalize* euthanasia. This is so because we may have good reasons not to criminalize euthanasia even if we think it wrong for us or others to perform euthanasia. Laws have all sorts of consequences that any responsible citizen will have to consider when deliberating and voting. One obvious such consequence is the use of public coercion – something that raises a host of independent moral issues. We do not have to think about those consequences in our private moral decisions. For example, the considerations relevant to someone's decision whether to become a prostitute are quite different from those relevant to legalizing or banning prostitution.

The corollary is far-reaching: Even if we knew our moral duties, we would remain ignorant about many of the effects of legally enforcing those duties. The very fact that political discourse is geared toward public policy – that is, toward the use of state coercion – turns every moral dispute into a dispute that is, to an important extent, causal. Legislation has complex consequences, so it is usually insufficient to invoke the moral wrongness of an action as a reason to prohibit it. The prohibition in question may promote evil behavior or outcomes. For example, someone who advocates prohibition of drug use on moral grounds should be attentive to the fact that the prohibition may encourage criminal behavior that he also condemns, even if he believes that, other things being equal, the ban would be morally justified. Even legal perfectionists – that is, people who want the state to coerce persons into leading virtuous lives – should accept this. Viewing the enforcement of morals as the main task of the law does not exempt one from causal analysis – unless, that is, legal perfectionism always overrides other moral concerns, such as alleviating poverty or reducing crime. Citizens should consider all the effects of the policies they are contemplating, and not just the answers to moral disputes posed in a legal vacuum. Here again, we can resort to The Display Test to determine the extent to which purely moral beliefs lead people to propose the legal enforcement of morality before audiences who would reject such measures if informed about their unpalatable consequences. The deep divides that we witness in public debates on euthanasia, affirmative action, and the other social issues that philosophers study under the head of applied ethics, *along with* the parties' reluctance to address facts that a typical audience would take to be against their proposals, are, again, best explained by the DF hypothesis. A version of the moral turn that appeals to the existence of purely moral positions ignores the fact that such positions often fail The Display Test.

Let us recap. We assessed the relative merits of the moral turn and the DF hypothesis as accounts of political positions that seem insensitive to consequences. The moral turn regards such positions as moral in nature, in a sense that exempts citizens from causal inquiry. As against this view, we argued that typical counterproductive political positions would lose their appeal should their unpalatable consequences be disclosed. Most political disputes are causally complex and for this reason are affected by rational ignorance and the forms of posturing that trade on it. We rejected, in particular, the attempt to ascribe counterproductive political speakers a belief in a distribution of distinct duties among various agents. This is untenable in areas of political morality where agent-neutral considerations are salient. Again, we rejected the idea of shared responsibility between political speakers and other agents (e.g., employers). The problem here is that the counterproductive speaker's selective sensitivity to causal analysis (of the sort found in economics, for example) is arbitrary. Indeed, citizens' ignorance and posturing are bound to affect even the attempt to use the law to enforce moral requirements. The enforcement of morality raises complex causal issues and moral concerns of its own. Given citizens' ignorance and the incentive to trade on it through various forms of posturing, public political morality should be seen as a narrower territory than overmoralized pictures of political discourse want us to believe. Political deliberation is much less about matters of principle than deliberativists want us to believe.[55]

---

[55] A caveat is in order. We have tried to show that the DF hypothesis is superior to the moral turn as an account of *everyday* political discourse, especially when public positions seem counterproductive. Our argument may not apply to many consequence-insensitive policy proposals advanced by philosophers and other scholars. Thus, by citing the works of Kymlicka and Blackburn at the outset we meant to illustrate how widespread the *moral turn* is in contemporary political philosophy. In deriving controversial policy proposals

6.8. A Note on Religious Morality

Religious beliefs involve yet another form of moral discourse failure.[56] A typical religious person (as someone different from a theist philosopher) subscribes to at least two sets of propositions.[57] The first includes the belief in the existence of God, typically asserted on faith. By definition, this belief is not supported by reliable scientific theories (if it were, it would not be necessary to appeal to faith). The second includes a moral code, originated in the commands of God. Religions differ here, especially on the weight they assign to the interpretation of sacred texts by prophets and commentators, but the idea is that moral principles are binding *because* they have been promulgated or revealed by God. Religious moral education often bears on political action. This is, of course, a central feature of theocracies and other regimes animated by religious fundamentalism, but it may play a substantial role in the public discourse of liberal democracies as well.

Religious educators typically teach rightful behavior. In answering the normal inquiry by the pupil of why she has to abide by a moral rule, the teacher offers a host of reasons embedded in the religious tradition. The nature and strength of those reasons will vary, but the will of God plays, in any case, a central role (otherwise, we would not call the tradition a religious one). The link between the first and the second sets of beliefs (the descriptive beliefs and the normative beliefs, as it were) can be quite complex. Modern religious traditions do not always emphasize the will of God as the reason to act morally, but certainly the fact that He created us and is so vastly superior to us in might, understanding, kindness, or

---

from abstract principles of political morality, those writers have made, we suspect, a *philosophical* mistake – they have taken for granted the moral turn. The moral turn may be so evident to some writers that they have not taken the trouble to defend it. Indeed, the moral turn has a good deal of initial plausibility, especially for people trained in contemporary moral theory. To that extent, they do not engage in discourse failure. The moral turn, when performed by scholars, may in many cases be a philosophical mistake of one of two kinds: Either writers jump too easily from abstract principles to concrete political proposals, or they hastily portray political positions of the ordinary citizen as moral. As we have argued, the latter spring from the interaction between rational ignorance and posturing. While the plausibility of the moral turn explains its popularity among academics, *which* specific policies will be more popular among them can often be attributed to the mechanisms of discourse failure we indicated in section 2.7.

[56] We are grateful to Jane Ackerman for helpful comments on a draft of this section.

[57] What follows is a stylized reconstruction of religious belief. Many people do not experience their religion in a systematic way, and there are of course important variations between faiths and between believers.

wisdom is an important ingredient in whatever mix of reasons are relevant to defend the moral code in question.[58]

Compare this form of moral learning with the kind of inquiry exemplified by secular moral philosophy. Secular moral inquiry is quite complex and sophisticated. There are many reasons for this (as we saw in our discussion of the failures in moral discourse), but one of them is the problem of ultimate justification – a highly complex question once arguments from authority are excluded. Moral philosophy is difficult and opaque. Religious morality, however, greatly simplifies our moral beliefs by postulating a *vivid* meta-ethical theory that tells us where to find the ultimate justification for those beliefs. All the hurdles of justification are swept aside by assuming that there is a God who has promulgated these principles to guide our behavior. Believers do not have to worry about the nature of justification and can thus concentrate on interpreting the divine commands so as to extract the proper guidelines for behavior. But even here religion simplifies things. The tasks of interpreting the often obscure or metaphorical messages of the sacred texts, and of ranking their importance in order to suppress conflicting commands, are eased by the availability of official pronouncements: the commentaries by prophets, the priests' official teachings, the pronouncements *ex cathedra* of the pope, etc. The very obscurity, vagueness, and length of the sacred texts lead believers to rely on authoritative interpreters. Arguments from authority combine with faith into a cognitive process that stifles critical thinking. For these reasons, religious moral education is a form of discourse failure. It relies on vivid theories that are easy for people to grasp: the belief in a supreme religious authority who in His infinite wisdom has decided what the moral rules and principles should be. Truth-insensitive processes are here especially reinforced by the appeal to faith and, to various degrees, the threat of afterlife punishment. Religious persons are relieved from reading abstract and difficult texts on meta-ethics. They do not have to decide the exact weight of deontological constraints and the principle of utility in moral argument, because they were taught that the religious tradition supplies all the answers. Religious claims are vivid because they involve the visible hand of God, straightforward causal mechanisms, and (as we saw in section 4.3) sometimes even bootstrap reasoning. They are easier to grasp than their competing opaque

---

[58] Of course, the more the role of God in moral teaching is diluted, the more it will resemble secular moral teaching, and the observations that follow in the text will be less applicable, whereas those made about moral error in section 6.6 will be increasingly relevant.

rival – secular moral theory. The intensity of religious beliefs is traceable to the privileged status of faith in religious justification. Herein lies the main source of religious discourse failure, because, by its very nature, faith is not supported by the most reliable theories of knowledge. Ironically, the complex attempts to demonstrate the existence of God throughout the history of philosophy by implication deny the epistemic credentials of religious faith.

We pass no judgment on the utility of religious beliefs; much ink has been spilled on that issue and we do not have a particular contribution to make.[59] We merely point out that, regardless of the social effects of religion, religious morality is, under our definition, a peculiar form of discourse failure. Nor do we mean to take sides on the *philosophical* issues about God's existence and attributes; our point is that *religious* discourse fails because faith is manifestly truth-insensitive. Indeed, religious discourse often displays extreme versions of the patterns of discourse failure already studied. Bootstrap arguments are the natural counterpart of faith. The sounder the critiques of religion are, the more prone believers are to see them as the Devil's clever tricks, for example. Their cleverness is a *temptation* that tries their faith and so makes reassertion of it both urgent and meritorious. Religious believers, perhaps more than any other user of bootstrap strategies, feel entitled to turn the very strength of a critique of religion against the critic.[60]

To be sure, deliberativists typically exclude religious reasons from the deliberative forum: As Rawls and others have urged, reasons offered in deliberation must be public reasons.[61] However, there is no practical way of excluding religion-driven *public* reasons in any realistic deliberative setting. For example, opponents of legalized abortion may appeal to a wide

---

[59] See the classic discussion in John Stuart Mill, *Nature, the Utility of Religion, and Theism* (London: Longmans, Green, Reader, and Dyer, 1874).

[60] For a study of "immunization" strategies against criticism of religion, see Hans Albert, *Das Elend der Theologie: krit. Auseinandersetzung mit Hans Küng* (Hamburg: Hoffmann und Campe, 1979). See also Hans Albert, *Treatise on Critical Reason*, op. cit., pp. 132–64. Because bootstrap religious arguments appeal to God's anger, salvation, and other facts in which the believer has a stake, persistent use of such arguments supports the widespread observation that religious beliefs are comforting – and, to that extent, prone to discourse failure. We do not defend a particular view about the kinds of beliefs it is comforting to entertain. It would be interesting to investigate how a theory of comforting beliefs may reinforce, qualify, or systematize the account of the patterns of political belief offered in this book. For a classical discussion of comforting beliefs, see Clifford, *The Ethics of Belief*, op. cit. (arguing that religious beliefs are comforting, ill-grounded, and morally objectionable).

[61] See note 17, Chapter 2.

variety of utilitarian and rights-based considerations, as they usually do. They will thereby comply with the public-reason requirement. Nevertheless, their *selection* of such considerations may well have been guided by religious beliefs. Religious discourse failure guides, then, the choice of public reasons. Because religious beliefs are widespread, it seems safe to conclude that they are a major source of discourse failure even in those deliberative fields where citizens comply with the requirements of public reason.

6.9. A Note on the Minimum Wage and Employment

The standard textbook model of the minimum wage predicts that it reduces employment. The number of workers whom firms are willing to hire varies inversely with the wage rate. At a higher wage, firms will hire fewer workers; at a lower wage, they will hire more workers. This is an application of the more general logic of price floors – that is, minimum prices set by law, usually on the grounds that prices would otherwise be "too low." Agricultural support prices are another example.[62]

In recent times, however, there have been attempts to use empirical data to undermine the standard view that minimum wage laws reduce employment. David Card and Alan B. Krueger use comparisons of employment growth at fast-food stores in New Jersey (where the minimum wage rose in 1992 from \$4.25 to \$5.05) and Pennsylvania (where the minimum wage was constant) to show that there is "no indication that the rise in the minimum wage reduced employment."[63] David Neumark and William Wascher call into question Card and Krueger's findings. By using payroll records from the same population, instead of (as in the Card-Krueger study) telephone surveys, they obtained data that "are generally consistent with the prediction that raising the minimum wage reduces the demand for low-wage workers."[64] In their reply, Card and Krueger defend their previous findings by using data from the Bureau of Labor

---

[62] See, for instance, Irving B. Tucker, *Macroeconomics for Today* (Cincinnati, Ohio: South-Western College Publishing, 1999), pp. 14, 90–2.

[63] "Minimum Wages and Employment: A Case Study of the Fast-Food Industry in New Jersey and Pennsylvania," *American Economic Review*, Vol. 84, no. 4 (September 1994), pp. 772–93, at p. 772.

[64] "Minimum Wages and Employment: A Case Study of the Fast-Food Industry in New Jersey and Pennsylvania: Comment," *American Economic Review*, Vol. 90, no. 5 (December 2000), pp. 1362–96, at p. 1363.

Statistics.[65] Russell S. Sobel investigates a related issue: the impact on the poor of the *level* at which the minimum wage is set. He estimates that minimum wages were always above the levels that "would be consistent with two frequently stated goals of public policy: the maximization of the total income of minimum wage workers and the level that would bring a typical minimum wage family out of poverty."[66] He argues that "endogenous features of minimum wage legislation, such as the level, the timing of changes, and the step process, are . . . shaped by pressures in the political process," and that "a simple interest group model can better explain the history of the minimum wage than can the levels that would achieve the stated goals of minimum wage policy."[67]

It seems fair, then, to draw three conclusions. First, current mainstream economics predicts that minimum wages will have an adverse impact on employment; indeed, in their 1994 article Card and Krueger observe that "the prediction from conventional economic theory is unambiguous: a rise in the minimum wage leads perfectly competitive employers to cut employment."[68] And in their 2000 piece they write that their "new findings run counter to *conventional wisdom.*"[69] Second, there is an ongoing empirical controversy about the accuracy of that prediction. Third, even if minimum wages had no definite impact on *employment,* a lower minimum wage would arguably increase the *total income* of minimum wage workers and help the worst-off worker's family *escape poverty.* In other words, there is strong theoretical support for, but ambiguous empirical confirmation of, the prediction that minimum wages increase unemployment, and in any event it seems likely that, in order to benefit the poor, they should be set at lower levels than those observed in the United States since their implementation by the Fair Labor Standards Act of 1938. Claims that minimum wage laws are counterproductive should accordingly be qualified to make room for the nuances that we observe in reliable discussions. This may lead to cumbersome formulations. At the very least, we would need such sentences as "the current minimum wage arguably defeats the

---

[65] "Minimum Wages and Employment: A Case Study of the Fast-Food Industry in New Jersey and Pennsylvania: Reply," *American Economic Review,* Vol. 90, no. 5 (December 2000), pp. 1397–1420.

[66] "Theory and Evidence on the Political Economy of the Minimum Wage," *Journal of Political Economy,* Vol. 197, no. 4, 1999, at p. 782.

[67] Op. cit., p. 782.

[68] Op. cit., p. 772.

[69] Op. cit., p. 1397, emphasis added.

purpose of helping the poor." However, such qualifications would leave our argument unscathed, for our theory of discourse failure explains better than the symbolic (Chapter 5) or the moral (this chapter) models the fact that deliberators in *actual* political fora almost invariably assert, *without qualification*, that minimum wages help the poor. Of course, the sharp disharmony between reliable economics and public political rhetoric subsisted during the many decades that preceded the foregoing empirical controversies, when the pessimistic stance held sway among economists.

6.10. Types of Discourse Failure: A Summary

Without trying to be exhaustive, we can say that discourse failure typically occurs in seven cases:

(1) When people explain a social situation by appealing to a visible hand whereas reliable social science appeals to an invisible hand (e.g., viewing economic prosperity as the result of public-spirited or otherwise virtuous[70] cooperation and not as the result of the workings of markets). See section 2.3.

(2) When people propose a zero-sum explanation whereas reliable social science offers a positive-sum explanation (e.g., viewing interest rates as the result of the greed of lenders, as opposed to viewing it as the result of the supply and demand of money). This zero-sum explanation is particularly persuasive when either benefits or losses are visible.[71] See section 2.3.

(3) When people propose a positive-sum explanation whereas reliable social science offers a zero- or negative-sum explanation (e.g., farmer subsidies seen as a cooperative social effort wherein everybody gains, as opposed to a redistribution in favor of farmers with net social losses). Positive-sum explanations are more persuasive when costs are hard to calculate. Typically, this occurs when costs are dispersed (as in the subsidy example) or when they involve counterfactual situations. An example of the latter category is

---

[70] It need not be altruistic cooperation. Explanations appealing to personal initiative and toil (perhaps because religion teaches that financial success is a sign of salvation) are also visible-hand (unless, that is, they derive from yet more basic invisible-hand theories, e.g. a theory of cultural evolution under which religious beliefs possess survival value for whole groups).

[71] The whale-hunting environmental example we discussed in section 2.3 is a case of zero-sum explanation with concentrated benefits and dispersed costs.

the *investment forgone* in pharmaceutical research caused by legal requirements for the testing of new drugs. See section 2.3.

(4) When people explain a social situation by appealing to obscure concepts (e.g., national interest or sovereignty) that, perhaps for evolutionary reasons, are so psychologically connected with certain policies (e.g., protectionism) that inquiring into the effects of those policies seems out of the question. See section 2.3.

(5) When people use persuasive definitions that obscure or conceal relevant similarities between institutions or events. See section 2.5.

(6) When people fail to address the complexity of normative issues. This includes appeals to religion. See sections 6.6 and 6.8.

(7) When people adopt positions at odds with reliable social science simply to avoid dissenting. See section 2.7.

These types of discourse failure exploit structural features of certain political positions, such as the distribution of costs and benefits of a certain policy. Given the rational ignorance hypothesis, appeal to such structural features has in turn rhetorical advantages in many settings (e.g., political competition). Notice that (6) relies on an extension of the rational ignorance hypothesis, originally formulated for factual contexts, to normative contexts.

Another type of discourse failure occurs:

(8) When people dismiss a view by using a bootstrap argument – that is, adducing the very fact that someone advances the view as evidence against that view. Bootstrap arguments exempt the speaker from costly inquiry into the merits of actual or possible objections to his political positions. See sections 4.3 and 6.8.

We saw that expressive (Chapter 5) and overmoralized (this chapter) theories of political discourse overlook discourse failure. All of the foregoing types of discourse failure stem from the fact that agents are sensitive to the personal costs and benefits of acquiring or spreading political information or views. Ingrained cognitive obstacles increase these costs.

7

Non-Epistemic Defenses of Deliberation

7.1. Deliberation as the Exercise of Autonomy

Theorists of deliberative democracy do not rely solely on the supposed epistemic virtues of deliberation. In this chapter we examine various non-epistemic defenses of deliberation. We will see that they are overly optimistic. Deliberation may be a valuable practice, but not in the institutional milieu assumed by deliberativists – to wit, majority rule *cum* wide redistributive powers. (We outline in Chapter 9 the institutional arrangements that hold out hope of overcoming discourse failure.)

Political deliberation can be defended by appeal to Kantian ideals.[1] There is surely independent value in people's thinking about moral matters for themselves. We enrich our individual moral reflection (our moral soliloquy, as it were) when we deliberate with others. Public deliberation is, on this view, the extension to the political realm of a valuable – indeed, central – human faculty. This argument is particularly eloquent against Platonic criticisms to democracy, because it precludes reliance on moral experts or philosopher-kings. Contrast this with science. For most of us most of the time, there is not much independent value in trying to figure out scientific matters by ourselves: We do well in deferring to doctors, physicists, and so forth. Moreover, it is ludicrous to expect to solve

---

[1] Thus, in his defense of deliberative democracy Robert Goodin points out that "democracy ... is essentially a matter of treating ... autonomous individuals with equal consideration and respect." Robert Goodin, *Reflective Democracy* (Oxford: Oxford University Press, 2003), p. 23. See also Nino, *The Constitution of Deliberative Democracy*, op. cit., p. 47. Nino believes that citizens of a democracy tend to select morally justified public policies, and for this reason political deliberation implements the Kantian principle of autonomy. Id., esp. pp. 117–21.

scientific problems by submitting them to massive deliberation. We do expect citizens, however, to reflect upon *right* and *wrong*, not because we think they are better judges of moral certitude than professional philosophers but because reflection is a morally valuable practice. The practice is valuable because the citizen autonomously weighs reasons for or against alternative policies, and others help him become aware of fresh reasons. The point is not that deliberators are likely to reach the truth but rather that deliberation is valuable quite apart from epistemic results.

We do not dispute the Kantian, autonomy-based insight in its more general form. To the extent that individual or social deliberation is an expression of our rational nature, it is a good thing independently of the wisdom of whatever policies may ensue from deliberation. *Intending to* approach the truth in dialogue with others is valuable in itself. We even concede that deliberation may sharpen our awareness of new or missed moral connections. But, unfortunately, the Kantian insight does not help the theorist of deliberative democracy.

One reason to doubt that political deliberation will inherit the worth of moral deliberation is that, as we saw in Chapter 6, political proposals do not follow from purely moral considerations. A political proposal always involves causal beliefs. We saw in Chapter 5 that support of political measures is not simply expressive of commitment to values or principles; it is usually performed *in the name of* values or principles. Someone who supports laws in the name of values or principles is committed to causal beliefs. If someone makes a political proposal in the name of a moral principle, he is committed to the belief that the proposal realizes the principle. Thus, someone who supports minimum wage laws in the name of helping the poor is conventionally committed to the causal belief that such laws help the poor.

We have also seen that, when we think about a moral issue in nonpolitical contexts, we usually think about what we should do in our individual lives. Should I give away 10 percent of my disposable income to alleviate poverty? Should I advise my friend to abort an unwanted pregnancy? As we indicated in section 6.7, no answer to such questions settles what the law should be like. Deliberators who are considering the enactment of a law must address an array of consequences that will ensue from legal enforcement. Will a welfare program alleviate poverty overall (i.e., taking into account, among other things, possible disincentives to investment and job search)? Will a ban on abortion help poor mothers overall? Will it diminish the number of abortions? Those questions remain unanswered even if we have strong views on the private morality of abortion. Purely moral issues become to a considerable extent causal issues in the transition from morality to law. To that extent, they are vulnerable to rational ignorance. Thus, someone who already thinks that abortion is immoral will not take the trouble to read the literature studying multifarious downsides of banning abortion.[2]

How to square, then, the intrinsic value of deliberation with the fact that people err systematically? Arguably, the Kantian insight assumes that in their exercise of their rational nature, persons can approach moral and empirical truths. The deliberativist might point out that there are contexts wherein we prefer that people make their own mistakes rather than achieve correct results by deferring to authority. Thus, schoolteachers are surely justified in asking pupils to do their homework by themselves even when they predictably will err, rather than have their parents do it. But notice that this is a *pedagogical* practice justified by the expectation that it will help pupils reach the truth by themselves in the long run. This practice does not lead to the multiplication of error. On the contrary, it trains students in the trial-and-error methodology characteristic of scientific inquiry. Contrast this with the pathologies of deliberative processes already discussed. Far from training citizens in the search for the truth, political deliberation magnifies error through the mutually reinforcing dynamics of rational ignorance and posturing. To the extent that there is here something like a trial-and-error process, it is guided by non-epistemic aims (increasing one's political power and obtaining various kinds of legislative benefits). But then, a crucial element in the Kantian insight is absent in realistic deliberative politics: Key actors do not even *intend to* approach the truth.[3]

Imagine someone who thinks hard, by himself, about trade policy. Moreover, he is public-spirited: He tries to think about which trade policy would be morally best. His thinking, alas, is blighted by vivid and unreliable beliefs ("Exports are good, imports are bad," "We need to protect our industries against foreign competition"). He then joins other citizens who have undergone the same process, and all of them deliberate on trade policy, with the result that he finds his views confirmed by public opinion. As we have seen, politicians and other suppliers of political "information" reinforce these mistakes. Citizens then vote and impose strong barriers

---

[2] Remember that in section 6.6. we extended the rational ignorance hypothesis (originally applicable to factual or causal information) to moral issues. If this extension is warranted, our point in the text holds a fortiori.

[3] We expand on deliberative sincerity in the next section.

on foreign trade, thus causing national and global impoverishment. But they reached this unhappy result in great part because they were *intentionally* misled. This fact alone should suffice to cast serious doubts on the Kantian credentials of political deliberation.

7.2. Sincerity in Deliberation

Deliberativists generally agree that citizens cannot legitimately give just any argument in the political arena. Citizens may not invoke solely their self-interest as a reason for supporting a policy; they must invoke the general interest. A public-spirited argument for a policy may take several forms. It may show that the policy will be to everyone's advantage; or it may urge that the policy be required by equality, civic virtue, or other ideals of political morality. Now the requirement of public-spiritedness poses a question: Must deliberators sincerely endorse those public reasons, or is it enough that they simply invoke them – that they simply throw them to the public forum, as it were?

Deliberativists tend to endorse the sincerity requirement.[4] It is unclear if this means that the speaker should believe what she says, or whether she should merely give reasons that she thinks are good ones for the *listener* to accept.[5] Be that as it may, both versions of the sincerity requirement

---

[4] See, for example, Jürgen Habermas, *Moral Consciousness and Communicative Action*, C. Lenhart and S. W. Nicholson, trans. (Cambridge, Mass.: MIT Press, 1991) p. 88; John Rawls, *Political Liberalism* (New York: Columbia University Press, 1991), p. 217. As we've pointed out, while the early Rawls can be properly described as a liberal contractarian in the Kantian tradition, Rawls's later work can be seen as part of the deliberativist movement. See also Christiano, *The Rule of the Many*, op. cit., p. 117. Nino might be understood to argue that insincerity would be innocuous if deliberative institutions induced citizens to respect certain formal constraints, such as generality (in a sense that excludes proper names or definite descriptions) and consistency, in their public positions. Nino nevertheless asserts that ideal deliberation is "a surrogate of the informal practice of moral discussion," which arguably presupposes sincerity. See Nino, *The Constitution of Deliberative Democracy*, op. cit., pp. 122–4. See also Gerald Postema, "Public Practical Reason: Political Practice," in Ian Shapiro and Judith Wagner DeCrew, eds., *Nomos XXXVII: Theory and Practice* (New York: New York University Press, 1995), p. 536.

[5] Gerald Gaus makes this important distinction in *Justificatory Liberalism*, op. cit., p. 139. See also Gaus, *Contemporary Theories of Liberalism*, p. 133. Gaus proposes the following principle of sincerity: "A reasoned justification must be sincere. Betty's appeal to reason *R* justifying *P* to Alf is sincere if and only if: (1) She believes she is justified in accepting *P*; (2) she believes that Alf is justified in accepting *R*; (3) she believes that *R* justifies *P* in Alf's system of beliefs." Id., p. 134. We think that this attenuated principle of sincerity excludes manipulation only if it requires Betty to disclose to Alf the fact (if it is a fact) that she does *not* endorse *R*.

rule out manipulation. The theory of discourse failure suggests, however, that the sincerity requirement is utopian. At the core of the discursive pathologies that we have identified is the mutually reinforcing interaction between citizens' ignorance and posturing, which is a form of insincerity. The expansion of deliberative fora (a central proposal of deliberativists) will simply reinforce the dynamics whereby insincerity spawns discourse failure.

It makes sense for deliberativists to require sincerity, because they need it to offset discourse failure. If *all* citizens (including politicians and rent seekers) said in public what they sincerely believed, even against their interest, discourse failure would obviously decrease. In such a world, people would not posture or argue in a self-serving or manipulative manner. Sincerity would not be necessary if the social rules for acceptance or rejection of positions were truth-sensitive (think about scientific seminars). Those seeking goals other than the truth, such as political or academic appointments, could not exempt their views from rigorous scrutiny. This would provide them with an incentive to pursue the truth. They would have to be instrumentally sincere. But deliberativists face a dilemma. In *feasible* democratic deliberative settings, discourse failure would be avoided by sincere deliberators, yet sincerity is unattainable in those settings, even instrumentally. On the other hand, deliberativists may avoid requiring utopian sincerity by advocating elitist deliberative settings, but then they would be sacrificing participatory democracy. If a society is truly deliberative and thus respectful of the sincerity requirement, it is not participatory; and if it is participatory, it cannot be truly deliberative.[6]

It would seem that theories of deliberative democracy have resources to defuse these worries. As we have already seen, deliberativists impose various constraints on deliberation: In Gutmann and Thompson's version, these are publicity, reciprocity, and accountability.[7] These requirements are meant to, among other things, secure impartiality. Let us assume, for the sake of argument, that citizens observe those constraints. Why, then, care about sincerity? The answer is that there is still ample margin

---

[6] "Democracy" is a notoriously plastic concept. Thus, Pettit suggests that democracy can be "conceived as a system for empowering the public reasons recognized among a people – their common valuations – rather than the will of the people conceived as a collective agent," where those public reasons are in turn those resulting from appropriate deliberation by "appointed boards and officials." Although this conceptual framework reconciles democracy with deliberation, our substantive point remains: Wide political *participation* (an ideal certainly cherished by deliberativists) cannot coexist with quality deliberation. See Pettit, "Depoliticizing Democracy," op. cit.

[7] See Gutmann and Thompson, "Why Deliberative Democracy Is Different," op. cit.

for hypocrisy and manipulation. Constraints on deliberation underdetermine substantive results. Even academics, who are expected more than anyone else to abide by the recommended constraints, often reach widely divergent and mutually incompatible results. Because feasible deliberation will be quite removed from ideal conditions, deliberators can muster public reasons for virtually any political measure while remaining within the recommended constraints. Constraints on the *kinds* of reasons will not prevent citizens with strong interest in the outcome from manipulating public arguments in self-serving ways.

Take, for example, the suggestion that a proper deliberative process requires the participation of everyone affected by a proposed policy. Thus, Ronald Dworkin (who, as a defender of a rights-based political morality, is more restrictive than typical deliberativists about which political matters should be left to majority rule) writes, "the political system of representative democracy . . . works better" at selecting policies for the sake of the general welfare than "nonelected judges, who have no mail bag or lobbyists or pressure groups, to compromise competing interests in their chambers."[8] This seems harmless enough, until we realize that it undermines the sincerity requirement. First, affected parties will have strong incentives to argue in a self-serving manner. If we want to enhance sincerity and impartiality, perhaps it would be better to entrust deliberation to *non*-affected parties. (We expand on this point in the next section.) Second, the suggestion overlooks the crucial fact that groups which might be affected by the policy under discussion have different organizational costs.[9] If the matter under discussion is, for example, public subsidies to the arts, both artists and art lovers will mobilize and take advantage of available deliberative fora. In contrast, taxpayers, whose expected individual benefits from blocking the subsidy are low, will remain uninvolved. Moreover, the taxpayer (or consumer) has a hard time estimating how a given proposal will affect him. Compare this with the ease with which those who stand to benefit from special-interest legislation will calculate their potential gains. The expansion of deliberative settings proposed by deliberativists could only aggravate the manipulative use of political argument. To the extent that legislation is disproportionately sensitive to well-organized special interests, a concern with sincerity should warn

---

[8] See Ronald Dworkin, *Taking Rights Seriously* (Cambridge, Mass.: Harvard University Press, 1977), p. 85.

[9] See Mancur Olson, *The Logic of Collective Action*, op. cit., and *The Rise and Decline of Nations*, op. cit.

us against placing much weight on what the most vocal parties have to say.[10]

7.3. Deliberation and Social Conflict

Writers sometimes defend deliberation as the best way to facilitate compromise in the face of strong and lasting disagreement.[11] Deliberation, they think, is instrumental to social peace. On one interpretation, this argument is trivial. It tells us that people who deliberate are not at war. The argument trades on the platitude that persons open to compromise are disinclined to engage in violent confrontation. If, in turn, proper deliberation is defined as deliberation conducted by persons open to compromise, then deliberation leads to peace only trivially. A more interesting version of the argument from peace may focus not on the connection between deliberation and absence of conflict but rather on the policies that promote peaceful citizenship in the first place. It may be claimed that deliberation teaches citizens to *accept defeat* in majoritarian politics. People can better learn to lose if they can make their case to their fellow citizens – that is, if they can deliberate. Deliberation has, on this view, a *cathartic* effect. It cushions the bitterness of political defeat and softens aggressive impulses.

The need to compromise may justify the restrictions placed by deliberativists on the kinds of reasons that citizens may advance. Most authors exclude, for example, religious reasons or reasons based on comprehensive worldviews[12] (call them *comprehensive reasons*). Arguably, this restriction helps achieve social peace. Because many comprehensive reasons can be divisive, deliberators would be well advised to limit the kinds of reasons they offer if they cherish agreement. Comprehensive reasons may be inappropriate as a tool for settling disputes.

Unfortunately, the argument from social peace overlooks the fact that there are two ways to counter aggressive impulses stemming from fear of political defeat. One is to prepare citizens for political defeat and exclude appeals to divisive views – the recommendations we just described. The other is to *reduce the number of losers*. If two people stand to gain from interaction, they will normally interact; by hypothesis, no one loses. The

---

[10] See Pincione, "Market Rights and the Rule of Law: A Case for Procedural Constitutionalism," p. 432, note 68 and accompanying text.

[11] See, for example, James Bohman, *Public Deliberation* (Cambridge, Mass.: MIT Press, 1996), pp. 84, 90–3; and Christiano, *The Rule of the Many*, op. cit., pp. 48–53.

[12] See note 17, Chapter 2.

contract serves as a model for such interactions. To be sure, some real-world contracts worsen the situations of third parties – they have negative externalities. Contracts may sometimes create losers. It is debatable how much government interference with freedom of contract, rather than spontaneous long-run market mechanisms, will minimize externalities. What *is* clear, though, is the massive amount of externalities embodied in majority rule. After all, majority rule means that the minority loses. The argument from peace must show that the externalities involved in majority rule are less severe than those involved in a contractarian society. It seems fair to place the burden of proof on this kind of deliberativist. A contractarian society can make only limited room for majoritarian politics, because dissenters may veto proposals inimical to their interests. To be sure, education and deliberation may help mitigate the frustration and resentment caused by political defeat. But it would be better to fight, if not eradicate, the disease responsible for those symptoms – namely, the very existence of losers in politics. This is in effect what the institution of contract does. If the deliberativist's concern is to reduce social conflict, he should favor an expansion of free markets rather than the nonconsensual redistributions characteristic of majoritarian politics.[13]

The deliberative democrat might reply that majority rule is needed to intervene in the market for the sake of justice. The one solution to the "loser problem" we should not accept, he can say, is precisely to expand free markets, where contracts operate from a baseline of unjust property entitlements. Deliberation is a better therapy for aggressive impulses because it raises hopes to remedy market injustices. While social justice requires majority rule to correct the outcomes of the free market, thereby turning some people into losers, deliberation tames losers and secures social peace. So even if the market secured social peace by preventing people from improving at the expense of others, justice would require intervention in the market. And even if free markets were inherently just, deliberation may be the only way to peacefully allow citizens to choose a conception of justice.

This reply misses our point about the connection between markets and peace. It does not matter, for present purposes, what a just baseline for market transactions is. Simply put, on *any* preferred baseline contracts make no room for losers. Assuming a just baseline, there is no reason why someone *concerned with social peace* would object to people's

---

[13] See Chapter 9 for a fuller development of this idea.

subsequently contracting as the *only* means to alter distributions. Thus, the deliberativist's concern with justice would be satisfied with allowing a once-and-for-all redistribution in accordance with his preferred ideal of justice – for example, a resource-egalitarian redistribution. From then on, he cannot consistently oppose free exchanges of the rights accorded in that baseline, if he is really concerned with social peace.[14]

The deliberative democrat might retort that the link between markets and peace fails, ironically, because of discourse failure. Some of those who do not compete well might feel, rightly or wrongly, that they are indeed losers in the market, the victims of injustice. Vivid, though perhaps wrong, zero-sum social theories might have made them feel that way. But whether or not they are justified (so the objection goes), they must be placated for the sake of social peace, and deliberation and education are appropriate ways of doing so. Majority rule brings those people hope of eradicating current injustices. Indeed, any society will have people who *feel* themselves disadvantaged by its rules, and so it cannot dispense with deliberation, coupled with majority rule, as tools with which to placate those feelings.

This response gets caught in a dilemma. Either deliberators are trying to communicate to one another their genuine beliefs, or they are not. If they are, the argument from social peace has to rest on the claim that the sincere exchange of information and arguments has soothing power. But this is a dubious claim: Communicating to others our genuine beliefs often hurts and angers them. It is not obvious that telling people what we really think will assuage their hurt feelings. The other horn of the dilemma drops the requirement that people deliberate honestly. Deliberators should use whatever arguments soothe the hurt feelings of losers. They see the exchange of ideas and information as a therapy. Deliberators say things not because they want to share their beliefs with others but because they want to placate them – if necessary, by misleading them. Their arguments will be sound only insofar as soundness calms and achieves peace. Needless to say, such utterances do not amount to deliberation, on any ordinary understanding of the term.[15]

---

[14] The deliberativist may insist that exchanges of the baseline rights must be prevented precisely for the sake of justice. But this is hardly compatible with his claim that, in the baseline, individuals had genuine *rights*, which rule out *paternalism*. For more detailed analysis, see Pincione, op. cit., esp. pp. 420–5. See also Eric Mack, "In Defense of the Jurisdiction Theory of Rights," in Guido Pincione and Horacio Spector, eds., *Rights, Equality, and Liberty* (London: Kluwer, 2000), pp. 71–98, esp. pp. 84–7.

[15] We criticize in section 7.6. the recommendation that deliberators should not always seek the truth.

Our appeal to free markets in this section served a local purpose: to show that if deliberation's purpose is to reduce social conflict, expanded markets do a better job than expanding deliberative fora under the current institutional framework. In Chapter 9, we will argue that free markets are the best milieu for ideal political deliberation itself, irrespective of how well they serve social peace.

7.4. Deliberation and Impartiality

As we indicated in the previous section, some writers argue that deliberation ensures impartiality because it takes into account everyone's interests – something that is less likely to occur in individual reflection.[16] The idea here is that collecting the opinions of as many citizens as possible, and especially of those affected by a prospective policy, ensures that political decisions will be as impartial as they can be. Everyone is heard, and everyone can contribute, however slightly, to the decision-making process. However, deliberating citizens will be less likely to be impartial than, say, the conscientious social scientist working in his study. He will normally take into account the *total* benefits and costs of alternative policies, however opaque such costs and benefits might be. In contrast, self-interest and rational error will prevent deliberators from being impartial, so the argument from impartiality is closer to vindicating elitism than to supporting deliberative politics as ordinarily understood. If we want impartiality, we'd better entrust policy analysis to the social scientist in his study than to citizens debating in the public forum, at least in societies that harbor institutions generally committed to reliable procedures for accepting and rejecting scientific views.

The deliberative democrat might respond that impartiality is not toward interests but toward viewpoints. He might concede that discourse failure blocks fair consideration of everyone's interests yet insist that deliberation improves the impartiality of the deliberative process with regard to the diverse points of view that compete for citizens' allegiance. The deliberative process will be impartial in the second sense if it gives fair hearing to all viewpoints, including partial ones in the first sense. Yet it is hard to see here the merits of deliberation over and above the merits of free speech. Given discourse failure, fair hearing is not likely to increase the quality of public policies. This is especially so if we expect those policies to be impartial in the first sense, and so attentive to their

---

[16] See Carlos Santiago Nino, *The Constitution of Deliberative Democracy*, op. cit., pp. 113, 119–20, 123, and 127–8.

hidden costs. If the deliberative democrat suggests that freedom to deliberate is a good thing, we completely agree. But then, the theory of deliberative democracy will not have made a contribution beyond the general arguments for free speech. In other words, the assertion "political deliberation is a good thing" is ambiguous. If it means that people should be free to deliberate, then, we think, it is obviously correct (we offered some reasons for this claim in section 4.5). If it means that deliberation will promote better laws and policies, then it faces the discourse failure objection.

The deliberative democrat might retreat to the following position: He might say that voting preceded by public deliberation is preferable to voting preceded by individual reflection (or no reflection at all). That is, democracy is taken as a normative given, and political deliberation is then offered as superior to soliloquy. This reply would defuse our first criticism of impartiality, because democratic theory upholds decision making by citizens and not by scientific or other elites, even if the latter are more impartial. This deliberative democrat concedes that public deliberation will be affected by discourse failure but insists that it is still more impartial than no deliberation at all. He might believe, for example, that exchanging ideas with others enhances sympathy with one another's interests. We do not dispute that political decisions should not be left to scientific elites. However, whether or not public deliberators affected by rational ignorance and error will reach better political solutions than individuals reflecting in solitude is far from clear. Perhaps the vote cast by a nondeliberating citizenry with a strong taste for serious study will lead to better policies than the vote cast by intense deliberators.

Sometimes deliberativists relax the requirement that deliberation should consist in reasoned argument. Gutmann and Thompson, for example, write that "deliberation...does not always have to take the form of a reasoned argument of the kind that philosophers tend to like.... Dispassionate argument that minimizes conflict is not always the best means for deliberation.... Matching reason to passion can often be a more effective way of representing one's constituents."[17] This vindication of immoderate, passionate speech crops up from time to time in the literature.[18] Yet such forms of "deliberation," which substitute screams and noises for reasons, is another symptom of discourse failure. More

---

[17] Gutmann and Thompson, *Democracy and Disagreement*, op. cit., p. 134.

[18] See, for example, some of the activities analyzed (and endorsed) by Michael Walzer in "Deliberation, and What Else?" in Stephen Macedo, ed., *Deliberative Politics: Essays on "Democracy and Disagreement"* (Oxford: Oxford University Press, 1999), p. 58.

often than not, emotional appeals serve the function of exaggerating the salience, and thus increasing the vividness, of an issue to the detriment of hidden, non-evident effects of a proposed policy – not to mention the nefarious role of passionate eloquence in the history of tyranny and demagoguery. Also, most of us applaud an impassioned speech not because it contributes to the *understanding* of the issue in a serious way but simply because we *antecedently* agreed with the substance of the speech.[19] Impassionate speech overrides the inner logic (section 3.1) that deliberation is supposed to activate, one that involves a disposition to change one's mind after honestly examining the opponent's reasons.

7.5. Deliberation, Participation, and Equality

Deliberation may be defended by relying on the idea of participation.[20] Participation (and deliberation as a component of it) is valuable, on this view, quite independently of political outcomes. This argument has two versions. On one view, the propensity to become involved in politics is a civic virtue, and public institutions must promote it. Citizens do not exhaust their participation in politics just by voting; they also must exchange their ideas in the political arena. On this view, the propensity to deliberate is both evidence and engine of civic virtue.

Supporters of this view will condemn, of course, the typical political careerist who primarily seeks power, money, or fame. It is obvious that there is little civic virtue in this. More interesting is the case of the citizen who genuinely wishes to improve the world by exchanging ideas with others. The deliberativist can praise this impulse, quite independently of whatever epistemic shortcomings political deliberation may have. Again, to say that this person ("the idealist") will ultimately fall prey of discourse failure would miss the point of praising as virtuous his drive to deliberate.

Thus stated, the claim is true but uninteresting. It comes very close to the truism that having a good will is good. If, however, the idealist seeks the best means to improve the world, why should he deliberate (given discourse failure), rather than, for example, acquire the knowledge necessary to identify the good policies – for example, by reading specialized books? It might be replied that it is just in human nature to seek the

---

[19] This is clear in Gutmann and Thompson's example, in which they praise a senator's passionate speech against renewing a patent for the Confederate flag. Op. cit., pp. 135–6. Surely they would not be willing to treat as a valuable form of deliberation an equally impassionate speech by a representative of the Ku Klux Klan.

[20] See, for example, Goodin, *Reflective Democracy*, op. cit., pp. 221–5.

opinions of others and to exchange ideas with them. But this aspect of human nature can be better channeled through serious and rigorous exchange of ideas with others. Yet, unfortunately, that cannot take place amidst the massive politics that characterizes modern democracies. The idealist would be better off pursuing virtue, then, if he tried to understand the problem he wishes to solve and exchange ideas with those similarly committed – something that, if we are right, should keep him *away* from most deliberative fora. Alternatively, the idealist might simply take direct action to improve the world (such as charity or community work) instead of getting together with others to discuss politics in the deficient ways that we have diagnosed.

Moreover, we disagree that involvement in politics under present conditions is a virtue. Competitive pressures in the political arena lead those involved in politics to posture, lie, and manipulate. People committed to deliberating in the manner prescribed by deliberativists will be quickly ostracized because their commitment to the truth will often clash with winning electoral tactics. If, on the other hand, they wish to win (maybe in order to do good things in government), they will engage in effective forms of discourse failure. This suggests the following generalization: The longer someone is *successfully* involved in politics, the less reason we have to think that his political discourse evinces the virtues prized by deliberativists.

The second version of the argument from participation claims that respect for persons calls for a deliberative attitude. Exchanging ideas with everyone before making collective decisions reflects equal concern for everyone. Deliberation is valuable in itself, even if it often leads to unsatisfactory outcomes. Indeed, modern democracies have been hailed as a great moral improvement over the *ancien régime* in great part because they abolished privileges and started a process of increased popular participation in political decision making. Democracy is obviously preferable to autocracy in terms of a public acknowledgment of human dignity – an acknowledgment that requires, in addition to universal franchise, a widespread deliberative disposition.

Yet it is far from obvious that deliberation *accompanied by majority rule* better realizes the value of equal respect than deliberation accompanied by other (nondictatorial) social choice rules – that is, qualified majorities or unanimity. Under any decision rule people may have freedom to exchange ideas with others, so additional argument is needed to show why majority rule is better than other rules on that score. In fact, in Chapter 9 we will argue that the kinds of incentives present in a contractarian society are likely to enhance the quality of deliberation, as compared with the low quality of deliberation that we observe under majority rule coupled with broad redistributive powers. Should the contractarian proposal be unfeasible, respect for persons may well call for both *universal franchise* and a *deliberative attitude*, but in any event deliberation would have no privileged relationship with *majority rule*. This version of the argument from participation does not lend specific support to majority rule.[21]

Characteristically, deliberative democrats propose governmental help to persons who are presumably marginalized from the political forum. Some propose that various disadvantaged groups should have access to the media to express their ideas publicly.[22] This position overlaps with those that see free speech as entailing positive, and not just negative, obligations on the part of society. On these views, the state must redress unequal opportunities for political speech that stem in part from private ownership of the media. Equal time on television for all political parties and regulations requiring that "representative positions" be equally included in political talk shows may be thought to derive from the more general idea that "expressing respect for persons...involves...seeking out their views and engaging them in discussion on the matter."[23]

Contrary to this view, we contend that discourse failure is a more fundamental source of *participatory inequality* than the lack of speech opportunities and that this suggests the need of institutional devices at variance with those advanced by deliberativists. Groups that are rarely seen as disadvantaged by deliberativists should command a greater share of the resources that society allocates to equalize political participation. Consumers and taxpayers suffer from well-known infirmities to voice their interests in the political arena. These groups are highly dispersed, and therefore each member stands to gain little from political activism aimed at blocking special-interest legislation (e.g., a specific tariff). More

---

[21] See also section 8.3. Democratic regimes are not, of course, majoritarian across the board. In paradigmatically democratic regimes, officials are chosen through procedures ranging from plurality rule to proportional representation, and decisions are taken by majorities or supra-majorities under a system of separation of powers. In the United States, for example, the composition of the Senate contravenes the principle of participation, understood here as "one person, one vote."

[22] See, for example, Christiano, *The Rule of the Many*, op. cit., pp. 88–93.

[23] Thomas Christiano, "The Significance of Public Deliberation," in James Bohman and William Rehg, *Deliberative Democracy*, op. cit., p. 252. Christiano does not address the institutional implications of the abstract duty to seek out the opinions of those affected by political decisions.

generally, the individual cost of participating in political activities may be high. As a result, political participation will be unattractive to consumers and taxpayers.[24] But this is not all. The analysis of discourse failure reveals that *theories* which tend to favor the interests of consumers and taxpayers suffer a rhetorical disadvantage in the political forum. For example, some economic theories show that protectionism decreases general welfare in the country that protects and that it redistributes resources from dispersed taxpayers toward special interests. Unfortunately, however, such theories are noticeably opaque.[25] So serious is this pathology that many consumers and taxpayers whose interests would be served by the findings of opaque theories do not themselves endorse those theories.[26]

Our view of the relationship between deliberation and equality is radically at odds with the intimations usually found in the literature. Thomas Christiano, for example, recommends enhanced deliberative procedures in order to "affect the *distribution* of the cognitive conditions of understanding among the citizens."[27] The idea is that persons with superior knowledge about factual matters and their own considered interests and values will have greater power than those who are ignorant or confused about those matters. This is certainly true, but more deliberation will often compound the problem. To see this, consider who are those endowed with superior knowledge about society and their own interests and values. Surely, vote-seeking politicians and well-organized groups[28] (henceforth, "group A") have much to gain from knowing the political means to advance their own interests and values. They internalize the benefits of learning the truth about how society works. At the other

---

[24] The asymmetry between dispersed costs and concentrated benefits goes a long way toward explaining the huge increase in tax revenue everywhere over the past hundred years. It also explains lobbying for tax *exemptions*. At a minimum, these models predict general increase in *non*-uniform taxes. On the logic of collective action underlying rent seeking, see generally Olson, *The Logic of Collective Action*, op. cit. On fiscal discrimination resulting from rent seeking, see James D. Gwartney and Richard Wagner, "Public Choice and the Conduct of Representative Government," in Gwartney and Wagner, eds., *Public Choice and Constitutional Economics*, op. cit., pp. 3–28, esp. pp. 17–25. For a survey, see Robert D. Tollison, "Rent Seeking," in Dennis C. Mueller, *Perspectives on Public Choice: A Handbook* (Cambridge: Cambridge University Press, 1997), pp. 506–25.

[25] See section 2.1. The political action of groups is hampered not only by their high organizational costs but also by the costs of apprehending and propagating opaque theories.

[26] See note 12, section 2.1.

[27] Id., p. 256.

[28] A group's investment in rent seeking is directly related to its members' individual expected gains and inversely related to its organizational costs, as explained in the literature cited in note 9, Chapter 1, and note 24, this chapter.

extreme, ordinary citizens ("group B") will tend to err in politics for the reasons we have given (see especially sections 2.2 through 2.5). The deliberativist's proposal assumes that public deliberation will help bridge the epistemic gap between groups A and B. But this is a mistake. Deliberation will allow members of group A to deepen and consolidate the mistakes made by those in group B. Members of group A benefit from knowing the extent to which those in group B will remain ignorant. One would expect them to pay pollsters and others in order to gauge public opinion. Suppose, for example, that polls identify globalization as the cause of an economic recession. Armed with this knowledge, a politician (who suspects the public to be mistaken) will make available to the public "evidence" that fits into a default vivid theory (section 2.3) and that the public will tend to endorse. Thus, they may say that the overseas manufacture by "slave labor" of tennis shoes has directly caused the closing of local tennis shoe factories. Generalizing from this observation, the ordinary citizen will mistakenly conclude that lowering the barriers to trade will increase domestic unemployment.[29] Having learned about the factory closings, the ordinary citizen will see his vivid yet mistaken beliefs (e.g., that an increase in imports increases unemployment) confirmed. Expanding deliberative practices is bound to consolidate rational ignorance and error.[30]

7.6. Is Discourse Failure Always Bad?

Discourse failure is a failure to achieve epistemic ideals. Political discourse fails because citizens advance unreliable claims. Someone may object, however, that the attainment of truth is not a paramount political goal. Philip Kitcher, for example, has argued that sometimes the search for the truth has bad effects, either on society as a whole or on vulnerable groups.[31] Seizing on this idea, the deliberativist may suggest that at least

---

[29] See supra, section 2.1. Our argument here does not turn, however, on the truth of mainstream economics on this point. It requires only that the citizen's beliefs result from a deliberative process that violates the rules of ideal deliberation. The citizen is mistaken in the sense that his beliefs do not stem from a reliable cognitive process. Such a process would surely require him to *consider* the views of mainstream economics on this matter and show why such views are wrong in order for him to be entitled to endorse the generalization indicated in the text.

[30] Our discussion of default views (section 2.3) reinforces this analysis.

[31] See Philip Kitcher, *Science, Truth, and Democracy* (New York: Oxford University Press, 2001), pp. 96–108 and 147–66. For a general defense of *lying* to sustain liberal values, see Ajume Wingo, *Veil Politics in Liberal Democratic States* (Cambridge: Cambridge University

some instances of discourse failure are not only innocuous but positively beneficial as well. He may argue that the goal of deliberation is to affirm and sustain common values and projects, and that sometimes these are better served by a public discourse that, at a minimum, does not offend anyone and, at a maximum, reinforces the public's enthusiasm for those values and projects. Sometimes this requires public endorsement of falsehoods. Imagine a state whose population is made of various national and ethnic groups. Suppose that some of those groups have a lower social and economic status, and that undercurrents of discrimination harm them in various ways. Finally, suppose that the early immigrants of those groups had bad work habits that put them, and to a considerable degree their descendants, at a disadvantage. These historical facts, let us assume, have been reliably established by scholarly work. Yet, our objector may urge citizens, and especially the government, to suppress these facts and replace them with a different story, one that attributes current inequalities to other factors, such as discrimination based on national or ethnic origin. He hopes that this false public discourse (displayed, for example, in public celebrations about the equally valuable contribution that all immigrants have made to the country) will help advance equality and counter discrimination. Even if under our definition this is discourse failure, the deliberative practices it involves are, on this view, intrinsically valuable as an expression of equal concern and respect for everyone, or at least valuable as a means to achieving social peace and self-esteem.

There are reasons to doubt this defense of discourse failure. Recall that discourse failure stems from the fact that politicians, rent seekers, and other groups stand to gain from widespread ignorance and error. So, far from promoting valuable social goals, as Kitcher's account suggests, the falsehoods that pervade public political discourse promote social outcomes that cannot be vindicated by any reasonable political theory. The public-choice literature has brought to the surface the strategies that political actors will adopt in a typical liberal democracy, and the resulting patterns of political decisions. Such decisions contravene widely held views about distributive justice. Rent seeking, and the special-interest legislation it induces, can serve as illustration. Such legislation can hardly be vindicated on egalitarian grounds, because the rich have

Press, 2003). According to Wingo, "political veils...have the ability to *hide, distort, and misrepresent*," and in liberal democracies "they serve to highlight core liberal democratic values and the core narratives of the polity." Op. cit., pp. 7–8. Gutmann and Thompson's defense of immoderate speech is also tantamount to vindicating discourse failure, as we indicated in section 7.4.

disproportionate rent-seeking power. Nor can it be vindicated on Rawls's difference principle, because special-interest legislation usually harms the worst-off. Moreover, such legislation clearly violates Lockean-Nozickean property rights, because it amounts to nonconsensual redistribution. Finally, those practices run afoul of utilitarianism: By definition, special-interest legislation does not provide public goods and so is not welfare-enhancing.[32] The kinds of cases exemplified by the foregoing discrimination story are relatively rare, as Kitcher himself concedes.[33] Our analysis suggests that in most situations, discourse failure does not serve any identifiable beneficial purpose. It is therefore hard to see what institutional devices will ensure that discourse failure will be confined to those rare cases in which it will further valuable goals.

But suppose, for the sake of argument, that, more often than not, discourse failure helps promote lofty goals. What kind of *deliberative* practices can possibly countenance such happy instances of discourse failure? Let us return to the discrimination story. Imagine a very conscientious citizen, one who is willing, at great personal expense, to enrich the deliberative practices of his society. He has internalized the value of robust deliberation to which the public culture of his community is committed, and, quite naturally, he thinks that he will best contribute to robust deliberation by finding the truth about an important public issue. He wants to make a significant contribution to citizens' understanding of the causes of the social and economic inequalities among various national and ethnic groups in his society. We may also imagine he is animated by a wish to eliminate discriminatory practices. He spends much time and resources doing the appropriate research for those purposes. After several years of inquiry, he finds out the truth (in our hypothetical, that the current underperformance of certain groups can be traced to a number of historical factors that include bad working habits and cultural features of their ancestors, and not so much to present discrimination or to differential innate abilities). He is now ready to offer his findings for consideration in the deliberative forum. What should deliberativists make of this person's contribution to public debate? It seems that, if their overriding concern is to foster equal respect to all national and ethnic groups, they are forced to conclude that this person is not contributing at all. But this seems to

---

[32] Drawing on his theory of collective action in *The Logic of Collective Action*, op. cit., Olson offers a historical case for the connection between special-interest legislation and economic decline in *The Rise and Decline of Nations*, op. cit.

[33] See Kitcher, pp. 102–3.

be a *reductio* of this version of deliberativism, because the behavior of the conscientious citizen we have imagined epitomizes, if anything does, deliberative virtue.

The deliberativist might retort that discouraging that kind of dissent (that is, well-grounded dissent with undesirable effects) need not damage healthy deliberative practices. He might invoke some accounts of scientific deliberation wherein some forms of dissent are discouraged. Thomas S. Kuhn's philosophy of science may seem to help his case. According to Kuhn, scientists take for granted certain fundamental theoretical propositions and work within the "paradigm" defined by those propositions. Sometimes they find it difficult to explain certain facts, but they take these "puzzles" as challenges to devise explanations within the paradigm. They reject explanations outside the paradigm as nonscientific.[34] The deliberativist we are imagining can treat false yet socially useful official lies as the fundamental propositions that define a scientific paradigm – in our example, the official story about the relative contributions of various national and ethnic groups. Accordingly, the historical findings of the conscientious citizen, at odds with the official story, should be treated as a puzzle to be explained within the prevailing paradigm. Deliberation about those findings will explain them away in terms consistent with the official story – for example, by questioning the authenticity of the relevant documents, or by pointing to flaws in the research design. In this way, the ideal of robust deliberation is saved: deliberation is encouraged within the limits established by the false but useful paradigm. Moreover, the ideal of equal respect is observed because the government claims no special epistemic authority in puzzle solving. On the contrary, political institutions encourage sincere efforts aimed at solving puzzles.

Nevertheless, there is an important difference between a Kuhnean paradigm and a prevailing form of discourse failure that constrains deliberation. In the former case, people sincerely uphold the paradigm, even though, unbeknownst to them, it may turn out to be inferior to an alternative paradigm. In the latter case, there is an epistemic elite, as it were, which knows that the prevailing theses are false and yet spreads them for the sake of what they believe to be higher values. This scenario conflicts with a defense of deliberation based on personal autonomy, because the public lacks the opportunity to assess all the evidence by itself. Still, the deliberativist may remain unmoved. He may give an *egalitarian* argument for constrained deliberation. Thus, in the foregoing discrimination case

---

[34] See Thomas S. Kuhn, *The Structure of Scientific Revolutions*, op. cit.

he may vindicate the concealment of historical truths on the grounds that deliberation based on certain irrevocable yet false premises is instrumental to equality. Deliberation may still be exalted as a puzzle-solving practice within the boundaries allowed by the accepted "paradigm."

But even conceding that massive social deceit is sometimes justified and that benign discourse failure is more frequent than we think it is, this defense of constrained deliberation faces an insurmountable conceptual difficulty. Theorists of deliberative democracy insist that deliberation is not to be confused with other forms of communication, such as those involved in bargaining and threats.[35] These practices share with deliberation some superficial traits: People ostensibly talk to one another, accept or reject proposals, pay attention to one another's assertions, and so forth. But, as deliberativists correctly point out, these practices lack a feature that deliberation has, namely the intention to find, together with our fellow citizens, the best reasons in support of a public policy. Deliberators see themselves as participants in a practice that serves epistemic objectives, in a broad sense that comprises the identification of the best factual and normative claims.[36] Deliberation is necessarily truth-sensitive when viewed from the standpoint of deliberators. The deliberativist we are imagining must claim, then, that *this* activity, defined by this point of view, is instrumental to equality. Conversely, the *non*-epistemic, "Kuhnean" defense of deliberation can intelligibly be asserted only by theorists like Kitcher, not by ordinary citizens, who, by hypothesis, must believe the false official story if social equality is to be promoted. It may seem that this concession is not fatal for an instrumental form of deliberativism: Deliberation, when conducted within appropriate informational constraints, is vindicated here as instrumental to a social value, such as equality. But the problem with this strategy is not that it is instrumental, or that it is instrumental to non-epistemic values, but rather that it is inconsistent. It in effect asserts that some political actors (a cultural elite) may violate deliberative requirements, such as sincerity. It is not a theory of deliberation all the way down.

The point can be made more vividly if we focus again on the conscientious dissenter. He has found on his own the information that

---

[35] See, for example, Christiano, *The Rule of the Many*, op. cit., pp. 117 and 248–53.

[36] Simon Blackburn makes the same point in relation to deliberation in the academy, *Ruling Passions*, pp. 299–300. The argument is structurally analogous to H. L. A. Hart's appeal to the "internal point of view" as a key to understanding the nature of a legal system. See *The Concept of Law* (Oxford: Clarendon Press, 1961), pp. 55–6, 79–88, 99–101, 105, 112–14, and 197.

the elite conceals from the public. From the point of view of bona fide deliberators, he is in a position to make a major contribution to public discourse. His fellow citizens should welcome his efforts to find the truth and to change, if necessary, their current views on the relative contribution of various ethnic and national groups and related issues. But the elite who had managed so far to manipulate people's beliefs will regret the dissenter's contribution, as will the non-epistemic, egalitarian "deliberativist" we are imagining. This shows why this position is not deliberativist all the way down. Not only does it claim that deliberation serves non-epistemic values; it also recommends exempting some (ironically for an egalitarian position, those strong enough to manipulate public debate) from the duty of sincerity. This problem should be especially acute for those deliberativists who prize *robust* deliberation, wherein citizens are exposed to the greatest variety of viewpoints.[37] The puzzle-solving model countenances discursive practices that cannot be recognized as deliberative.

---

[37] For a recent defense of deliberative robustness, see Sunstein, *Why Societies Need Dissent,* op. cit., esp. pp. 104–6 and 209–13.

8

Deliberation, Consent, and Majority Rule

8.1. Consent and Reasonableness

In this chapter we examine the relationships between political deliberation, consent, and majority rule. To what extent can deliberation generate consent to social policies? What is the connection between deliberation and majority rule? Some defenses of deliberative democracy rest on the idea that laws enacted after due deliberation conform to everyone's reason. Such laws reflect a reasonable consensus that, at a minimum, excludes imposing some people's will on others.[1] An obvious worry here is how to make room for voting – and thus losers – in a deliberative democracy, given that a vote normally freezes deliberation well before the ideal convergence expected by theorists of reasonable consensus.[2] On the view we want to examine now, deliberation cushions the conflict between political coercion and consent of the governed[3] – a vexed conundrum of liberal political philosophy.[4] We argue, however, that dissenters are coerced into accepting the majority's decision, and that prior

---

[1] Thus, for example, Joshua Cohen writes that "deliberation aims at rationally motivated consensus." Joshua Cohen, *Deliberation and Democratic Legitimacy*, in Alan Hamlin and Philip Pettit, *The Good Polity: Normative Analysis of the State* (Oxford: Blackwell, 1989), p. 23. For a criticism of this view, see Jeremy Waldron, *Law and Disagreement* (Oxford: Clarendon Press, 1999), pp. 91–3.

[2] See Gaus, *Contemporary Theories of Liberalism*, pp. 122–5.

[3] See Peter Singer, *Democracy and Disobedience* (Oxford: Oxford University Press, 1974), p. 50; and J. Jenkins, "Political Consent," *Philosophical Quarterly*, Vol. 1, 1970, pp. 60–6.

[4] The very consistency of the notion of government by consent has been debated for centuries. See John Plamenatz, *Consent, Freedom, and Political Obligation* (New York: Oxford University Press, 1968).

deliberation does nothing to justify that sort of coercion. We also examine the obscure relationship that deliberation bears with majority rule in the theories defended by deliberativists and conclude that the encouragement to deliberate presupposes unnecessarily coercive politics, given more consensual alternatives.

How can deliberation expand the consensual basis of laws and policies? Some writers argue that appropriate deliberation helps citizens realize that there are several reasonable *and* mutually incompatible views on an issue.[5] Thus, Gutmann and Thompson hope that deliberative processes animated by the values of reciprocity, publicity, and accountability will incline citizens toward the adoption of viewpoints and policies that everyone will regard *as reasonable.*[6] In a similar vein, Elster says that deliberation may help citizens converge on reasonable viewpoints because it seems conceptually impossible to express selfish arguments in a debate about what *the public good* requires. He further contends that it is psychologically impossible to express other-regarding preferences (as required by the rules governing proper deliberation) "without ultimately coming to acquire them."[7]

Selfish arguments are certainly out of place in debates about the public good because appealing to one's own interests as an *ultimate* consideration is irrelevant to determining what the public good requires. Still, anyone can disguise self-interest with public-spirited rhetoric, and this is compatible with excluding self-interested arguments from the public forum. The theory of discourse failure points to several ways in which simulation may succeed. Consider how easy it is for special interests to hide the social costs of the policies they support. It may seem that Elster's remark (that expressing other-regarding preferences makes people acquire those preferences) defuses the worry about self-serving appeals to the public interest: People who have acquired other-regarding preferences will obviously not be motivated to disguise personal advantage as common advantage. We cannot properly assess this thesis without pertinent psychological research, but it is certainly wrong when applied to professional politicians, lobbyists, and other political careerists. They build their entire careers on their ability to mask self-interest with sanctimonious public-spirited

---

[5] See references in note 1, Chapter 6.

[6] See Gutmann and Thompson, *Democracy and Disagreement*, op. cit., pp. 52–7.

[7] Jon Elster, "The Market and the Forum: Three Varieties of Political Theory," op. cit., p. 12. Joshua Cohen defends the psychological thesis in "Deliberation and Democratic Legitimacy," in Elster and Aanund, eds., op. cit., pp. 76–7, originally published in Alan Hamlin and Phillip Pettit, eds., *The Good Polity*, op. cit., pp. 17–34.

rhetoric. Moreover, social pressures to express other-regarding reasons will likely lead political actors, including many ordinary citizens, to refine their concealment techniques, rather than acquire other-regarding preferences.

Let us assume, however, that deliberation takes place under institutions that effectively screen out unreasonable positions, *and* that citizens believe that this is the case. Citizens would then regard the deliberation's outcome, however this is identified, as reasonable. Because not all parties will accept the same viewpoint, the argument from reasonable consensus must downplay the distinction between accepting a viewpoint and believing that a viewpoint is reasonable. On this view, consensus on a viewpoint may be reached even among citizens who reject that viewpoint, provided that they find it reasonable. So, the argument from reasonable consensus must assume something along the following lines:

(a) Citizens regard a viewpoint as reasonable if, and only if, they believe that it can be given a plausible defense.
(b) Citizens may reject viewpoints that they regard as reasonable.
(c) If citizens regard as reasonable a viewpoint (and the policies, laws, etc. based upon it), then they have reached a reasonable consensus on the policies, laws, etc. grounded on that viewpoint.[8]

Admittedly, (a) is vague because it does not specify what a "plausible defense" is. We can nevertheless dispense with the specification, because, as we shall shortly see, the argument from reasonable consensus would founder even if we had a precise understanding of plausibility.[9] Item (b) captures a common fact of experience: We often reject reasonable positions. Philosophers, for example, often reject views supported by plausible or even masterly arguments. Vexed philosophical problems (e.g., whether there are external objects, how mind relates to body) are not problems about which philosophers remain agnostic or hesitant. Thus, we find firmly convinced realists and phenomenalists in epistemology, and firmly convinced dualists and materialists in the philosophy of mind.

---

[8] Rawls's insistence that "overlapping consensus" encompasses only *reasonable* "comprehensive doctrines" suggests that he endorses (c). See *Political Liberalism*, p. 144. Likewise, Gutmann and Thompson argue that "reciprocity" (which they view as constitutive of genuine deliberation) requires *mutually acceptable* moral reasoning and reliable methods of empirical inquiry. These authors accordingly stress the role of reciprocity in fostering "agreement." See Gutmann and Thompson, *Democracy and Disagreement*, pp. 252–94.

[9] In the next paragraph, however, we offer the beginnings of a characterization of "reasonableness."

Typically, however, those persuaded of one view think it worthwhile to *keep exploring* possible defenses of opposite views. They see rejection as provisional and typically feel pressures toward further probing into rejected views. The proposition (c) is, of course, the key claim in this attempt to show that deliberative democracy fosters consensus.

Let us say that a view is *reasonable* when it is worth exploring, even after rejection. It is common for good scholars to regard rival views as reasonable, as witnessed by the great pains they sometimes take to scrutinize the other side. They sincerely attempt to reinforce as much as possible the views they reject, exploring reformulations, possible weaknesses in their own views, and so on. Similarly, citizens who voted against a policy may agree that it rests on reasonable grounds. It is crucial for the argument from reasonable consensus to claim that deliberation, by making our opponents aware of our reasons for supporting a policy, increases the likelihood that they will end up regarding it as reasonable.

We can now see how deliberativists can be led to hold (c), the claim that perceived reasonableness amounts to consensus. When I reject a policy (law, decree, etc.), I have one of two objections against it: that it is unreasonable or that it is reasonable yet, on inspection, unacceptable. In the latter case, I have to inspect the view because, being reasonable, it is supported by plausible arguments. The result of the inspection may have been negative so far. Stronger arguments may have tipped the balance against the policy. But the fact that the policy is reasonable prevents me from rejecting it irrevocably. Because I may revise my rejection of a view that I regard as reasonable, there is some tension between saying that I am *coerced into* doing certain things and saying that I find it reasonable to do such things. Consider the following dyad:

(i) *A* is coerced into doing *X*.
(ii) *A* believes that he may have a reason to do *X*.

The argument from reasonable consensus needs to assume that (ii) undermines (i). The idea is that the more strongly an agent believes that he should do *X*, the less strongly will he be coerced into doing *X*.[10] So, the argument goes, in a deliberative democracy, minorities are mildly coerced, as it were, into abiding by majorities' dictates. This is so because

---

[10] We could have stated the argument from consent more precisely by stipulating thresholds of strength of the reasons underlying a viewpoint for it to qualify as plausible (or reasonable). Because nothing turns on introducing such precision, we prefer the less cumbersome formulation in the text.

deliberation filters out unreasonable viewpoints, so everyone ideally ends up recognizing that the arguments supporting majoritarian policies are plausible. Deliberation enhances, to various degrees, the reasonableness of a political proposal in the eyes of those who reject it. Deliberation reconciles coercion with consensus.

Unfortunately for this argument, whether or not B coerces A into doing X is independent of how reasonable A views his doing X. Someone is being coerced into doing something whenever his decision not to do it is changed by another's threat.[11] I am coerced into doing A regardless of the strength of the independent reasons I might have had to perform A. A strong reason to betray my wife (my love for another woman, for example) does not *in the least* render less coercive a gangster's threat to kill my son unless I betray my wife. Or consider date rape: The fact that the woman is attracted to her date makes no difference to the question of whether she was coerced into sexual intercourse. Coercion may well be an all-or-nothing concept.

The argument from reasonable consensus assumes that the coerced person has no inclination whatsoever to perform the coerced act. But this is false: I may be inclined to punch Joe in the nose yet have decided not to do it. I will still be coerced into punching Joe, against my own decision, if threatened by your gun to my head. This is true even if I enjoy punching Joe in the nose. Admittedly, my opposition to doing X will weaken as the strength of my reasons for doing X increases, other things being equal. The stronger my reasons to do X vis-à-vis my reasons to refrain from doing X, the less I will regret to be coerced into doing X. The word "regret" is here important. It involves a comparative assessment of the values that I attach to the alternatives. But the fact that my opposition to doing X is weak is entirely compatible with my being coerced into doing X.[12] I may have decided not to do X even though the decision was close. A balance of reasons generates in me a disposition to behave in a certain way, and correlatively a disposition not to act in other ways. These dispositions

---

[11] Some authors require that the threat be illegitimate (typically, because it threatens violation of the addressee's rights) for it to be a case of coercion. Thus, we want to condemn "money or life" robbery but not other kinds of threats that intuitively do not violate rights. For an argument along these lines, see Robert Nozick, *Anarchy, State, and Utopia*, op. cit., pp 262–5. In the present context, however, we can drop the illegitimacy requirement without weakening the point we are making – namely, that coercion (understood as a credible threat) changes the agent's decision.

[12] Whether one can possibly be coerced into doing things one was already willing to do is a matter of linguistic convention. Nothing in our argument turns on taking sides in this issue.

may be more or less strong, depending on the balance of reasons. By contrast, coercion works normally as an all-or-nothing concept: Either I am coerced into doing something or I am not. More important for present purposes, I can be coerced into doing things that the balance of reasons is *slightly* tipped against. If a gunman threatens to kill me unless I give him five dollars, I am still being coerced even if I was only slightly disinclined to give him the money in the first place.

We can now see why the thesis that in a deliberative democracy minorities are mildly coerced is mistaken. Even if we concede that deliberation selects reasonable viewpoints, the claim that minorities *voluntarily* (i.e., without coercion) abide by majoritarian decisions is unwarranted. At best, deliberative processes will get minorities to mildly *oppose* majoritarian policies. Majoritarian policies may look more or less reasonable to the minority. Still, the fact that the minority nonvoluntarily abides by such laws admits of no degrees. The state still sends the police to those who refuse compliance.

Can the deliberativist protest that saying that deliberative democracy is coercive is a purely verbal move? Can he say that all he means is that political coercion is more acceptable when people mildly oppose it? He might concede that minorities do not voluntarily abide by majorities' decisions but insist that the coercion involved here is less objectionable because of the mildness of the opposition. We have been assuming, for the sake of argument, that deliberative democracy selects policies on grounds that minorities acknowledge as reasonable. If losers acknowledge the reasonableness of the democratic outcome, they will be less opposed to it. On this view, politics does embody social coercion, but deliberation makes coercion more acceptable to political minorities because it reduces the strength of their opposition. Isn't this fact enough to show that we ought to promote deliberation?

Not so. The mild-opposition argument faces insurmountable obstacles. If discourse failure is as widespread as we argued, citizens will not converge on *objectively* reasonable viewpoints, even though they themselves believe their positions to be reasonable. Imagine someone arguing that the United States should withdraw from NAFTA because "it causes a loss of American jobs." Imagine, further, a NAFTA supporter replying, "The loss of jobs is more than offset by new jobs in export industries and by consumer gains." Let us grant that, as a result of deliberation, each deliberator will end up believing that the position of the other is reasonable. Yet the grounds offered by the NAFTA opponent in this example are unreasonable: Given the *status quaestionis* in reliable economic theory,[13] his argument is not worth exploring. The disagreement here is not like, say, those between Rawlsians and utilitarians or between reliable positions on the effects of the minimum wage on employment.[14] It follows not only that the protectionist is mistaken but also that the free trader's belief in the reasonableness of the protectionist position is mistaken as well. But then, should protectionism earn majoritarian support, the losing minority would *not* be *consenting*, even mildly, to the policies enacted by the majority.[15] This is so because error vitiates consent. Discourse failure not only dooms the prospects of approaching the truth through political deliberation but also excludes the sort of consent that is central to the argument we are examining. It is commonplace in normative theories of consent (as embodied, for example, in the law of contracts) that certain types of error, along with fraud and duress, vitiate consent.[16] So there should be, after all, a liberal worry here – how deliberative democracy is supposed to fit properly in a recognizably liberal political morality – that is, a morality that embraces the ideal of government by consent?

As we have seen, the idea that deliberation makes losing minorities accept democratic outcomes tries to reconcile majority rule with reasonable consensus. We now see, however, that the deliberativist cannot invoke this reasonable consensus to mount a liberal case for deliberation (a case wherein the ideal of government by consent is central), and that in any event epistemic considerations are fatal to the claim that majority rule leads to reasonable consensus when preceded by deliberation. Indeed, the argument in this section also reaches even appeals to freedom that cannot easily fit classical forms of liberalism. Some writers argue that an appropriate conception of freedom should allow us to say that we can be made free by being coerced into doing certain things. Central to these arguments is a notion of the agent's genuine will, autonomy, or positive freedom, possessed by her higher self, in contrast with the first-order desires of her lower self.[17] Coercion liberates the will from the ignoble

---

[13] See section 2.1.

[14] We briefly review the current literature on minimum wages and employment in section 6.9. We characterize reliable social science in section 4.1.

[15] We will see in section 8.4 that it is often problematic to say that even majorities consent to the policies they vote for.

[16] Surely, the high opportunity costs for the average voter of becoming aware of even elementary propositions of reliable social science render such errors excusable. For fuller treatment, see section 4.6.

[17] A classical source is Rousseau, *Du Contrat Social*, Book 4, Chap. 2. See also the discussion of the attempt to reconcile freedom with coercion in Isaiah Berlin, "Two Concepts of

impulses of the lower self, so that genuine freedom can be realized. For present purposes, we do not have to address this line of argument. We just point out that it is unavailable to the deliberativist who values reasonable consensus (as something different from sheer bargaining). No genuine will can be formed through a process that involves systematic error. So, even if *coercion* could be reconciled with freedom by enabling the citizen to follow the dictates of her higher self, *deliberation* will misrepresent those dictates.

8.2. Deliberation, Justice, and Rights

Even if we assume that citizens' propensity to compromise is an essential feature of ideal political deliberation, difficulties remain. Compromise can yield unjust outcomes. As Jon Elster observes, "a little discussion can be a dangerous thing, worse in fact than no discussion at all."[18] To see this, consider the following case:

Once upon a time two boys found a cake. One of them said, "Splendid! I will eat the cake." The other one said, "No, that is not fair! We found the cake together, and we should share and share alike, half for you and half for me." The first boy said, "No, I should have the whole cake!" Along came an adult who said, "Gentlemen, you shouldn't fight about this: you should *compromise*. Give him [the boy who claims the whole cake] three quarters of the cake."[19]

Elster notes that the outcome resulting from the decision procedure that the adult suggested to the boys "is socially inferior to that which would have emerged had they both stuck to their selfish preferences."[20] More deliberation may detract from justice: Staking selfish claims would have led to a better result.

The deliberativist might reply that the compromise suggested to the boys amounts to exploitation of the unselfish boy by the selfish boy, and that, to that extent, it is ruled out by any attractive conception of deliberation. Indeed, deliberativists may take this case to illustrate their belief that

Liberty," in his *Four Essays on Liberty* (New York: Oxford University Press, 1969); Spector, *Autonomy and Rights*, op. cit., pp. 12–22; and Charles Taylor, "What Is Wrong with Negative Liberty?," in Alan Ryan, ed., *The Idea of Freedom: Essays in Honour of Isaiah Berlin* (Oxford: Oxford University Press, 1979).

[18] Elster, "The Market and the Forum: Three Varieties of Political Theory," op. cit., p. 14.
[19] R. Smullyan, *This Book Needs No Title* (Englewood Cliffs, N.J.: Prentice-Hall, 1980), cit. by Elster, op. cit., p. 15.
[20] Ibid.

a presumption of equality should constrain proper deliberation.[21] The reason why in the cake example bargaining is better than compromise is that bargaining over unowned things is, in this example, tantamount to distributing things under a presumption of equality.

This response, however, removes much practical significance from the deliberative model. If the deliberative pathologies we have identified in this book are ineradicable, theories of deliberative democracy must be understood as regulative ideals, goals that we ought to approach as much as possible.[22] Yet, how can we be confident that such an approximation to ideal deliberation, *short of full realization*, will not promote forms of exploitation akin to those we noticed in the cake example? Deliberative democrats typically want to neutralize inequalities that either hinder proper deliberation (by, for example, raising the costs of political participation for certain groups) or distort it (by, for example, allowing the rich to be overrepresented in the media). But why would partial improvements on real-world deliberation display *lesser* hindrances to, or distortions of, deliberation than in the cake example? After all, the cake example assumes an initial equality in property rights (neither boy has differential property rights), something lacking in actual democracies. Moreover, in the cake example the boys know all the relevant facts, whereas (as we saw in sections 2.1 through 2.5) in actual political deliberation special-interest proposals will have discursive advantages in a world of rationally ignorant citizens – an outcome that can hardly be vindicated on egalitarian grounds. It seems safe to conclude that attempts to improve on current deliberative practices often will not promote justice. Compromising will not neutralize the deficiencies of opposing claims. These deficiencies were fueled in turn by earlier rounds of deliberation that, through discourse failure, gave those claims rhetorical advantages. Like the selfish boy, those who benefit from discourse failure enter deliberation with objectionable advantages.

Deliberativists sometimes argue for a more modest role for deliberation. They suggest, for example, that we have a duty to seek out the opinions of those whose lives would be affected by our decisions. Failure to do so would be unjust, because "the person who has no say is likely to have his interests neglected."[23] Those who will be affected by the decisions of

---

[21] For the place of equality in deliberation, see, for example Bohman, *Public Deliberation*, op. cit., chapter 3, and Christiano, *The Rule of the Many*, op. cit., pp. 91–3.

[22] We addressed defenses of deliberation as a regulative ideal in section 4.6.

[23] Christiano, op. cit., p. 253.

others have a right to be heard. The hope is that robust deliberation will induce the decision maker to take seriously into account how his decisions will affect others. But is deliberation the best method for registering how our decisions affect others? A system of exhaustive and well-defined private property rights demonstrably internalizes all externalities, including those that worry the deliberativist.[24] Conferring enforceable rights is surely a better way to protect people's interests than merely giving them a say in decisions that might affect them. As we expand the areas of social life governed by private-property rights, we correspondingly reduce the areas of social life subject to majority rule. There is an insurmountable tension between the consensus-based ground for deliberation and majoritarian politics. Admittedly, at first blush a well-defined system of property rights cannot accommodate those who prefer to live under a different system of property rights. Whether this is so, and to what extent, are questions we leave for Chapter 9.

8.3. Deliberation and Majority Rule

How does majority rule make its entrance in theories of deliberative *democracy*? Those theories aspire to improve on traditional views of constitutional democracy, where the majority can enact various kinds of public policies as long as it respects rights. In those traditional versions of constitutional democracy, winning majorities do not really have to justify public policies to losing minorities, as long as those policies respect rights. It is just a matter of gathering votes, forming alliances, and so forth. Deliberativists reject this practice because it eschews civic deliberation. They see deliberation as a way to enhance the legitimacy of democratic decisions by allowing citizens to reason with one another about the merits of their respective views. Political deliberation, for them, enriches the democratic process.

Deliberativists, then, are careful to distance themselves from sheer majoritarianism. They do not want to appear as endorsing majority will *tout court*. They want to exclude two possibilities. First, majoritarian decisions that were not preceded by appropriate deliberation lack full

---

[24] See Demsetz, op. cit.; Garrett Hardin, "The Tragedy of the Commons," *Science* 162, 1968, pp. 1243–8; Robert C. Ellickson, *Order without Law: How Neighbors Settle Disputes* (Cambridge, Mass.: Harvard University Press, 1991); David Schmidtz, *The Limits of Government: An Essay on the Public Goods Argument* (Boulder, Colo.: Westview Press, 1991), pp. 15–32; and Michael Heller, "The Tragedy of the Anticommons: Property in the Transition from Marx to Markets," *Harvard Law Review*, Vol. 111 (1996), p. 621.

legitimacy. Thus, political deliberation must be public, officials should be accountable, and everyone must have had fair chances of being heard by others. Second, certain outcomes ought to be beyond the reach of majorities if the conditions that make deliberation possible are to be preserved. A majoritarian decision that gravely impinges on basic human rights is illegitimate even if the deliberation was conducted in the appropriate manner.[25] This view is consistent with the claim that deliberation has a role in creating new, less momentous rights or in clarifying their scope (or, for that matter, the scope of basic human rights themselves). But at some point citizens have to vote, whether or not they have observed the procedural and substantive constraints just indicated. While the connections between deliberation and the adoption of binding policies by majority rule are, as we will see, obscure, deliberativists invariably presuppose that majority rule is in place. Majority rule, and not the merits of the arguments presented, dictates the political decision. Can the theory of deliberative democracy provide a unified account of deliberation and (constrained) majority rule?

One might think that deliberativists can criticize as unjust a decision adopted by majority rule. They may treat proper deliberation as a necessary but not a sufficient condition for political legitimacy. The argument requires only one abstract guiding idea in institutional design, such as the idea of equal concern and respect. This idea grounds the selection both of a certain process of deliberation and majority rule. Majority rule might lead to outcomes inconsistent with the idea of equal concern and respect, such as a discriminatory law. If so, the guiding idea, and not the process, prevails. The law ought to be struck down.

It is unclear, however, how exactly the deliberative process connects with majority rule in this argument. One can endorse deliberation without endorsing majority rule. Deliberation may be intrinsically desirable. For example, deliberation may help realize the ideal of equal concern and respect; it may give us an opportunity for persuasion by exposing others to the reasons given by those with whom they disagree; and it may reflect our nature as creatures capable of rational argument. However, these reasons are consistent with adopting *unanimity* rule, a three-fourth majority rule, or any other voting rule short of dictatorial ones. Adoption of simple majority rule does not obviously follow from whatever merits attach to deliberation.

[25] See section 8.6.

Some writers have said that unanimity rule and other supra-majoritarian rules ought to be rejected because they are biased toward the status quo.[26] But this position trades on the negative connotations in the idea of preserving the status quo. We can just as plausibly characterize the unanimity rule as embodying consensus – a term enjoying a better press than "privileging the status quo." Similarly, describing majority rule as an opportunity for majorities to enroll minorities in the majority project, or to steal from powerless minorities, might lead us to dismiss majority rule. In both cases, the dismissal would be too quick.

We can, of course, imagine a status quo that is unattractive as a baseline for the operation of the unanimity rule. But the status quo is not always objectionable. If the status quo is unjust, we should indeed favor a rule that allows change. But if the status quo is just, we should prefer a more conservative rule. The selection of a status quo depends on general views about justice. We can say, for example, that the status quo is unjust because it fails to work for the benefit of the worst-off.[27] The deliberative democrat might wish to require that the justice of the status quo *itself* be determined by deliberation. But this is an obscure requirement. "To be determined by deliberation" cannot mean something like "to be unanimously agreed upon after appropriate deliberation" without committing the deliberativist to the very status quo she is suspicious about. And, of course, the less stringent the required majority, the less authoritative the status quo will be *whatever* people did to be in the position they occupy in it. In real-world status quos, people have valid claims on resources, on any plausible theory of distributive justice. People have made differential productive efforts, or freely gave birthday presents to others, and so forth, in exercise of whatever property rights a just (egalitarian, libertarian, etc.) distribution conferred on them.[28] Moreover, "the outcome of deliberation" typically comprises a variety of mutually inconsistent viewpoints.[29] Hence, we cannot dispense with normative judgments that lie *outside deliberation* if we want to identify and evaluate the result of deliberative processes and choose the optimal rule of social decision.

[26] See Carlos Santiago Nino, *The Constitution of Deliberative Democracy*, op. cit., pp. 117–19.

[27] This is, of course, at the heart of Rawls's difference principle. See *A Theory of Justice*, op. cit., pp. 53 and 57–65.

[28] See Nozick, *Anarchy, State, and Utopia*, op. cit., pp. 198 and 219–20; and Loren Lomasky, *Persons, Rights, and the Moral Community* (New York: Oxford University Press, 1987), pp. 132–5.

[29] We expand on this in the next section.

Is there another way to establish a privileged connection between deliberation and simple majority rule? The ideal of equal participation is of no avail here. In terms of equal participation alone, majority rule is no better than other rules for collective decision making. Equal participation requires universal franchise, which underlies all nondictatorial social choice rules, from simple majority to unanimity.

Perhaps the fact that deliberative democrats tend to remain silent on the precise nature of the connection between majority rule and deliberation is not fatal to their main enterprise. They may stress the importance of deliberation in a good polity, while assuming that a standard feature of it is majority rule. On this view, deliberation may be flawed, but, given majority rule, it is still better for citizens to deliberate than not to do it. But why? If the claim here is that deliberation is *valuable*, in a sense of "valuable" that lacks practical implications, it is, we think, dubious. We can easily imagine that rain is valuable for a farmer, even if he is impotent to bring it about. The same for negative value: A drought has negative value for the farmer, even if he cannot stop it. Political deliberation has, if we are right, negative social value, even if its pathologies are ineradicable. If, on the other hand, the claim that deliberation is valuable is geared toward practical proposals, we have at least two recommendations. First, the expansion of *existing* deliberative fora and the creation of new ones *under current institutional constraints* should be discouraged. More deliberation would just provide further opportunities to those who already benefit from discourse failure, including the politicians in charge of implementing those measures. The fact that discourse failure is, at its core, a mutual interaction between the posturing of many politically active citizens and the rational error of the rest makes it likely that adverse selection will plague deliberative fora: Posturers will disproportionately make them up. Second, citizens genuinely interested in quality deliberation should join groups that observe rules for serious deliberation. The hopes of expanding these genuine deliberative practices to the population at large are, unfortunately, dim.

Another way to make this point is to recall that, on the one hand, citizens' ignorance and, on the other, politicians' and other political actors' posturing are mutually reinforcing.[30] Citizens' ignorance is ineradicable because it rests on the fact that the individual citizen's vote is nondecisive to the political outcome. (Recall that various proposed shortcuts to the acquisition of accurate political information are bound to fail.

---

[30] See especially section 2.3. Here ignorance includes error.

See section 4.4.) Moreover, posturing is the natural response of those who stand to gain from widespread ignorance. Thus, we would expect a higher incidence of posturing among vote-seeking politicians, rent seekers who need the approval of majorities for special-interest legislation, and citizens who advance their reputations or material gains by communicating to the relevant circles that they stand on the "right" side of sensitive political issues. These agents, unlike the voter *qua* voter, internalize the benefits of their political activities. The interaction between ignorance and posturing is unavoidable as long as (i) the citizens' decisions to become well informed have no significant impact on policies, (ii) public beliefs about society significantly diverge from the most reliable views, and (iii) the state wields wide redistributive powers, and so is in a position to affect individuals in many and changing ways. The pathologies spawned by the combination of these three factors cannot be eradicated within the framework of deliberative democracy. The only way to alleviate the problem is to abandon majority rule in favor of a supermajority rule or otherwise curtail governmental redistributive powers. We will see in Chapter 9 how citizens can form societies free of discourse failure in ways that best realize both the liberal concern for consensual politics and the deliberativist concern for enhanced deliberative practices.

8.4. Vote Indeterminacy

Given certain configurations of preferences in the electorate, majority rule yields indeterminate outcomes. This phenomenon is reflected in the so-called *voting paradoxes*.[31] The idea is that voters will reach, through majority rule, different outcomes, depending on the order in which the options were presented to them. Those who set the electoral agenda, then, can in effect control the electoral outcome. This is well known. But there is another kind of indeterminacy: Electoral outcomes may vary with alternative ways of framing the question submitted to the vote. Even if the agenda-setting problem could in practice be satisfactorily solved,[32] deliberativists cannot simply say that majority rule leads to the most acceptable political outcome, for outcomes are indeterminate in the following way: Suppose that, in the aftermath of a terrible terrorist attack,

---

[31] See, for example, Alan M. Feldman, *Welfare Economics and Social Choice Theory* (Boston: Martinus Nijhoff, 1980), pp. 162–4.
[32] See Cooter, *The Strategic Constitution*, op. cit., pp. 43–46.

voters are asked to approve a financial package to fight terrorism over-seas. Suppose also that this policy will result in increased anti-American sentiments worldwide, which in turn will make more organizations willing to finance anti-American terrorism in the United States. Alternatively, we may suppose that the proposed policy, while overall effective in fighting terrorism, will detract funding for health care, education, or other goals valued by many citizens. There is no guarantee that those who would vote for the policy as presented would still do so if those costs became transparent. What is the electorate *doing*, then? Is it accepting the increase in anti-Americanism and increased terrorism in the United States, or the cuts in social programs, for the sake of fighting terrorism overseas? Or should we say, rather, that they were misled into thinking that fighting terrorism would not carry such bad consequences? Because voters are likely to change their votes should they become aware of relevant consequences of adopting a proposal, majoritarian outcomes will vary with the ways in which the issues submitted to the vote are framed.

Vote framing has an important corollary for democratic theory. A political proposal involves a number of causal consequences that the public will often have trouble detecting. If so, the proposal to which voters are presumably consenting is indeterminate, especially when they are unaware of those consequences. If consent means anything close to binding consent (as in the law of contracts), citizens are seldom consenting to the policies they vote for. Discourse failure is also a failure of consent. The incentive to err and lie in politics betrays the ideal of democracy and, more generally, the ideal of government by consent.

Someone may protest that the requirements we impose on genuine majoritarian consent (e.g., approval of proposals with full disclosure of consequences) overlook the role of civic deliberation. In a free-speech environment, everyone has opportunities to supply information about the relevant consequences of the proposed policies. Citizens will in turn autonomously evaluate the evidence for and against the policies. The objector does not disagree with our insistence that consent be appropriately informed. He simply claims that citizens should determine, by their own lights, what the relevant consequences are. In this way, opacity becomes innocuous. Deliberative democracy is about enabling citizens to fill the gaps in political proposals. This reply attempts to circumvent, then, the epistemic critique of deliberative democracy based on the theory of discourse failure. The deliberativist is now using a non-epistemic notion, *autonomous* balance of reasons, to steer the debate away from concerns about the accuracy of citizens' beliefs about society. Autonomous balance of reasons is, in this view, the mark of the kind of consent that matters for the legitimacy of a social order.

This reply faces several difficulties. First, as we observed in section 8.1, discourse failure might vitiate to some degree citizens' consent given through the vote. To be morally significant, consent has to meet certain epistemic conditions. This idea is at work in the law of contracts, where certain informational deficiencies void a contract for lack of consent. The theory of discourse failure casts serious doubts on the validity of citizens' consent in typical democracies, because it underscores serious epistemic deficiencies in political discourse. Epistemic deficiencies are relevant to the moral dimension of consent. It is hard to see how an autonomous balance of reasons can have moral authority if the only available reasons are vitiated by discourse failure.

Second, my consent to an action is morally relevant when that action affects *my* interests or rights. My consenting to behavior that affects *your* interests or rights is either irrelevant or unintelligible (unless, say, you are a child and I am your parent). But democratic vote in a redistributive setting does not express consent in this sense. Because democratic vote is directed toward the adoption of socially binding policies (that is, toward the use of state coercion), it is consent, if at all, to a course of behavior that affects the rights or interests of *other autonomous agents*. The electorate ("the people") is not a super-being capable of consenting. (Voting for a policy that generates losses to the defeated minority is not like my consenting to the doctor's amputating *my* right arm to save *my* life.[33])

Third, respect for autonomy requires that citizens not only be able to strike their own balance of reasons for and against a political proposal but also that they be able to *frame* political proposals in accordance with their considered judgments about the relevance of various political dimensions. Take a particularly important question such as, "Should *A*, rather than *B*, be elected president?" In the usual context of wide redistributive powers, that question is highly opaque with respect to the specific policies citizens are consenting to by voting for either candidate. The

---

[33] Nozick alerts against the tendency in utilitarian ethics to personify social entities. We are making here a similar point against the tendency to personify electorates. See Nozick, *Anarchy, State, and Utopia*, op. cit., pp. 32–3. For an analogous line of reasoning in the critique of state sovereignty, see Fernando R. Tesón, *Humanitarian Intervention: An Inquiry into Law and Morality*, third ed. (Ardsley, N.Y.: Transnational Publishers, 2005), chapter 3.

deliberativist, as we have seen, would rest content with enabling citizens to reach a considered answer to that question. He will insist that they simply balance the reasons for and against either candidate. Opacity is here the price of autonomy. However, if we are concerned with autonomy, the requirement that citizens weigh solely the merits of the candidates does not go far enough. Why not enhance citizens' autonomy by enabling them to decide what *kinds of questions* will be submitted to their vote? The argument from autonomy takes for granted governmental institutions with broad redistributive powers – a setting in which the questions presented to the electorate are notoriously indeterminate with respect to political contents that matter to most citizens. Yet autonomy presumably requires that citizens choose among options formulated in ways that matter to them. One way to do this, which we will discuss in Chapter 9, is to allow citizens to choose among voluntary communities that differ, inter alia, in their ways of *framing* the political proposals submitted to the electorate. Some citizens may believe, for example, that the question "Should *A* or *B* be elected president?" is the wrong one. They may prefer to be asked whether, say, a certain tax should be levied to finance a social program. Others may prefer to be asked whether they wish to contribute to the program on condition that enough people contribute. Our point is that a wholehearted endorsement of autonomy should enable citizens to select among different institutional designs. If that is the choice, the relevant questions will be different.

We end this section with a caveat. Political deliberation is largely sterile (if not harmful) because it takes place in the electoral context. We do not denigrate deliberation generally.[34] Of course, deliberation is plagued with discourse failure in non-electoral contexts as well: Recall, for example (section 2.6), our remarks about posturing and other truth-insensitive communicative attitudes in the academic world. But the problem is compounded when deliberation takes place with a view to a binding vote, because electoral politics places a premium on persuasive, truth-insensitive strategies. These in turn reinforce, through the processes already explained, widespread beliefs that are already affected by discourse failure. For these reasons, the idea, popular among political theorists, that the shortcomings of democracy can be overcome, at least in part, by having a robust debate preceding a binding vote is open to serious doubt.

---

[34] We have nothing to add to the standard reasons why it would be disastrous to establish censorship, even if intended to eliminate discourse failure. See section 4.5.

8.5. The Courtroom Analogy

Some writers have suggested that deliberation is valuable for reasons akin to those that make the judicial process valuable.[35] The analogy is instructive because it gives us opportunity to further discuss the roles of truth, impartiality, consent, and sincerity in deliberation. Concededly, in a lawsuit, the parties' arguments do not track the truth except incidentally: They want to win, not to seek the truth. To that extent, they will engage in discourse failure. A prosecutor's career may depend on the number of convictions he secures. Lawyers are contractually bound to try to persuade courts that the law is on their client's side. Yet, a well-designed judicial process will take advantage of the biases of both parties and help the truth prevail. It makes sense to say that a process is epistemically reliable despite its components' being epistemically unreliable.[36] Deliberative theorists might try to construct a parallel argument for the democratic process. In an appropriate institutional setting, discourse failure can, they might say, spread political truth or make political outcomes valuable. To be sure, the judge has no clear analogue in democratic politics, where no independent authority is expected to transform unreliable deliberative inputs (e.g., presidential campaigns) into reliable outputs (an enlightened public opinion). But this is precisely the challenge that the deliberativists we are imagining purport to meet. They propose institutional frameworks that will make discourse failure work for lofty goals. In the judicial process, the rules of evidence and other procedural restrictions force the parties to supply facts and arguments that help the judge, whose impartiality is in turn ensured by appropriate rules, make a sound decision. Similarly, even though in a deliberative democracy many people commit discourse failure, appropriate rules for political debate and decision making may ensure sound political outcomes. The parliamentary rules of order may be an example, but one may think of additional, or different, constraints to make the multifarious interests and views in a modern democracy converge toward political literacy. Some deliberativists, for example, suggest that the state should adopt measures to remedy the inequality in the possibilities of

---

[35] See, for example, Gutmann and Thompson, *Democracy and Disagreement*, op. cit., p. 45 (challenging "the contrast between the principled decision making of courts and the prudential lawmaking of legislatures"). For a critique of the analogy, see Christopher Schroeder, "The Law of Politics: Deliberative Democracy's Attempt to Turn Politics into Law," *Law and Contemporary Problems*, Vol. 65 (2002), p. 95.

[36] See Nozick, *Invariances*, op. cit., pp. 94–5.

public expression of views.[37] Alternatively, deliberativists might simply trust the ability of a free press to spontaneously perform the screening functions they cherish.

The courtroom analogy may also serve the purpose of justifying coercion against those who are outvoted in the democratic process.[38] Liberal views of society presume that coercion has to be reasonably justified. The deliberativist position we are now examining attempts to rebut the presumption against coercion by resorting to the idea of fair hearing. The losing minority cannot claim that coercion against them is unjustified if they have been given a fair hearing. In criminal cases, for example, prosecutors must make compelling cases (indeed, they must prove them beyond a reasonable doubt). The defendant, in turn, has many opportunities to counter the prosecutor's claims. Only then a conviction is justified: It has met the presumption against coercion. Political coercion, the deliberativist may suggest, can be similarly justified. Just as coercion against the criminal defendant is justified only when he has received a

---

[37] See, for example, Nino, *The Constitution of Deliberative Democracy*, op. cit., pp. 164–5 (arguing that the "disadvantages of the market mechanism for providing access to public communication" can be overcome by a combination of public and private expression channels, where "control of the mass media must be distributed among diverse political units"). Unfortunately, Nino fails to indicate why discourse failure will not affect, or be the consequence of, such control. Similar difficulties surround Owen Fiss's defense of various forms of regulation of speech "to enhance robustness of public debate." Thus, he points out that "the state may have to act to further the robustness of public debate in circumstances where powers outside the state are stifling speech. It may have to allocate public resources – hand out megaphones – to those whose voices would not otherwise be heard in the public square. It may even have to silence the voices of some in order to hear the voices of others." See Owen Fiss, *The Irony of Free Speech* (Cambridge, Mass.: Harvard University Press, 1996), pp. 3–4. We do not deny that, *in theory*, some kinds of speech regulation might enhance the robustness of public debate. Rather, we claim that, in the real world, such political decisions *will* both be affected by discourse failure and reinforce it. (At the very least, they seem to have a dubious record for the diversity of views. See Thomas W. Hazlett, "The Dual Role of Property Rights in Protecting Broadcast Speech," *Social Philosophy and Policy*, Vol. 15, 1998, pp. 176–80. Hazlett's reservations hold a fortiori for societies that place a lower premium on free speech.) We show in Chapter 9 how more consensual institutions hold out hope for robust debate. For related issues, see section 7.5.

[38] Unanimity rule is no exception. If a proposal is vetoed, unanimity rule entails that the forms of coercion embodied in the status quo (e.g., property law and criminal law) remain unaltered. Of course, this does not affect our critique (section 8.1) of the thesis that deliberation renders majority rule consensual. To be sure, all choices presuppose a legal milieu – at a minimum, a legal liberty to decide within a certain range of alternatives. But some choices are more fundamental than others. The institutional arrangements we will propose in Chapter 9 make consent operate at a more fundamental level: the choice of legal systems.

fair hearing, so coercion against losers in the democratic process will be justified only when they have received a fair hearing in deliberation.

The courtroom analogy, however, fails on all fronts. The rules that neutralize discourse failure in the courtroom are absent in political debate. This should not surprise us: The restraints typical of the judicial process are impossible to establish in politics. The differences are too many and too important.[39] Judges and parties in judicial proceedings operate under rules that force them to handle all relevant information and to take plausible objections seriously. Constitutional guarantees of stability, as well as various procedural and substantive legal requirements, foster judicial impartiality. In addition, courtroom rules ensure reasonable accuracy of information (think, for example, about the judicial standards for admitting expert testimony[40]). None of this happens in political deliberation. Not only do deliberating citizens handle inaccurate information, but they also operate under conditions that spread discourse failure. No impartial arbiter assesses the evidence furnished in the deliberative forum. In politics, there is no such thing as the certification of expert witnesses. Discourse failure operates unchecked, as it were. (Needless to say, we do not have much hope that authorizing the state to appoint "epistemic arbiters" will diminish discourse failure or would be otherwise desirable.) It is true, as we have conceded, that in the courtroom the parties will engage in one form of discourse failure – namely, things said out of self-interest. However, they are typically free from another, perhaps more insidious form of discourse failure: the one that stems from rational ignorance. The parties to a lawsuit have incentives to be well informed, as they internalize many benefits and costs of winning or losing. Thus, it is to their advantage to make the best possible legal case – to research the law responsibly, to bring credible witnesses, and so forth. Significantly, the lawyer's chances of winning a case will improve if she addresses all the arguments offered by her opponents. Contrast this with a usually winning strategy in politics: Just ignore what your opponent says. Political actors, unlike parties in the judicial process, externalize the costs of implementing their mistaken views. If they happen to be wrong, others pay. In sum, unlike what happens in the courtroom, in the deliberative forum there is guarantee neither of fair hearing nor of accountability for moral or epistemic mistakes.

---

[39] See Schroeder, "The Law of Politics: Deliberative Democracy's Attempt to Turn Politics into Law," op. cit., esp. pp. 103–25.
[40] See Goldman, *Knowledge in a Social World*, op. cit., pp. 304–11.

We conclude that the attempts to portray deliberation as functionally equivalent to the judge's well-informed and impartial reasoning have failed. It seems reasonable, therefore, to make the burden of proof rest here with the deliberativist. As far as we can see, no forces *within redistributive majoritarianism* are capable of transforming inputs affected by discourse failure into valuable outputs, in the way we see in the courtroom. Indeed, the judicial analogy suggests (ironically for theorists of deliberative democracy) a Platonic way out of such pathologies: appointing unelected rulers invested of the power to assess the merits of citizens' proposals. Like deliberativists, we reject this solution; unlike them, we will favor consensualist alternatives (Chapter 9).

8.6. Substantive Principles and Deliberative Politics

Writers have advanced various views on the relationships between substantive moral principles and deliberation. Some regard substantive principles as inputs to deliberation. Gutmann and Thompson explain this position:

> The principles and substantive conclusions that deliberative democrats put forward do not preempt actual deliberation.... [T]he principles and conclusions must be subjected to the rigors of actual deliberation; that is part of what it means to treat them as politically provisional. Deliberative democrats offer their arguments not as philosophical constraints on democratic politics, but as moral contributions to democratic deliberation.[41]

For these authors, "the principles and substantive conclusions" are basic liberty, equal opportunity, and fair opportunity. They put forward these principles as "key components of the content of deliberation."[42] A possible objection is that if the substantive principles are beyond deliberation, they lack adequate foundation within the theory. Viewed as constraints on deliberation, they surely must be justified on nondeliberative grounds. Deliberation is to that extent irrelevant, or at least not as central as the authors intend it to be.[43] Gutmann and Thompson's reply, in the quoted passage, is that those substantive principles are not "philosophical constraints on democratic politics." They are instead "moral

---

[41] Gutmann and Thompson, "Why Deliberative Democracy Is Different," op. cit., p. 178.

[42] Id., p. 167. Gutmann and Thompson distinguish those principles from "the standards that regulate the conditions of deliberation": reciprocity, publicity, and accountability. Ibid. For present purposes we do not need to introduce this distinction.

[43] See Frederick Schauer, "Talking as a Decision Procedure," in Stephen Macedo, ed., *Deliberative Politics* (New York: Oxford University Press, 1999), p. 20.

contributions to democratic deliberation." We do not see how these remarks make the difficulty disappear. Why are basic liberty, equal opportunity, and fair opportunity privileged within the theory of deliberative democracy? What is *deliberative* about these principles and not about the others competing with them in the political arena (for example, Rawls's difference principle, or the principles of self-ownership, utility, or equality of resources)?

Some deliberativists think that the very idea of deliberation can bear the burden of justifying basic rights. Carlos Nino suggests that a host of classical liberal and welfare rights are justified because they make deliberation possible. People who suffer government censorship, or who starve, cannot deliberate.[44] We will not quarrel with this claim, yet showing a conceptual connection between rights and deliberation does not justify either of them. If deliberation is not a valuable thing, it cannot justify rights. Nino's argument is plausible only if one sees rights as preconditions of *ideal* deliberation (even then, it sounds contrived to say that the reason why, say, official torture is wrong is that it precludes the victim from deliberating). We saw in section 7.6, however, that feasible deliberation under current institutional constraints leads to policies that no attractive political morality can vindicate.

There is a general difficulty with the attempt to derive rights from deliberation. If persons have rights, we may not subject the interests or choices protected by those rights to democratic decision, however inspired by deliberation it is, and even if deliberation approaches the ideal. The deliberativist may nevertheless retort that deliberation is appropriate among those who would be greatly affected by someone's decision. The idea is that those affected by my possible decision should have a say in whether society should allow me to make that decision. But this is surely wrong. If four men propose marriage to Jane, the fact that her decision will gravely affect the interests of the four men generates no reason to defer the selection of Jane's husband to a collective decision by the five (e.g., by majority rule). Jane has an exclusive *right* to decide on that matter.[45] It seems, then, that at least some rights cannot possibly derive from political deliberation (or vote). Moreover, as shown by the right to choose a consenting spouse, some rights that are beyond the reach of deliberation and vote are not prerequisites for deliberation either – it seems possible to conceive of free, open, and informed deliberation in a milieu in which spouses are selected by majority rule.

---

[44] See Nino, op. cit., pp. 138–41.
[45] See Nozick, *Anarchy, State, and Utopia*, op. cit., pp. 268–9.

If some rights are neither prerequisites for appropriate deliberation nor created (or specified) by it, an unqualified version of the impartiality argument for deliberative democracy, which we criticized on other grounds in section 7.4, collapses. It is simply wrong to give equal weight to all important interests in situations involving rights. The four men who propose marriage to Jane have an important interest in the question of who is going to marry her, yet even if some of the other three will be more affected by Peter's marrying Jane than Peter and Jane would (individually or jointly) be by her marrying any of them, this will not in the least weaken Jane's right to choose Peter. Nor is the marriage example idiosyncratic. If I have a right that you not take my wallet, it is preposterous to suggest that all persons affected by your taking my wallet (for example, your children, or your favorite charities) should vote on whether you should do it. Once we understand what it is to have a right, it becomes clear that political deliberation may be seriously inadequate as a basis for public policy. As the examples show, deliberation as a way to redistribute resources is affected by whether or not citizens have private property rights. The same analysis applies to free speech, equal protection, the freedom against arbitrary arrest, and the other traditional liberal rights. This is not to say that we can freely tinker with the language of rights to insulate our own preferred values and principles from majoritarian preferences. The point here is that, *if* people have rights, deliberation's role must be limited. Perhaps some kind of ideal deliberation, or deliberation *about long-term and general constitutional rules*,[46] holds out hope of discovering what rights really are, which rights we possess, and how weighty they are. Deliberation about long-term and general constitutional rules arguably replicates the impartiality constraints reflected both in contractarian theories of the state and theories of deliberative democracy. What the language of rights *does* rule out is *ordinary* political deliberation as the process by which *basic* rights are created and specified.

Treating basic rights as constraints on the deliberative process, or on the outcome of deliberation, or on both is a more promising line of argument.[47] Basic rights are off the deliberating table. They are, in

---

[46] For a seminal investigation of how rational individuals approach constitutional choice, see James M. Buchanan and Gordon Tullock, *The Calculus of Consent*, op. cit., esp. chapters 5 and 6.

[47] Sometimes Gutmann and Thompson seem to hold this view. But this interpretation is complicated by the fact that, as we have seen, they insist that rights and principles be subject to revision through the deliberative process. See Gutmann and Thompson, "Why Deliberative Democracy Is Different," op. cit., pp. 175–9.

some sense, moral truths established by philosophical theorizing, not by popular deliberation. On this view, political deliberation may serve only to apply basic rights to specific situations, or to derive nonbasic rights. Deliberation might help translate an abstract right to equality into more concrete rights and principles, apt to settle particular differences among citizens. For example, the abstract right to free speech cannot, without further specification, provide the answer to whether or not a journalist is entitled not to reveal confidential sources even in a criminal proceeding. On this view, deliberation furnishes the requisite interpretation.

Close inspection of those interpretive processes reveals, however, that they are plagued with discourse failure. Making abstract political concepts more concrete requires causal beliefs. Take again the free-speech example and assume that the core value behind free speech is pluralism, understood as citizens' having easy access to the widest array of information and ideas. Assume also that legislators must strike a balance between a constitutional right to free speech, so understood, and the protection of other constitutional rights through the criminal law. Finally, let us add the heroic assumption that deliberation reached a discourse failure–free verdict on the appropriate mix between protection of free speech and of those other rights.[48] That mix might consist, for example, in a tradeoff among pluralism, extent of the journalists' privilege, and protection of other rights through the criminal law. Here deliberation helps derive concrete principles. Unfortunately, even under such implausibly favorable conditions, citizens are unlikely to learn what they need to assess which legislative proposal will achieve that mix. They would have to engage in complex analysis of the incentives that alternative policies would create for the relevant actors to behave in ways that will bring about the preferred mix.

---

[48] This assumption is heroic on two counts: (a) it relies on a clear-cut response to the question of what the outcome of deliberation is (an assumption we disputed in section 8.4), and (b) it ignores discourse failure in the deliberative process, especially when, as it is reasonable to assume, such abstract constitutional rights, and their balancing against one another, allow for a variety of contestable views, and so self-serving argumentation. On the contestability of constitutional rights, see Pincione, "Market Rights and the Rule of Law: A Case for Procedural Constitutionalism," op. cit., passim.

9

Overcoming Discourse Failure

Voluntary Communities

9.1. A Contractarian Society

In this chapter we tentatively suggest a remedy for the discursive pathologies that afflict typical liberal democracies. Throughout this book we
have examined and rejected many attempts to cope with discourse failure that took for granted majority rule and wide governmental redistributive powers. The shortcomings of those proposals suggest that discourse
failure cannot be eliminated short of a radical redesign of political institutions. We saw in Chapter 2 that discourse failure is the result of the
combination of three factors: rational ignorance, posturing, and redistributive politics. Because, as we extensively argued, the first two factors cannot be eradicated under redistributive politics, getting rid of
redistributive politics suggests itself as the only way out of discourse
failure.

In this chapter we offer a proposal in that direction.[1] We defend a contractarian society – that is, a society in which people allocate resources
through voluntary exchanges, not through majority rule. We will call this
society the Framework Contractarian Society (FCS). We remain neutral
with respect to initial allocations of rights and duties. (Right-) libertarians, for example, uphold strong rights of self-ownership – that is, rights
of exclusive control over one's own body and mental powers – and regard
external resources as unowned and subject to appropriation, provided
that, roughly put, others are not thereby made worse off. Alternatively,

---

[1] We think that our proposal draws independent support from various attractive ideals of
political morality. At a minimum, it may reconcile deliberation with influential ideals that
cannot be realized under current institutions (see section 7.6).

(left-) libertarians hold that external resources are initially owned in common and so allow private appropriation on the condition that the others be compensated. Egalitarians favor a starting point of initial equality of welfare or resources. Some versions of egalitarianism dispute even the idea that, in the baseline, people should have *private*-property rights rather than some form of communal ownership rights. Still other egalitarians ("luck egalitarians") hold that the morally relevant baseline ought not to be sensitive to factors that are beyond people's control.[2] The FCS is compatible with any of these proposals, provided that the property rights they recognize are consensually transferable.

The FCS excludes some starting points. For example, it excludes the Hobbesian state of nature, wherein no one has rights, and distributions of exclusive control of resources where "owners" have no legal power to exchange those resources. It is, however, compatible with welfare or positive rights (e.g., a right to unemployment benefits), provided the right-holder may freely exchange those rights at any time. Thus, *X*, a well-paid worker, may sell now her potential right to unemployment benefits (perhaps *X* wants to risk future uncompensated unemployment in order to buy more things now).

In this contractarian society, individuals may form voluntary subsocieties, groups in which persons could join with others of their choice. Individuals who join these communities will have ample rights of exit. We will call these groups the Voluntary Communities (VCs). The FCS would retain central powers for two purposes: to enforce contracts and the right of exit from the VCs, and to protect basic civil rights to life and personal security, by force in extreme cases, in case one of the VCs goes wrong in any of the ways we indicate below.[3]

---

[2] For brief discussions of these views, see (on versions of libertarianism) Peter Vallentyne, "Libertarianism," *The Stanford Encyclopedia of Philosophy* (Fall 2004 Edition), Edward N. Zalta, ed., URL http://plato.stanford.edu/archives/fall2004/entries/libertarianism/; (on resource vs. welfare equality) Kymlicka, *Contemporary Political Philosophy*, op. cit., pp. 75–87; and (on luck egalitarianism) John Roemer, "Equality and Responsibility," *The Boston Review*, April/May 1995 issue, available at http://www.bostonreview.net/BR20.2/roemer.html.

[3] Our argument here is strongly influenced by Nozick's proposal for a "framework for utopia" in chapter 10 of *Anarchy, State, and Utopia*, op. cit. Our polemical impetus is, however, different from Nozick's. While Nozick intends his argument to make the ideal of a minimal state (i.e., a state confined to the protection of libertarian rights) inspiring, we resort to (something like) a framework for utopia to bring home why discourse failure can be overcome only at the expense of the redistributive powers presupposed by theories of deliberative democracy.

Those who place a high premium on ideal deliberation, consent, and personal autonomy should be attracted to this proposal, especially if they are convinced by our diagnosis of discourse failure. However, ours will not be an all-things-considered defense of the FCS. Thus, readers who accept our theory of discourse failure may conceivably reject the proposal in this chapter. Perhaps they imagine an institutional design for reducing discourse failure different from the ones we have dismissed, or perhaps they favor the use of coercion to further certain ideals of human or communal excellence and so dislike the very idea of the FCS, or some of the VCs that it allows.

9.2. Contracts and Truth

Several considerations support our contractarian proposal, but the main one for present purposes is this: Discourse failure stems from the combined effect of rational ignorance and posturing *in the context of institutions that allow wide governmental discretion to redistribute resources.* Citizens would be more likely to become informed if political actors could not use the state for private purposes, such as material gains, personal power, or glory. Political discourse fails because many citizens remain ignorant and many others trade on that ignorance. Rational ignorance and posturing are mutually reinforcing. If we eliminate the institutional structures that generate these pathologies, people will not err or lie as often as they do in typical redistributive societies.

Why would that happen? Because, under our proposal, areas of social life where truth will flourish will expand. In the FCS, individuals will gain by educating themselves before engaging in market exchanges. Standard economic analysis applies here. A consumer will cease to invest in information about prices and qualities of products when his marginal cost and benefit of doing so are equal. Likewise, citizens will be well informed about the effects of their transactions because they will internalize the benefits of becoming informed and the costs of remaining ignorant. In contrast, in current democracies citizens internalize the costs, but not the benefits, of becoming politically literate. On the other hand, those who enjoy real, honest political deliberation will have ample opportunities to form deliberative communities whose members prize truth. In the FCS, citizens who stand to lose from redistributive measures will be able to veto them: Only contracts determine distribution there. On the other hand, those who wish to live in a redistributive community may do so by joining with like-minded individuals. In that community there would be no perverse incentives of the kind found in current *coercive* redistributive societies, in which most people can at best exercise their exit rights at a prohibitive personal cost (e.g., by emigrating). We saw how such incentives translate into discourse failure. In contrast, in those VCs the quality of deliberation will improve. A contractarian society that allows individuals to voluntarily join a variety of institutional arrangements is more attractive to those who cherish the deliberativist's ideal than present institutional arrangements.

In addition, our proposal gives ideal deliberation a true chance. Recall (section 8.4) that majority rule over distributive issues often results in the indeterminacy of the questions submitted to voters. Deliberativists recommend that citizens deliberate about issues exogenously submitted to them. The voluntary scheme defended here enables citizens instead to pick the *kinds of questions* on which they want to vote. They may, for instance, prefer to join VCs in which members vote for transparent subsidies, taxes, and regulations, on a case-by-case basis, rather than for politicians endowed with generic redistributive powers. Even more, citizens will be able to select the *political institutions* that, by their own lights, generate the electoral questions they deem relevant. We conjecture that competitive pressures will improve the deliberative quality of some VCs: They will admit members who offer reliable signals of commitment to serious deliberation, and these in turn will want to join those VCs. We should also expect those VCs to expand membership as a means of expanding the diversity of views that quality deliberation demands. And, of course, those who dislike deliberative politics will find opportunities to fine-tune their selection of VCs – a fine-tuning that current states, with their nonconsensual memberships, exclude.[4]

Our critique of the epistemic argument for deliberative democracy rests on the proposition that the incentives under which political actors operate will, more often than not, lead them away from the truth. This is not meant to deny that sometimes people pursuing noncognitive goals will reach the truth. In the judicial process and scientific practices, for example, those seeking prestige or wealth usually make, as a side effect, epistemic contributions. Yet, political deliberation will fail to approach truth within the institutional frameworks that deliberativists take for

---

[4] VCs will in turn admit new members under mutually agreed conditions. In general, however, VCs will want to expand membership up to the point at which they have economies of scale in the production of public goods. But the fact that beyond that point VCs restrict entry need not leave people's communitarian preferences unmet; on the contrary, it provides incentives to latecomers to form new, similar VCs.

granted. Truth[5] will not emerge as a side effect of the interaction among majority rule, wide redistributive powers, and the associated incentives to err and posture. In contrast, in a contractarian society, in which people are free to exchange well-defined property rights, individuals approach the truth even if they pursue non-epistemic ends, such as monetary profit. Thus, citizens-consumers will get accurate information about the transactions they contemplate. They alone will bear the cost of erring. Sometimes producers of knowledge, such as scientists, stand to gain prestige from genuine discoveries – that is, *true* propositions. And, of course, if their discoveries are marketable, they can become rich too.[6]

Our proposal may seem at odds with our endorsement in section 4.5 of Alvin Goldman's view that free markets do not necessarily promote truth. Not so. We agreed with Goldman that deregulated speech markets do not necessarily promote truth, but we reached this conclusion (as, we think, he did) *against the backdrop of majority rule over distributive policies* – that is, current liberal democracies. A major source of discourse failure is precisely the operation of majority rule for redistributive purposes. The free market for speech involved in the FCS will not be affected by the perverse incentives we have identified, because people will have limited possibility of political or social gain by distorting the truth. The FCS allows individuals with similar interests and values to create communities that, in their own eyes, will best further those interests and values. One can predict the creation of religious, multicultural, artistic, socialist, academic, and other communities. Selective[7] and self-selective processes will ensure that VCs be populated by members well informed about and committed to the principles or values underlying those communities.

9.3. Contracts and Compromise

Our proposal mitigates the problem of compromising among citizens who hold conflicting values – a central theme of deliberativism. We

---

[5] We refer here to factual and moral truths, in the philosophically noncommittal sense indicated in notes 7 and 8, Chapter 1.

[6] See Goldman, p. 260. We explore the connections between the contractarian-consensual principle and the incentives to become *politically* informed in section 9.6.

[7] We should note that, in a fully contractarian scheme, a person becomes a member of a VC by mutual agreement between him and the VC (or its contractually determined representatives). One cannot enter a community by unilateral decision. More on membership in sections 9.4 and 9.5.

suggested in section 7.3 that enlarging markets, and so reducing the scope of politics, is a more promising route toward social peace than deliberative compromises. An objector might say that the FCS cannot accommodate the individual who prefers *not* to live in a contractarian society – say, someone who prefers to live in a religious or centrally planned community. He may complain that the contractarian society turns him in effect into a loser by precluding *ab initio* the formation of the kind of community he cherishes. Deliberativists repeatedly suggest that deliberation is a plausible way of settling *this* kind of dispute. For example, the deliberativist may defend the welfare state as a compromise between free marketeers and socialists. The former would have retained private means of production while the latter would have succeeded in securing payments from rich to poor. Or consider moral and religious differences. Some people support gay marriage; others reject it, still others do not care. The argument we are considering might treat civil unions between homosexuals as a compromise between the rival views.

But this is just the bright side of compromising. If compromise is not reached, under majority rule one group will end up imposing its views on the other. And even when compromise is reached, both parties will still be partly dissatisfied: the socialist would perhaps see the welfare state as insufficiently egalitarian, whereas the free marketeer might regard it as too inefficient or too restrictive of private property. Similar analysis holds for the gay marriage issue. So in either case some people will remain dissatisfied. The argument from compromise must assume that the dissatisfaction brought about by compromise is offset by the partial satisfaction that both parties obtain – something that is open to question.

If, however, we remove the assumption that society must reach a collective decision binding on all parties, people with different values will be free to voluntarily join with others who share those values. Thus, in the contractarian society that we imagine here there is no need for compromise because no one can *impose* his goals (moral or otherwise) on others. In our scheme, VCs acknowledge ample exit rights, while entry is a matter of agreement between the VC's representatives and the prospective new member. In this sense, people who join a religious community, for instance, freely submit to its rules. By the same token, they should be allowed to leave the community if they wish to do so (for example, if they have lost their faith and no longer accept the communal restrictions). Someone concerned with compromise should take steps in this contractarian direction rather than insist on the expansion of deliberative fora in the context of nonconsensual political institutions. Notice an interesting asymmetry here. A purely contractarian society (such as the FCS) makes room for voluntary arrangements to form collectivist communities (i.e., communities in which decisions to use resources are centralized, as in certain religious or socialist communities). In contrast, a collectivist basic framework precludes to various degrees the operation of contracts. As a result, while people can voluntarily transform their contractarian society into a collectivist society, the reverse is unlikely.[8] So our proposal better addresses the question of conflicting values and ideals of social or individual excellence by allowing citizens to freely form VCs organized along their preferences.

Some VCs will still face decision-making problems, such as framing or agenda manipulation (see section 8.4). There is no guarantee that these problems will be completely eradicated under our scheme. However, the fact that membership is voluntary will arguably reduce *nonconsensual* manipulation. Moreover, because voluntary communities will reduce the need to compromise about some issues, no one will ever be forced to endure an arrangement he thinks intolerable, whether or not it resulted from manipulation.

9.4. The Paradox of Contract

Are there moral limits to the creation of communities? To avoid free riding on whatever public goods they supply, the communities we propose should provide for sanctions for breach of their rules, and members will not be allowed to evade those sanctions by invoking their general right to exit.[9] It is difficult, however, to provide general criteria for striking the balance between the members' general right to exit and their contractually acquired duties. In any event, those difficulties are not peculiar to our proposal. They concern any political morality that prizes personal autonomy and freedom of contract – any liberal view – and are vividly brought out by a well-known paradox of contractual freedom – namely, whether a contract whereby someone sells himself into slavery is binding.[10] We will not discuss these complexities in detail, but the following

---

[8] See G. A. Cohen, *Self-Ownership, Freedom, and Equality* (Cambridge: Cambridge University Press, 1995), pp. 105–6.

[9] See Ilya Somin, "Revitalizing Consent," *Harvard Journal of Law and Public Policy*, Vol. 23, 2000, p. 753, esp. pp. 761–71.

[10] See the classical discussion in John Stuart Mill, *On Liberty*, in John Stuart Mill, *On Liberty, with The Subjection of Women and Chapters on Socialism*, Stefan Collini, ed. (Cambridge:

remarks may indicate the direction that a more thorough discussion should take.

People may have three kinds of preferences regarding others. Suppose I am a Catholic but do not care if others are Catholic. This is a *personal* preference in Dworkin's sense,[11] and it poses of course no problem for the contractarian framework we are here considering. But suppose that not only am I a Catholic, but that also I can be happy, or realize my life plan, only if those around me are also Catholic. I want to live in a homogenous Catholic community. This is an *external* preference in Dworkin's sense, because the behavior of others is essential to the satisfaction of my preference. Whatever one thinks about this kind of preference, it is fair to say that current liberal democracies have some trouble accommodating it. I do not value religious diversity, yet I am forced to pay taxes to promote values and practices to which I object. The contractarian framework can better accommodate my preference by allowing me to seek like-minded persons and form with them a voluntary Catholic community. Our proposal allows the satisfaction of the external preference without coercion. Let us call this a *communal* preference. Communal preferences can be satisfied by voluntary arrangements between like-minded people. Imagine, however, someone whose preference is either to *force* others into Catholicism, or that everyone in the world become a Catholic, no matter how much coercion is needed to achieve this end. Let us call this a *totalitarian* preference. For this individual it will not be enough to join a voluntary Catholic community, because what he wants is to coerce others (as an end or as a means); he does not simply want to live in a religiously homogenous society. By definition, a totalitarian preference cannot be satisfied by voluntary arrangements. The FCS cannot honor totalitarian preferences, because doing so would defeat the very basis on which the FCS rests. Yet, our proposal is as tolerant as any proposal can be in a world in which some people have totalitarian preferences. It allows individuals to satisfy their communal preferences. Members of those communities will deliberate in ways that are generally proscribed by theorists of deliberative democracy. Thus, a Catholic VC will allow its members to use religious

Cambridge University Press, 1989), pp. 102–3. Mill resolves the paradox by saying that selling oneself as a slave is null and void, because it defeats the very purpose of not interfering with someone's liberty. This view raises a number of complex questions about interference and liberty that we will not pursue here.

[11] See Ronald Dworkin, "DeFunis v. Sweatt," in M. Cohen, T. Nagel, and T. Scanlon, eds., *Equality and Preferential Treatment* (Princeton, N.J.: Princeton University Press, 1977), pp. 77–81.

arguments in deliberation, even to justify public coercion. In contrast, most deliberativists disfavor such appeals to religion, because religious views are comprehensive views and thus beyond public reason.[12] There will be, then, a tendency for strong believers in comprehensive worldviews to abandon communities in which public reasons prevail in political discourse. In doing so, they will contribute to the strength of the deliberative practices that deliberativists cherish – and such practices will, *ex hypothesi*, be available to anyone who cherishes them.[13]

Notice that under our proposal, deliberative communities will have resources to protect their deliberative practices. The admission contract may contain rules for deliberation that deliberativists favor, such as those requiring the exclusive use of public reasons in political argument. So, two mechanisms operate to facilitate the flourishing of ideal deliberative communities. Those who resent ideal deliberative practices will be free to leave those communities and form, or join, VCs that adopt their preferred deliberative practices (e.g., based on comprehensive views). And those who are unwilling to play by the rules of ideal deliberation may be denied entry.[14] This conclusion should not offend liberal sensibilities. Protecting deliberative practices by restricting membership is already recognized in liberal societies: Think about church services, during which certainly dissenters are not allowed to interrupt the minister in the middle of the sermon, regardless of the relevance and merit of the dissenters' objections. We conjecture that one major reason why even the most liberal-minded persons do not object to these practices is that they occur in an environment where people enjoy unrestricted exit rights: Thus, people are neither forced to attend nor to remain in church services.

The framework we are defending does not assume that consent is carte blanche for grave mistreatment of individuals. This apparent limitation upon contractual freedom can be conceptualized in various ways. One is to develop a theory of inalienable rights – that is, rights that cannot be validly relinquished by the individual (we will not pursue this line of argument here, except for a brief remark at the end of section 9.7). Another line of argument rests on the idea of a public good (see section 2.3). The recommendation that public goods be coercively supplied by the state

---

[12] See, for example, John Rawls, *The Law of Peoples*, op. cit., pp. 131–2.

[13] None of this implies approving or promoting a particular kind of community, or any view about whether it is smart or foolish to have strong communal preferences.

[14] Restrictions to entry by VCs are consensual in a way that current immigration controls are not. The former stem from contract; the latter, from laws.

does not contradict the consensualist principle reflected in the FCS. By definition, individuals prefer to contribute to the production of a public good rather than not have it at all, yet they prefer even more intensely to free ride on the productive efforts of others. As in other cases of market failure, having government provide the good is in theory a possible solution. Most important, this solution is consensual in the sense that it channels, rather than thwarts, people's preferences. One such public good is the market order itself and the basic human rights to life, security, and property that it presupposes. In the absence of those rights, people will free ride (e.g., by stealing) on the productive efforts of others: This was Hobbes's point when he described the state of nature where persons would find themselves in a stateless society.[15] In the language of the theory of public goods, the market itself satisfies the conditions of nonrivalrous consumption and non-excludability. The state provides *this* good by preventing murder, torture, and deprivation of physical liberty and property, and by supplying fair-trial services and enforcement of contracts. But we cannot decide here to what extent members of voluntary communities may forgo some of those rights, and conversely, when the FCS may forcibly intervene in those communities to avoid grossly illiberal treatment on persons who have consented to it.[16] Each case will have to be decided on its merits by the FCS's courts, which will develop increasingly refined, principled ways to trade off the consensual formation of communities and the consensual reasons to coerce their members into the production of public goods. We cannot anticipate what those principles will be, in much the same way that it is impossible to predict the lines along which common-law adjudication will evolve. We do submit, however, that something like common-law courts will have to be in charge of settling these issues, if the discourse failure of political processes is not to be reinstated in the FCS.[17]

Judges sensitive to the moral importance of consent will adopt doctrines that help people overcome collective action problems. Their decisions will in practice overlap with those reached on the basis of moral

---

[15] See Thomas Hobbes, *Leviathan* [1651], Chapter 13.

[16] For a defense of forcible intervention to protect basic human rights, see Fernando R. Tesón, *Humanitarian Intervention*, op. cit., passim. The problem in the text is different, however, as it concerns mistreatment of persons who have consented *ex ante* to it.

[17] Recall (section 8.5) that we acknowledged the epistemic virtues of some real-world judicial procedures. For a historically grounded speculation about the directions that common-law adjudication without centralized legislative powers will take, see Bruce Benson, *The Enterprise of Law* (San Francisco: Pacific Research Institute, 1990).

(as distinct from efficiency-based) considerations about the limits of actual consent. Judges will develop intellectual techniques to distinguish free riders from individuals who honestly do not wish the good to be provided – that is, who do not behave opportunistically. Imagine a Catholic VC in which the authorities have established a penalty of prison for blasphemy. Outrageous as this practice may seem to more secular sensibilities (and certainly to the authors of this book), we conjecture that FCS judges will strike the balance at a more permissive point than current liberal democracies do. They will tend to tolerate those harsh penalties, but they will also require due process of law, short prison terms, humane treatment of prisoners, and other humanitarian measures. Remember that the convicted person in this example consented to the rules of this community, in much the same way as cloistered monks and nuns, and volunteers, accept strict disciplinary codes. The general point is that, in the absence of centralized legislation, the FCS will give rise to increasingly refined judicial distinctions among the legal effects of various types of consent. To the extent that judges formulate increasingly fine-tuned discriminations between free riders (who in principle should not be exempted from the rules of the VC) and honest holdouts (whose contracts to form bizarre communities should be enforced), even illiberal ways of life will reflect the value of consent.

9.5. Further Objections and Replies

Someone might object that our proposal does not improve on redistributive liberalism, because people can currently form religious and other groups under the standard constitutional principles of freedom of association and religion. However, our proposal allows for a number of practices that current forms of liberalism rule out. These include having an official religion; funding religious or ideologically prone schools through taxes; expropriating production for common use without compensation; paternalistic societies in which, for example, bans on red meat are as strong as current bans on certain drugs; anti-paternalistic societies in which no food or drug, however dangerous, would be prohibited; and so on.

People who share false or objectionable beliefs or attitudes would be allowed to form their own communities. Thus, people who believe in astrology or black magic could voluntarily join *political* communities of like believers. We may imagine such communities adopting public policies by consulting the alignment of the stars, or the rulings of the witch doctors. What about people who voluntarily join communities whose

members value racial or religious homogeneity?[18] We think that much
of the evil these people have inflicted throughout history can be traced
to their ability to seize the machinery of the state, and from the fact that
their victims could not exit except at a very high cost in a world composed
entirely of states. Under our proposal, those who hold these objectionable beliefs and attitudes would wield limited power over others, as entry
into and permanence in those communities would be voluntary. Thus,
these groups would have been effectively disarmed because they could
not coerce the unwilling. More generally, the revulsion we feel toward discriminatory preferences derives in significant part from our experience
in current noncontractarian societies. Under our proposal, many illiberal
arrangements would fail for lack of membership if people had a right of
exit whose limits will stem only from the foregoing need to dissuade free
riders. Given what we know about the basic needs of human beings, the
opportunities for human flourishing that alternative ways of organizing
society offer, and the massive migrations, sometimes at inordinate risks
or personal costs, toward more liberal societies, it seems safe to speculate
that tyrannical regimes would have a hard time finding customers. (How
many people would sign up to live in a VC like present-day – 2006 – North
Korea?) Thus, we establish two conditions for tolerating illiberal communities: They have to be entirely voluntary at their origin, and they have
to provide unrestricted rights of exit for those who genuinely ceased to
demand whatever public goods they were offered by those communities.

Because VCs might impose various kinds of entry restrictions, it may
seem that, for all the appeal of the idea of VCs, our proposal fails to
expand people's opportunities to choose the society in which they would
like to live. But this appearance vanishes as soon as we realize that opportunities for joining the preferred type of community are responsive to
people's preferences and ideals. The contractual nature of the VCs will
generate an indefinite process of community emergence and extinction.
Strong "secession" rights are likely to result from the combined operation of the background right to exit and the conditions for cessation of
membership contractually established – to attract cooperative members,
communities will strive to reduce exit costs (e.g., by waiving claims on fees
or performances that the member agreed to in the admission contract).
In any event, we speculate that the FCS's judiciary, *ex hypothesi* committed
to contractual freedom, will set limits on how the current generation may

---

[18] We (the authors of this book) would definitely not join certain VCs – certainly, none of
the above. We avoid, however, such autobiographical remarks.

shape the world in which future generations will have to live – future generations cannot consent to anything we do now. Accordingly, the FCS may choose to retain a piece of territory. Even within that territory, however, individuals will possess weak "communitarian" rights: They may decide to form voluntary associations with like-minded individuals over those tracts of land they acquired in conformity with the market rules operating within the FCS. Such rights are, in a sense, weaker than those giving rise to VCs, because the associations formed in the FCS's territory may not in turn restrict freedom of contract itself or change the basic criminal law.[19]

We may be accused of solving the discourse failure problem only trivially. Presumably, everyone knows that the pathologies of political rhetoric will disappear if politics itself does. But notice that "political rhetoric" admits of at least two meanings, and neither helps the objection. In one sense, the expression refers to the activity of talking about politics generally. In this sense, there is no reason why, under our scheme, people will refrain from discussing political issues. For example, they may wish to speculate about the political design of VCs they contemplate to form or join. Or they may be interested in discussing how a noncontractarian society will work, and whether and how to get there. Our proposal makes pointless, however, the kind of political rhetoric found in modern democracies – that is, rhetoric aimed at winning political power in *nonconsensual* communities: the current states. As we have argued at length, those who want to avoid discourse failure will welcome this development. In a second sense, "political rhetoric" refers indeed to discourse aimed at winning political power. In our proposal this will still be possible in some VCs – that is, in those communities whose members *consensually* adopted (something like) a political structure. True, a speaker may still use discourse failure to convince others to join a certain type of VC, or that forming it is worthwhile. Crucially, however, that speaker will confront persons who have every incentive to learn about these prospective communities, because each one's choice *is decisive* on the outcome – here: becoming a member.[20] For this reason, we would not expect levels of discourse failure as high as those we find in current societies.

---

[19] For a discussion of the philosophical aspects of self-determination and secession, see Tesón, *A Philosophy of International Law*, op. cit., pp. 127–56.

[20] Contrast this situation with that in which voters have to decide how much to invest in political information, as explained in section 2.2.

An objector might deny our claim that people can form VCs uphold-ing *any* conception of justice that they prefer, for what can prevent the rich from forming their own VCs, thus escaping their justice-based duties toward the least fortunate? In that case, the objection goes, the poor would not have succeeded in joining a society they prefer, namely a redis-tributive society, because the rich would have placed themselves beyond the reach of the tax laws that (presumably) implement morally required redistribution. This objection, however, is guilty of the form of discourse failure we dubbed "the moral turn" in section 6.1. It describes the sit-uation (the rich joining their own VC) in static, rather than dynamic, terms. In that VC, the rich would still need things, such as cars (possibly Mercedes and Jaguars), food (perhaps gourmet food), and so forth. Either those goods are produced locally or are beyond the VC's bor-ders. If they are produced locally, the rich would have to hire workers, in which case they would admit people who presumably are not rich. If those goods are instead produced outside the VC, the rich would buy them there, with the aid of trade agreements with other VCs. In doing so, by application of the law of comparative advantages, they will contribute to the prosperity of the VCs where the goods in question are produced.

The objection we are imagining describes the situation too coarsely. If our objector contemplates a situation in which the rich themselves will make the cars and grow the vegetables, we can ask if someone will clean the toilets or serve coffee in those factories. If the answer is yes, then *someone* other than the rich will presumably be needed to perform those tasks, and so forth. The more finely grained we describe the situation, the more apparent it is that the rich will admit people who are not rich, or will establish trade relations that will likely promote, in opaque ways, the welfare of the less rich.

One natural worry, given the charge of utopianism that we have leveled against theories of deliberative democracy,[21] is that the voluntary scheme proposed here is utopian too. Recall, however, why the kind of utopianism that affects deliberativism is unattractive. The deliberative proposal can-not function as a regulative ideal because it is counterproductive. In gen-eral, more deliberation reinforces discourse failure.[22] This is not the case with the proposal in this chapter. While a fully consensual society seems unattainable and in that sense is indeed a utopian ideal, it *does* function as a regulative ideal. Current societies can incrementally expand freedom

---

[21] See especially sections 2.2 and 4.6.
[22] See section 4.6.

of contract, thus allowing greater internalization of informational costs and benefits, and in that way help reduce discourse failure. They can also allow citizens to exit from the services provided by the modern welfare state, letting citizens cease to be both (potential) beneficiaries of and contributors to those services.[23] Therefore, while we can infer that a society has reduced discourse failure from the fact that that society resembles the FCS, we *cannot* infer the degree to which a society reduces discourse failure (or realizes other goals dear to deliberativists) from the size or number of its deliberative fora.

9.6. Discursive Advantages of Voluntary Communities

The deliberative practices that people adopt in the VCs will be free from the pathologies associated with redistributive politics. Thus, high levels of taxation justified with the rhetoric of public goods but in reality benefiting special interests cannot be sustained for a long time if citizens have the right to exit. In its most general form, discourse failure stems from the fact that majority rule massively externalizes the costs of political decisions. I, a farmer, may not take a thousand dollars from your pocket. Most probably, I would be held criminally or civilly liable for that behavior. However, if I persuade government, or the majoritarian coalition that elected it, to subsidize farmers, I can have someone else – the government – take the money from you. I will not be held liable by you or by anyone else. I have externalized the costs of my behavior. This phenomenon (the external costs of majority rule over distributive issues) has been widely discussed in the public-choice literature.[24] As elsewhere in this book, our focus here is on the *discursive* attitudes grafted onto this process. Political actors present rent-seeking behavior as warranted by moral concerns (thus, farmers are described as "depositories of American values"). This characterization is often accompanied by false social theories (e.g., mercantilism). Special interests trade on citizens' ignorance and the patterns of beliefs that are associated with it.[25] And they do this helped by the fact that moral concerns are more likely to

---

[23] See Somin, "Revitalizing Consent," op. cit., passim.

[24] See the classical discussion in Buchanan and Tullock, *The Calculus of Consent*, op. cit., esp. pp. 119–262. See also Cooter, *The Strategic Constitution*, op. cit., pp. 58–60; and Gwartney and Wagner, "Public Choice and the Conduct of Representative Government," op. cit., pp. 17–18.

[25] See section 2.2.

guide behavior in the polling booth because the cost of virtue is low there.[26]

To the extent that our proposal is based on consent, it preempts the externalization of costs described previously. Discourse failure associated with that mechanism will not arise. Could there be other forms of discourse failure in a contractarian society? Sure. Sellers will tend to exaggerate the quality of their products and services, in much the same way that candidates tend to exaggerate the virtues of their electoral platforms. But the analogy between current societies and the FCS stops there. Sellers have a contractual obligation to deliver the products they sell. Moreover, buyers will fully internalize the benefits of shopping around, comparing prices and reputations, and so on. The market will tend to correct asymmetries in information.[27] At the very least, much would be gained if discourse failure were limited to the problems raised by asymmetries of information. It is true that asymmetries of information are a source of market failure. In actual markets people will refrain, out of fear of undisclosed defects, from buying things that they would have bought in a fully transparent market. But government regulation has costs of its own. Even assuming that the government intervenes to address a genuine market failure, regulation raises the cost of goods and services by preventing consumers from choosing their preferred combination of risk and price.

Our proposal bypasses these problems. It allows risk-friendly citizens to live in a community where they can get lower prices for what they demand even at the risk of disappointment. Thus, in an unregulated economy I might choose to consult, say, an advanced medical student for a physical condition that I have. I might think that he has enough knowledge to provide good health care, yet he will charge me less because he is not a licensed physician. I decide to run the risk. You might think that this is an unreasonable risk to bear and prefer to pay higher medical fees but be reassured that health care is provided only by professionals licensed by the state. These are the kinds of considerations that will motivate citizens to join VCs. Some would choose to join an unregulated community, thus accepting the risk of deregulation in exchange for lower prices. Others would choose to join a regulated community, wherein everyone

---

[26] See section 1.2.

[27] See Gillian Hadfield, Robert Howse, and Michael Trebilcock, "Information-Based Principles for Rethinking Consumer Protection Policy," *Journal of Consumer Policy*, Vol. 21, 1998, p. 131.

voluntarily assumes the costs (in terms of higher doctor fees) of regulation. And, when selecting VCs, potential members will have an incentive to learn about the communities they plan to join (and, correspondingly, some others will have an incentive to supply the relevant information in the free markets upheld by the FCS).

A contractarian society would be free, then, of the kinds of discourse failure that plague current redistributive societies. Opportunities to lie will be constrained by competitive pressures and judicial remedies for fraud. Because in current societies a single citizen has virtually no impact on the direction taken by redistributive policies, even citizens who are willing to benefit others have no incentive to acquire the information they would acquire if they could make separate decisions concerning how to benefit those groups. In a market society they do have such incentives because they themselves bear the costs and benefits of becoming well informed about alternative charitable endeavors. Moreover, persons who ask for charity, including charitable organizations, are subject to competitive pressures (they must, that is, convince donors that they are more deserving, or more efficient in reaching out to the genuinely deserving, than others). A related point is that discourse failure will not distort the public's beliefs about the extent to which they are helping the needy – a distortion encouraged by the black-box mechanisms involved in current welfare states. As a result, both the demand and the supply of charity will in all likelihood increase.

Unlike the all-encompassing, coercive framework provided by redistributive democracy, our scheme allows persons interested in deliberation and redistribution to join like-minded citizens in voluntary communities. Crucially, discourse failure will be reduced in those communities as well. They will be formed by individuals who value ideal deliberation. Contrast this with current redistributive democracies, where the *deliberative unit* is arbitrary, in the sense that it includes persons inclined toward serious exchange of ideas along with many others who are not so inclined. The ideals espoused by deliberativists would have a better chance of becoming reality if selective and self-selective pressures gave rise to communities in which members would not posture, argue in self-serving ways, disregard objections to their views, and so forth.

The role of deliberation and redistribution in these voluntary communities helps identify the exact target of the criticism in this book. We have discussed several epistemic and moral shortcomings in the deliberative practices that are feasible in modern democracies. Our point is not that making *such* democracies less deliberative would improve things.

We are certainly not suggesting that it would be good for people to vote without deliberating. Nor are we suggesting that nondemocratic arrangements fare any better: Indeed, nondemocratic regimes display a record of manipulative political discourse that is unparalleled by the worst deliberative practices we observe in liberal democracies. At a minimum, such regimes tend to give rise to a public political discourse pervaded by fear and obsequiousness, in addition to the other forms of discourse failure we have discussed in this book. Our point is that the combination of majority rule and wide governmental powers to redistribute resources degrades deliberation. The FCS countenances whatever distributive patterns are adopted by the VCs (including those patterns favored by deliberativists[28]). When carried out in VCs, deliberation and open exchange of ideas recover the high premium put on them both by traditional liberal thinking and by deliberativism. (Recall that those who are more comfortable with less liberal practices may form their own voluntary communities, provided they are consensual in the sense indicated here.) Majority rule and redistribution are perfectly legitimate if adopted by one such community.[29]

---

[28] For example, Nino holds that appropriate deliberation presupposes a host of welfare rights. See *The Constitution of Deliberative Democracy*, op. cit., pp. 43–66, 139, and 222. In *The Ethics of Human Rights* (New York: Oxford University Press, 1991), Nino embraces redistributive policies that implement "an egalitarian expansion of personal autonomy," which is mandated by his theory of rights, pp. 302–3, at 302.

[29] Are there any concrete proposals that could conceivably get current democracies closer to our consensualist approach? The political obstacles are daunting, but we offer here a few suggestions, none of which is original per se but take on a new light when understood as ways to reduce discourse failure.

1. People may be allowed to opt out of various coercive redistributive schemes. This may include, where appropriate, the use of vouchers for education, health care, and so forth. (For a recent proposal along these lines, see Ilya Somin, "Revitalizing Consent," op. cit., pp. 753–805.) These programs would create incentives for citizens to become better informed about the services they are buying and would neutralize, to a degree, the posturing by politicians and rent seekers. Once they lost access to the redistributive apparatus of the state, such groups would have less to gain by spreading inaccurate views about society.

2. Tax reform may also help democracies move to a more consensual society. For example, replacing in-kind welfare benefits with a negative income tax, or a minimum guaranteed income, might motivate citizens to internalize the cost of acquiring information about consumption alternatives. The forms of discourse failure attendant to in-kind provision would thereby be reduced. This argument differs, then, from the classical defense of the negative income tax by Milton Friedman, *Capitalism and Freedom* (Chicago: University of Chicago Press, 1962), which rests on efficiency and political feasibility. It also differs from defenses of the minimum guaranteed income (e.g., Philippe van Parijs in *Arguing for Basic Income: Philosophical Arguments for a*

9.7. Loose Ends

Two final remarks. First, the fact that the FCS recognizes contract as the only source of changes in people's rights and duties does not preclude the emergence of relationships of friendship and family. To the extent that personal relationships are consensual, the FCS is perfectly hospitable to them (with allowances made for children). Similarly, the FCS allows for the development of various subcultures, with, again, a proviso that participation in them be consensual. Thus, we understand the value of cultures in individualistic terms, as the result of voluntary exchanges over time. This conception of a culture has the important twin consequences that members may validly decide to leave it, and that ways of life and cultural patterns may not be coercively imposed on persons.[30]

Radical Reform [London: Verso, 1992]) that appeal to a principle of equal division of external resources.

3. Liberalization of trade and immigration would also help reduce discourse failure, as it would, again, increase the internalization of informational costs across national borders. People would have lower emigration costs and so could choose which society to join. Persons could thus freely choose among different political and economic systems, and thus between various redistributive schemes.

To be sure, all of these measures are highly imperfect, not the least because they will surely be blocked by those who benefit from keeping opaque the costs of policies in current societies. But perhaps historical experience can help here. Moves from less to more consensual societies (moves toward freedom) have occurred, not as the result of political deliberation, but for exogenous reasons. Here are a couple of well-known examples:

1. The democratization of Eastern Europe was not the result of citizens' deliberating and improving policies but, at least in part, of the United States' posing a credible threat to the Soviet Union, which in turn deterred the Soviet elites, seeking self-protection, from a return to Stalinism as a way to compete militarily with the United States.

2. Germany and Japan moved toward freedom, not as a result of deliberation, but of military defeat.

These facts may suggest that perhaps the move toward a consensual society can occur only as the result of various kinds of crises. There is reason to be pessimistic, however. Sometimes even many decades of massive discourse failure and ensuing crises may be impotent to move society toward more consensual arrangements. Thus, the reverse development in Argentina since 1945, which culminated in the 2001 financial collapse, did not seem to move society in that direction; moreover, it fueled discourse failure (consider the current [2006] Argentine administration's rhetorical and diplomatic gestures toward Fidel Castro's and Hugo Chávez's regimes). In any event, political deliberation by itself, for the reasons we discussed, cannot achieve that goal.

30 For a defense of this consensualist conception of community in the context of international law, see Fernando R. Tesón, *A Philosophy of International Law* (Boulder, Colo.: Westview, 1998), pp. 127–56.

Second, we have explored how far the idea of consent can go in accommodating central elements in the liberal tradition, such as the importance of personal autonomy, freedom of contract, and basic individual rights. We undertook this exploration because a more consensual society holds out hope of overcoming discourse failure. We did not mean to suggest, however, that consent is the only thing that should matter in a complete theory of political morality. For example, on some readings of Kant, persons are not morally entitled to consent to any treatment whatsoever that others may inflict on them. However, a fully developed Kantian theory of rights might well reach conclusions similar to the ones we have suggested here on the basis of unqualified consent and a recognition that sometimes (as in public goods production) coercion overcomes collective-action barriers to the expression of genuine consent.[31]

---

[31] For a generally Kantian approach to political philosophy with an emphasis on international relations, see Fernando R. Tesón, *A Philosophy of International Law,* op. cit.

Index

abortion, 58, 142, 168, 169, 170, 178, 184
academics, 29, 57, 58, 59, 60, 61, 62, 63, 64, 89, 95, 171, 176, 188
accountability, vii, 187, 205, 223, 224
Ackerman, B., 15, 95
Ackerman, J., 176
ad hoc judgments, 129
ad hominem argument, 82–3
Adda, J., 23
affirmative action, 45, 93, 142, 146, 166, 168, 175
Afghanistan, 54
Africa, 37, 54
Albert, H., 104, 178
altruism, 24, 81, 149
analytic philosophy, 54
ancien régime, 195
Anderson, E., 124
antebellum South, 48, 49. *See also* slavery
Apter, D., 16
Argentina, viii, 32, 39, 104, 246
argumentum ad populum, 43
Aristophanes, 33
Aristotle, 108
asymmetries of information, 243
Aumann, R., 121
autonomy, 2, 4, 5, 47, 50, 113, 183, 184, 201, 210, 219, 230, 234, 245, 247
    deliberation as exercise in, 183–6
axioms of preference, 67

Bach, K., 31, 76
bankers, 51, 52
Bartels, L., 106
Bartosek, K., 54
Bayesian logic, 120–2
Becker, E., 8
belief
    epistemic and instrumental related, 65–82
    epistemically rational, 16, 72, 73, 74, 75, 76, 77, 78
    instrumentally rational, 69, 70, 71, 72, 73, 75, 76, 77, 78, 126, 133, 136, 140
    self-induced, 69
    See also default belief; political belief
Bennett, S., 14
Berg, J., 68
Berlin, I., 210, 211
Bernecker, S., 31, 72
Bhagwati, J., 9, 94
Blackburn, S., 44, 146, 147, 169, 175, 202
Bohman, J., 1, 149, 189, 196, 212
bootstrap argument, 34, 102–5, 177, 178, 182
Bovens, L., 118
Brennan, G., 6, 111, 135
Brennan, T., 46
Bricmont, J., 88
Buchanan, A., 81
Buchanan, J., 91, 109, 111, 226, 242
Bunge, M., 155
Buscaglia, E., 104
Bush, G. W., 22, 56, 62

Cambodia, 54
Campbell, D., 66
Candaele, K., 161
capital punishment, 58, 150–1, 152, 161, 162, 165, 168
capitalism, 34, 45, 47, 55, 120
Card, D., 179, 180
Castro, F., 48, 54, 59, 60, 246
Catholicism, 235
causal complexity, 150, 168
causation, 30, 35
censorship, 56, 108, 220, 225
charity, 80, 81, 132, 138, 147, 148, 159, 195, 244
China, 54
Christiano, T., 1, 13, 14, 15, 108, 149, 155, 186, 189, 196, 197, 202, 212
Chu, R., 68
Chu, Y., 68
civil libertarianism, 166
Clark, F., 37
Clifford, W., 69, 178
Clinton, B., 62
coalitions, 57, 59, 63
coercion, 3, 7, 36, 50, 104, 114, 152, 154, 167, 174, 204, 208, 209, 210, 211, 219, 222, 230, 235, 247
    deliberative democracy as, 206
cognitive dissonance. *See* cognitive psychology
cognitive psychology, 40–4
    accessibility, 40
    framing effect, 40
    reinforces discourse failure thesis, 43–44
Cohen, G., 47, 234
Cohen, J., 65, 204, 205
collective action, 49, 197, 200, 237
Collingwood, R., 66
common law, 47, 237
communism, 44, 45, 54, 55, 56, 57, 60, 112
    academics on, 53–7
communitarian, 240
communitarian values, 56, 231. *See also* preference: communal
comparative advantages, 9, 10, 11, 24, 90, 92, 104, 144, 241
compromise. *See* conflict, social; contract

concentrated versus dispersed losses and gains, 27
Condorcet. *See* Jury Theorem
confirmation, 9, 42, 84, 180
conflict, social, 4, 190, 192
    deliberation and, 189–92
consent, 2, 5, 204, 207, 210, 218, 219, 221, 222, 230, 236, 237, 240, 243, 247. *See also* government by consent
    deliberation as, 204–11
conservatism, 56, 57
consistent agent, 133, 134, 135, 140
constitution, 213. *See also* democracy: constitutional
constitutional rights, 227
constraints on deliberation, 188
consumer, 109, 188, 209, 230
contract, 46, 190, 219, 234, 236, 239, 242, 246, 247
    and compromise, 232–4
    paradox of, 236–8
    and truth, 230–2
Converse, P., 23
Cooper, R., 23
Cooter, R., 46, 57, 104, 217, 242
Copp, D., 124
Corbett, J., 37
corruption, 91
counterproductive positions, 5, 81, 116, 126, 132, 134, 136, 137, 138, 140, 141, 144, 145, 147, 148, 150, 151, 152, 154, 155, 159, 160, 161, 166, 168, 170, 175, 180, 241. *See also* self-defeatingness
Courtois, S., 54
Coverse, P., 16
Cowen, T., 25, 121, 147
criminal law, 222, 227, 240
Cuba, 47, 48, 49, 50, 54
    as a slave society, 47–50

Daniels, N., 98
deadweight loss, 22
Deardorff, A., 9
DeCamp Wilson, T., 42
decision theory, 66, 67, 68, 69, 126, 127, 128, 129, 130, 131, 134, 137
    characterized, 66–7
default belief, 157
    characterized, 31

default beliefs, 31, 35

deliberation, vii, viii, 1, 2, 3, 4, 7, 13, 14, 15, 16, 19, 20, 28, 35, 62, 65, 66, 72, 74, 81, 85, 90, 91, 92, 93, 94, 95, 98, 99, 100, 101, 102, 105, 108, 111, 112, 113, 114, 115, 116, 117, 118, 121, 122, 123, 125, 128, 139, 142, 143, 145, 147, 148, 149, 154, 155, 156, 159, 170, 171, 172, 173, 174, 175, 178, 183, 184, 185, 186, 187, 188, 189, 190, 191, 192, 193, 194, 195, 197, 198, 199, 200, 201, 202, 203, 204, 205, 206, 207, 208, 209, 210, 211, 212, 213, 214, 215, 216, 218, 220, 221, 222, 223, 224, 225, 226, 227, 228, 230, 231, 233, 236, 241, 244, 245, 246

bad reasons in
as conducive to truth
courtroom analogy
deliberative institutions
and equality, 194–8
as fair hearing
and free speech, 108–13
and impartiality, 192
and majority rule, 213–17
as a regulative ideal
and rights, 211–13
sincerity in, 186–9

deliberative democracy, vii, 1, 2, 4, 5, 7, 13, 14, 23, 53–64, 87, 92, 101, 102, 108, 114, 117, 142, 145, 161, 165, 168, 170, 183, 184, 187, 193, 202, 204, 207, 209, 210, 212, 213, 214, 217, 218, 221, 224, 225, 226, 229, 231, 235, 241. *See also* deliberation
defined, 1–2
distinguished from traditional liberal views, 2–3

deliberative polls, 15, 95, 96, 97

Delli Carpini, M., 16, 85, 106

democracy, viii, 1, 2, 5, 7, 13, 17, 19, 35, 44, 45, 65, 78, 83, 102, 104, 116, 118, 119, 120, 142, 145, 148, 183, 187, 188, 193, 199, 204, 209, 213, 218, 220, 221, 226, 244. See voting. *See also* Bayesian logic; deliberation: majority rule; Jury Theorem

Democratic Party, 21, 98, 120

Demsetz, H., 30, 50, 213

deontological agent, 158

deontological constraints, 150, 158, 159, 161, 164, 177

deontological ethics. *See* deontological constraints; Display Test

desert, v, 50

Detroit, 144

Dickhaut, J., 68

Dinopoulos, E., 11

discourse failure, vii, viii, 4, 13, 17, 18, 21, 25, 26, 27, 29, 31, 33, 34, 35, 36, 38, 39, 43, 44, 45, 46, 47, 48, 49, 50, 53, 54, 55, 58, 59, 61, 62, 63, 64, 70, 71, 72, 76, 78, 79, 80, 81, 82, 83, 86, 87, 89, 90, 92, 93, 94, 95, 96, 97, 99, 101, 102, 103, 107, 108, 109, 111, 112, 113, 114, 115, 116, 117, 118, 119, 122, 123, 124, 134, 138, 139, 141, 142, 143, 148, 152, 155, 156, 157, 159, 161, 166, 170, 171, 172, 176, 177, 178, 179, 181, 182, 183, 187, 191, 192, 193, 194, 195, 196, 199, 200, 201, 202, 205, 209, 212, 216, 217, 218, 219, 220, 221, 222, 223, 224, 227, 228, 229, 230, 231, 232, 237, 240, 241, 242, 243, 244, 245, 246, 247

actual policies distinguished from, 35
characerization and forms of, 13–21
defined, 16–17
discourse failure about, 39
discourse failure (DF) hypothesis, 145, 147, 149, 150, 151, 152, 154, 157, 158, 160, 161, 164, 165, 167, 168, 175
moral turn as, 142–50
obscurity and vagueness as sources of, 29–32
political art as, 35
protectionism as, 8–13
single fact activating, 32–3
symbolism as, 141
testing theory of, 83–6
types of, summarized, 181–2
usefulness of, 198–203
and voluntary communities, 242–5

Display Test, vi, 29, 58, 149, 150, 151, 152, 153, 154, 155, 156, 157, 160, 161, 162, 164, 168, 169, 175
defined, 151–2

dissent, 55, 59, 108, 201. *See also* academics

Dixit, A., 9

Donnelly, J., 54

Downs, A., 14, 15
Dreier, P., 161
Dretske, F., 31, 72
drugs, 96, 114, 115, 182, 238
Dryzeck, J., 108
Dukeminier, J., 47
Durfee, J., 37
Dworkin, R., 2, 145, 188, 235

Ebeling, R., 80
Eblacas, P., 37
Eccles, J., 66
economics, viii, ix, 9, 12, 19, 20, 29, 39, 47, 52, 57, 58, 62, 67, 83, 84, 88, 89, 90, 91, 94, 98, 105, 107, 120, 123, 143, 144, 167, 175, 180, 198. *See also* comparative advantages; minimum wage laws
    extension to new domains, 28
    hostility to, 29
    international, 8–13
    Keynesian, 57
education, vii, 21, 28, 44, 51, 81, 107, 114, 142, 146, 176, 177, 190, 191, 218, 245
Edwards, J., 8
egalitarianism, 146
Eisenstein, S., 33
Ekelund, R., 111
Eldestein, J., 54
elite, 170, 201, 202, 203
Ellickson, R., 213
Elster, J., 1, 65, 149, 205, 211
enforcement, 153, 154, 165, 174, 175, 184, 237
    costs of, 153–4
    ignored in moral argument, 173–5
environmental protection, 36–8
    car fumes, 37
    contamination of rivers, 37
    global warming, 37
    oil spillages, 37
environmentalism, 36, 37, 38, 83, 101
epistemic argument, 3, 15, 80, 113, 172, 231
Epstein, R., 30, 69
equality, viii, 2, 3, 5, 49, 50, 62, 64, 145, 91, 146, 169, 186, 197, 199, 202, 212, 225, 227, 229. *See also* deliberation
Erikson, R., 106

error, vii, 15, 16, 17, 19, 42, 78, 82, 87, 91, 93, 95, 103, 107, 112, 114, 116, 118, 119, 123, 138, 139, 141, 172, 173, 177, 185, 192, 193, 198, 199, 210, 211, 216
    duty to overcome, 113–15
    failure to connect, 171, 172
    moral, 170–3
essentialism, 44, 50
Estlund, D., 1
Europe, 54, 246
    Eastern, 54, 246
euthanasia, 143, 168, 169, 173, 174, 175
evildoing, direct involvement in, 161–6
evolutionary theory, 30, 53, 58, 156, 157, 182
exploitation, 67, 144, 160, 161, 162, 163, 164, 211, 212
expressive behavior. *See* symbolism
externalism, 76
externalities, 101, 144, 190, 213

Fair Labor Standard Act. *See* minimum wage laws
farm subsidies, 22, 52
farmers, 22, 27, 33, 51, 52, 53, 100, 153, 181, 242
Feigl, H., 66
Feldman, A., 217
Feyerabend, P., 93
Fiorina, M., 106
Fishkin, J., 1, 15, 95, 96, 97
Fiss, O., 222
Foley, R., 72, 76, 77
framing, 40, 42, 70, 120, 217, 218, 220, 234. *See also* cognitive psychology; voting
free speech, 3, 7, 13, 108, 112, 113, 169, 192, 196, 222, 226, 227
    and collective tragedies, 112
    marketplace of ideas, 108–112
    reasons for, 112–113
free trade, 8, 9, 10, 11, 12, 13, 17, 20, 33, 39, 79, 91, 94, 101, 103, 104, 117. *See also* comparative advantages; protectionism
Hecksher. *See* Hecksher-Olin Theorem
Freeman, E., 66
Friedman, M., 51, 147, 245
Friedman, R., 147
Frisch, M., 54

game theory, 9, 22, 23, 27, 36, 38, 55, 57, 58, 59, 61, 62, 70, 157
  coordination game, 55, 57, 60
  negative-sum games, 27, 181
  positive-sum games, 27, 181
  zero-sum games, 4, 22, 27, 28, 34, 36, 39, 122, 181, 191
Garrett, A., 66
Gaus, G., ix, 2, 3, 14, 65, 80, 131, 155, 186, 204
Gawande, K., 12
geocentric theory, 20
Germany, 59, 112, 246
Gilbert, D., 42
Gillens, M., 95
Gilovich, T., 40, 41, 42, 43, 69
God, 176, 177, 178. *See also* religion
Golam Azan, H., 22
Goldman, A., 15, 16, 17, 19, 20, 83, 108, 109, 110, 111, 112, 117, 223, 232
Goodin, R., 1, 13, 15, 80, 118, 119, 120, 121, 147, 183, 194
government by consent, 210, 218
government failure, 58, 111, 112
Gray, J., 80
Grayling, A., 122
Green, D. P.
Greenspan, A., 8
Griffin, D., 40, 69
Grossman, G., 11, 23
Guevara, Che, 59
Gulag, 56
Gunn, R., 37
Gutmann, A., 1, 2, 14, 108, 142, 145, 154, 187, 193, 194, 199, 205, 206, 221, 224, 226
Gwartney, J., 197, 242

Habermas, J., 2, 65, 154, 155, 186
Hamlin, A., 204, 205
Hansen, W., 12
Hanson, R., 121
Hardin, G., 213
Hardin, R., 14
Hart, H., 31, 202
Hausman, D., 67
Havana, 60
Hayek, F., 30, 80, 155
Hazlett, T., 222
Hecksher-Olin Theorem, 10, 11, 12

heliocentric theory, 20
Heller, M., 213
Helpman, E., 11, 23
Hobbes, T., 237
Holmes, O., 108
Honoré, T., 31
Hoon, H., 10
Hume, D., 66
Hutchison, F., 66
Huxley, A., 33

ideal deliberation, 7, 225, 226, 236, 244
immigration, 56, 236, 246
impartiality, viii, 5, 187, 188, 192, 193, 221, 223, 226
  deliberation and, 192–4
  toward interests or viewpoints, 192–3
imperialism, 34, 59
interest rate, 26
internalism, 76
Internet, iv, 116
investment in information and reflection (IIR), 69

Jenkins, J., 204
Johnson, P., 54
Jones, O., 30, 117
Jost, T., 53
Joyce, J., 122
Jury Theorem, 117–120
justice, 2, 4, 23, 27, 36, 46, 80, 90, 131, 146, 147, 165, 166, 190, 191, 199, 211, 212, 215, 241. *See also* deliberation

Kahneman, D., 40, 41, 69
Kamm, F., 158
Kant, I., 2, 247
Keater, S., 16, 85, 106
Keith, T., 33
Kelsen, H., 30, 47
Keohane, R., 99
Kirkpatrick, J., 55
Kitcher, P., 198, 199, 200, 202
Kletzer, L., 10
Klick, J., x, 53, 121
Kliemt, H., 111
Krakowjak, M., 37
Kramer, M., 54
Krier, J., 47
Kripke, S., 45

Krouse, R., 145
Krugman, P., 11
Kuhn, T., 87, 93, 201
Ku Klux Klan, 194
Kymlicka, W., 145, 146, 147, 169, 175, 229

Ladha, K., 118
Laffer curve, 99
Lakatos, I., 87
Laslett, P., 1
Latin America, 54
Lau, R., 16, 106
law. *See* enforcement
law reviews, 89
law schools, 63, 89
  international law professors, 63
left and right, 63–4
  left-of-center positions, 56, 57, 58, 60, 61
Leiter rankings, 89
Lenhardt, C., 155
liberalism, 2, 210, 238
  practices excluded by, 238
libertarianism, 56, 229
Lindert, P., 10, 23
List, C., 119
lobbying, 5, 7, 11, 12, 15, 18, 51, 79, 104,
  107, 188, 197, 205
Locke, J., 2, 62
Lomasky, L., ix, 6, 215
Luque, R., 32
Luttbeg, N., 85

Macedo, S., 149, 193, 224
Mack, E., 158, 191
Mackuen, M., 106
majority rule, 2, 3, 5, 13, 18, 45, 101, 102,
  118, 183, 188, 190, 191, 195, 204, 210,
  213, 214, 215, 216, 217, 222, 225, 228,
  231, 232, 233, 242, 245
  deliberation and, 213–217
Malia, M., 54
marginal analysis, 67
market failure, 2, 26, 36, 37, 38, 57, 58, 90,
  101, 127, 237, 243. *See also* asymmetries
  of information; externalities
Martin, R., 66
Marx, K., 120, 213
Matusz, S., 10
McCarthyism, 56
McKelvey, R., 105
McPherson, M., 67, 145

media, vii, 32, 37, 85, 96, 107, 115, 116, 196,
  212, 222
median voter, 25, 101
Meehl, P., 66
meta-ethics, 177
Mexico, 34
Mill, J. S., 3, 13, 42, 108, 112, 149, 178, 234,
  235
  as deliberativist, 3
  and free speech, 3, 13, 108–13
minimum wage, 28, 123, 124, 126, 127,
  128, 132, 134, 136, 137, 138, 139, 140,
  143, 144, 149, 153, 157, 161, 162, 164,
  167, 168, 179–81
  Fair Labor Standards Act, 180
Mitchell, G., 43
Mitchell, W., 58
moral balancing, 150–151
moral turn, 142–50, 151, 152, 154, 156,
  158, 159, 160, 161, 164, 166, 167, 168,
  175, 241

Nader, R., 94
NAFTA (North American Free Trade
  Agreement), 12, 209
Nagel, E., 156
Nagel, T., 158, 164, 235
Namolin, L., 54
narratives, 89, 199
National Public Radio, 54
nationalism, 147
NATO (North Atlantic Treaty
  Organization), 16
Nellermoe, J., 37
Neuman, W., 85
Neumark, D., 179
New York Review of Books, 54
New York Times, 8, 54, 55
Newcomb's Problem, 127
Nicholsen, S., 155
Nino, C., 1, 2, 13, 14, 142, 155, 183, 186,
  192, 215, 222, 225, 245
Nisbett, R., 23, 42
Norman, V., 9
North Carolina, 8
North Korea, 50, 54, 163, 239
Norton, D., 66
Norton, M., 66
Nozick, R., vi, viii, 2, 30, 45, 50, 60, 61, 78,
  115, 124, 126–9, 130, 131, 140, 147,
  158, 208, 215, 219, 221, 225, 229

on circular reasoning, 78–9
on intellectuals, 60–1
on rent control, 45–6
on symbolism, 124
on utopia, 229

O'Brien, J., 68
Obeng, K., 22
Olson, M., 111, 188, 197, 200
opacity, 9, 24, 25, 28, 29, 30, 35, 36, 37, 38,
    41, 44, 46, 47, 52, 58, 62, 69, 70, 73,
    80, 81, 87, 90, 91, 92, 96, 99, 100, 101,
    102, 104, 106, 107, 116, 117, 120, 153,
    157, 177, 192, 197, 218, 219, 241, 246.
    See also vividness
Ordeshook, P., 105
overlapping consensus, 169, 206

Paczowski, A., 54
Page, B., 1, 16, 84, 85, 105
Panne, L., 54
Papineau, D., 122
Parfit, D., 158
Parisi, F., 53
Parker, G., 5
participation, vii, viii, 3, 81, 93, 114, 138,
    171, 173, 187, 188, 194, 195, 196, 212,
    216, 246
deliberation as enhancing, 194
patriotism, 24
Paul, J., 59
peace, social. *See* conflict, social
persuasive definitions, 44–50
Pettit, P., 23, 143, 187, 204, 205
Pham, M., 23
philosophy. *See* analytic philosophy
physicians, 51, 53, 114
Picasso, P., 33
Pildes, R., 124, 126
Pincione, G., 63, 82, 112, 189, 191, 227
Plamenatz, J., 204
Plato, 183, 224
political art. *See* discourse failure
political belief, patterns of, 21–39
political satire, 34
political science, viii, 83, 88, 89, 90, 107
politicians, vii, 8, 13, 15, 18, 19, 21, 25, 26,
    31, 35, 39, 53, 76, 80, 82, 83, 84, 85, 91,
    95, 96, 98, 106, 107, 110, 111, 113, 122,
    123, 132, 138, 139, 154, 155, 157, 170,
    185, 187, 197, 199, 205, 216, 231, 245

Pope, 177. *See also* religion
Popper, K., 66, 87, 93, 103, 155
pornography, 56, 168
Posner, R., 47, 89
Postema, G., 186
posturing, 18, 44, 53, 79, 82, 94, 97, 118,
    121, 140, 145, 149, 150, 154, 168, 170,
    175, 176, 185, 187, 216, 220, 228, 230,
    245
characterized, 139–40
poverty, 24, 26, 32, 34, 53, 112, 113, 147,
    160, 164, 169, 174, 180, 184
preference, 36, 49, 67, 68, 69, 70, 109,
    235
axioms of, 68
communal, 235
intransitivity, 67, 68
totalitarian, 235
price, 25, 28, 32, 46, 50, 51, 52, 84, 91, 104,
    107, 149, 152, 179, 220, 243
Prisoner's Dilemma, 90, 127
professions, 51, 52
prostitution, 56, 174
psychology. *See* cognitive psychology
public good, 36, 49, 109, 205, 236
public reason, 14, 179, 236
publicity, 187, 205, 224
Pugel, T., 10

Quattrone, G., 41

Rabinowicz, W., 118
rational choice, viii, 4, 5, 6, 29, 43, 69, 70,
    78, 80, 82, 90, 91, 131, 139
extension beyond economics, 28–9,
    91
and morality, 82
and political discourse, 7
testability of, 78–9, 129
rational ignorance, 14, 15, 16, 18, 19, 28,
    43, 44, 53, 73, 81, 85, 94, 95, 97, 114,
    121, 127, 138, 139, 141, 143, 144, 145,
    149, 150, 151, 159, 161, 168, 170, 172,
    173, 175, 176, 182, 185, 193, 198, 223,
    228, 230
extended from facts to theory,
    16
as obstacle to deliberation, 13–14,
    19
and shortcuts, 107
and symbolism, 138

rationality, vii, 4, 5, 6, 14, 15, 17, 19, 41, 43,
    65, 66, 67, 68, 69, 70, 71, 72, 73, 74,
    75, 76, 77, 85, 106, 123, 126, 127, 128,
    129, 131, 132, 135, 137, 140, 141,
    159
  epistemic and instrumental, 65–78
Ratliff, W., 104
Rawls, J., 2, 14, 142, 145, 146, 154, 169,
    178, 186, 200, 206, 215, 225, 236
Reagan, R., 56, 59, 98, 99
reasonableness, 206, 207, 208, 209, 210
  and consent, 204–11
reasons
  agent-neutral, 158, 162, 163, 164, 165,
    175
  agent-relative, 158, 159, 163
  comprehensive, vii, 58, 59, 89, 142, 169,
    170, 189, 206, 236
  reciprocity, 187, 205, 206, 224
Redlawsk, D., 16
regulative ideal, 113, 116, 117, 212, 241.
    See also deliberation
Rehg, W., 1
reliabilism, 31, 72, 74, 76
reliable social science, 13, 17, 18, 28, 30,
    35, 43, 45, 57, 58, 62, 63, 69, 70, 71,
    73, 81, 83, 84, 85, 86, 87, 88, 89, 90,
    91, 92, 97, 99, 105, 115, 117, 122, 155,
    156, 181, 182, 210
  operational tests for, 87–90
religion, 54, 56, 156, 168, 176, 177, 178,
    181, 182, 236, 238
  and moral justification, 176–9
rent control, 46, 47, 84, 91, 144, 165
rent seeking, 5, 11, 22, 197, 200, 242
Republican Party, 21, 57, 98, 120
responsibility, moral, 79
  split, 166–8
Revesz, R., 38
Ricardo, D., 9
right
  inalienability of, 236–8
rights, 2, 13, 38, 45, 46, 47, 50, 53, 54, 55,
    62, 79, 106, 151, 157, 158, 160, 163,
    165, 169, 179, 188, 191, 200, 208, 212,
    213, 214, 215, 219, 225, 226, 227, 228,
    229, 231, 232, 233, 236, 237, 239, 245,
    246, 247. *See also* constitutional rights;
    deliberation
  human, 50, 53, 54, 55, 79, 214, 237

inalienability of, 236
property, 45, 46, 47, 145, 169, 190, 212,
    213, 226, 229, 233, 237
robust deliberation, 1, 13, 108, 110, 200,
    201, 203, 213, 220, 222
Rodgers, D., 59
Roemer, J., 229
Rorty, M., 104
Rosario, city of, 32
Roseberry, L., 59
Ross, L., 23
Rousseau, J., 117, 210
Ryan, A., 211

Sabin, J., 98
Sachs, J., 11
sacred text, 176, 177
Sakano, R., 22
Schauer, F., 224
Scheffler, S., 146, 158
Schick, F., 68
Schiffrin, S., 166
Schilpp, P., 66
Schmidtz, D., 80, 84, 131, 147, 153, 154,
    213
Schroeder, C., 221, 223
Schwartz, S., 45
science, viii, 3, 4, 13, 17, 18, 20, 30, 35, 43,
    57, 58, 62, 63, 69, 70, 71, 73, 83, 84,
    85, 87, 88, 90, 91, 92, 93, 97, 105,
    115, 117, 155, 156, 157, 181, 182, 183,
    201, 210. *See also* reliable social
    science
scientific progress, 92, 93, 112
secession, 239, 240
Segerstrom, P., 11
self-defeating reformer (SDR), 125, 128,
    134, 135, 136, 139
  rationality of, 132–7
self-defeatingness, 137, 138, 139,
    150
  as symbolism, 123–4
shortcuts, *See* rational ignorance
Sierra Club, 38
signaling, 55
Simmons, R., 58
sincerity. *See* deliberation
Singer, P., 204
Siqueiros, D., 34
Skolimowski, H., 66

slavery, 48, 49, 50, 234
in Cuba, 47–50
draft as, 49, 50, 176
Slovic, P., 40
Smart, J., 158
Smith, A., 24
Smith, V., 68
Smullyan, R., 211
Sobel, R., 180
social conflict. *See* conflict, social
social science. *See* reliable social science
socialism, 55
Sokal, A., 88
Somin, I., 14, 105, 106, 116, 234, 242, 245
Soviet Union, 16, 50, 53, 54, 246
Sowell, T., 94
special interests, vii, 23, 29, 45, 96, 111, 116, 188, 196, 197, 199, 200, 205, 212, 217, 242
Spector, H., ix, x, 158, 191, 211
Srinivasan, T., 9
Stalin, J., 53
Stamm, K., 37
status quaestionis, 17, 28, 90, 97, 209
Stevenson, C., 44
Stimson, J., 106
Sugden, R., 55, 104
Sunstein, C., 47, 55, 124, 126, 203
supply and demand, 22, 25, 28, 181
symbolism, viii, 123, 135, 141. *See also* discourse failure; self-defeatingness
interpreted using standard rationality assumptions, 129–32
in politics, 124–6
social or subjective, 125
symbolic rationality, 126–9

taxation, 36, 50, 84, 242
taxpayer, 22, 27, 188
Taylor, C., 211
teachers, 51, 63, 74
Tesón, F., i, iv, x, 63, 117, 219, 237, 240, 246, 247
Thatcher, M., 56, 59
Thompson, D., 1, 2, 14, 108, 142, 145, 154, 187, 193, 194, 199, 205, 206, 221, 224, 226
Thomson, J., 171, 172
Thornton, M., 96
tolerance, 164, 169

Tollison, R., 111, 197
trade, 8, 9, 10, 11, 12, 13, 13, 16, 20, 21, 23, 24, 30, 34, 35, 38, 39, 56, 80, 90, 94, 95, 101, 103, 104, 108, 110, 116, 117, 121, 175, 185, 198, 227, 230, 237, 241, 242, 246. *See also* comparative advantages; protectionism
truth, vii, viii, 3, 4, 7, 12, 14, 15, 17, 19, 20, 45, 61, 62, 63, 70, 71, 72, 73, 75, 76, 77, 83, 85, 91, 92, 93, 95, 99, 101, 103, 107, 108, 109, 110, 111, 113, 115, 117, 118, 119, 120, 121, 123, 139, 145, 149, 155, 178, 184, 185, 187, 191, 195, 197, 198, 200, 202, 203, 210, 220, 221, 230, 231, 232. *See also* deliberation
veritistic value, 99, 109, 110, 111
Tucker, I., 179
Tullock, G., 91, 226, 242
Tversky, A., 40, 41

Ulen, T., 46
unanimity rule, 214, 215, 222
unemployment, 10, 12, 16, 20, 24, 25, 28, 32, 48, 90, 96, 97, 104, 144, 156, 157, 160, 161, 162, 164, 165, 167, 180, 198, 229
Unger, P., 153, 154
United Nations, 54
United States, iv, viii, 8, 11, 12, 13, 27, 39, 54, 57, 59, 84, 98, 104, 108, 147, 180, 196, 209, 218, 246
utility, 6, 31, 41, 84, 126, 127, 128, 129, 130, 131, 132, 133, 134, 136, 139, 177, 178, 225
causal, 128, 132
evidential, 127
symbolic. *See* symbolism

Vallentyne, P., 229
Vietnam, 54
virtue, 10, 54, 59, 74, 81, 101, 113, 114, 125, 148, 149, 169, 186, 194, 195, 201, 243
civic, 149, 194
vividness, 24, 28, 38, 42, 94, 99, 138, 194. *See also* cognitive psychology
vivid theories, 23–5
voluntary communitied (VC), 229, 230, 231, 232, 233, 234, 236, 239, 240, 241, 242, 243, 244, 245

von Neumann, J., 67
voting
  framing, 120, 217, 218, 220, 234
  strategic, 120
  universal franchise, 195, 196, 216. *See also*
    Bayesian logic; democracy; Jury
    Theorem
vouchers, 53, 245

Wagner, J., 186
Wagner, R., 197
Waldron, J., 118, 204
Wall Street Journal, 54

Walzer, M., 193
Watkins, W., 66
welfare state, 44, 55, 145, 146, 147, 233,
    242
Wenar, L., 46
Werth, N., 54
whale hunting, 37, 38, 181
Williams, B., 158
Wingo, A., 198

Zalta, E., 229
Zangwill, N., 33
Zhou, R., 23